GLAD FARM
A MEMOIR

Second Edition

Catherine Marenghi

Glad Farm: A Memoir

Second edition

Published in the United States of America

ISBN-13: 978-1544629735
ISBN-10: 1544629737

Biography & Autobiography / Personal Memoir

To Stephen
and, most especially,
to Steven

ACKNOWLEDGMENTS

The author gratefully acknowledges those who participated in this story and its publication. Some people may be surprised by their inclusion in this memoir; others, by their omission. A few of the names have been altered. My narrative choices were not motivated by a desire to hurt or exclude anyone; my intent was only to tell my story as faithfully as I can.

I owe a particular debt to Steve Eisner and Jon Reisfeld, whom I met at the When Words Count writers' retreat in Rochester, Vermont. They were the first to suggest to me, in 2013, "You should write a memoir."

My talented son Steven Pfau has provided insightful editorial comments on several drafts of this work, as well as many years of unflagging encouragement for my writing. Lana Echard at Tate Publishing has been both a skilled editor and a supportive reader. Paul Gillin has shared his writing expertise and warm encouragement. Deborah Schneebeli, Carmen Peralta, Linda Arnold, Liane Davis, Margaret Pantridge, Anita Diamant, Rachel Ekstrom, Meryl Moss, the women of my book club—Catherine Dee, Maureen Farrell, Joyce Galonsky, Edith Harmon, Rebecca Kinchley, Linda Lengyel, Sharon Scofield—and so many others in my extended family have lent me their wisdom, support, and precious time.

Special thanks go to President Jimmy Carter who, in an act of immense kindness and generosity, took the time to answer my letter—although I was a stranger to him. I had written to express my admiration for Mr. Carter's work with Habitat for Humanity. I said I had written a book about rising up from poverty, noting that he above anyone would understand the power of a decent habitat in shaping a person's destiny. To my delight, he replied, in a personal handwritten note, that he would be willing to write a few words for my book jacket—only after reviewing a draft, of course! As a postscript, he added, "I, too, was raised in a house with no indoor plumbing."

Because our houses define us, because they inhabit us in more ways than we inhabit them, a significant portion of the proceeds of this book will be donated to Habitat for Humanity.

TABLE OF CONTENTS

You can't put the past behind you.
It's turned your flesh into its own cupboard.
Not everything remembered is useful,
but it all comes from the world to be stored in you.

From *Citizen: An American Lyric*
by Claudia Rankine

1

THE NEW HOUSE

1986

This was the day a house would be born.

This was the day. A day like tall windows with sunlight streaming through. A perfect January day, with a sky so clear it could blind you with its blue light.

This was a day like New Year's Day. Out with the old, in with the new. The old house, the unspeakable old house, would soon be over and done with. Rickety, shoddy, one-room structure, still standing after forty New England winters, it was a house never meant to be seen, never meant to be lived in. But it *was* lived in, by a family of seven no less. Set back far from the road at the end of a long dirt driveway, mercifully hidden behind a stand of sugar maple trees, it would soon be bulldozed, bashed in, and forgotten. A new house would rise on the same acre of land, but this one close to the road, where people could see it, drinking in the full light of day.

A house would fall. A new house would rise to take its place. And I would be there to see it.

As I drove west out of Boston that morning, the Mass. Turnpike rimmed with grizzled snow on both sides, the winter sun was glaring through a windshield streaked with a fine lace of road salt. I drove intently, as if guided by a taut string stretched between two pushpins on a map. Boston at one end, and the other a place I never spoke about, a strange place I once called home.

13 Prairie Street, Milford, Massachusetts. A lonely scrap of earth on the outskirts of a fading mill town. I spent the first seventeen years of my life there, and my mother and brother had never left it. There was a time when I couldn't wait to get away from it. Now I couldn't get there fast enough.

This was the day a house would be born.

As I turned onto Prairie Street, I could see Ma and Jerry up ahead, standing at the foot of the driveway, as if too impatient to wait indoors. I soon joined them, the three of us standing together in the bitter cold, saying nothing, our faces all turned in the same direction, wearing the dumbstruck expressions of immigrants about to embark on a foreign shore.

And then we heard it, the rumbling of two giant trucks turning onto Prairie Street, all decked out in festive red flags to trumpet their oversize loads. Each one carried a section of the new house on its back.

My mother gasped softly. "Here it comes!"

It was a factory-built wonder, clad in cream-colored vinyl with black shutters, fully finished inside. The pieces were interlocking, like a giant doll house, ready to be hoisted by crane and dropped onto the waiting foundation. And before we knew it, in a matter of hours, there it was: the long-awaited dream house, all snapped together, clean and perfect, beckoning us to step inside.

Ma was giddy as a child, snapping instant pictures with her favorite Polaroid, invariably getting her thumb into every shot. The camera whirred and clicked as it spat out glossy photos one by one. She took pictures of everything—the brass doorknobs, the beige wall-to-wall carpet, the closets with folding doors, the powder blue porcelain toilet and matching sink. And why? She had gone without these basic niceties most of her life. She was chronicling her entrance into the modern world.

She was trading her outhouse for a flushing toilet. Her wood-burning stove for a shiny electric range. Aluminum pails of drinking water hand-carried from the well, for hot and cold running tap water. And who could believe it—there was even a dishwasher! Anyone passing by on the street that day would have had no idea what a crowning achievement it was for this particular family to step into this simple split-level house.

My mother, Myrtle Ann, still had a youthful appearance for a woman of sixty-six years. Her naturally dark hair, with only a single streak of gray, was always parted on the side and pinned neatly behind her ears with two long hairpins. She wore a plain cloth coat, and her face was framed by a silky flowered kerchief tied tightly under her chin. She wore no makeup, ever, and her only ornament was a plain gold wedding band that she still wore, decades after her husband's passing.

Her thick wrists were ringed with at least a dozen rubber bands; she collected and saved them on her wrists, a frugal habit, just as she always saved endless chains of safety pins by fastening them to her brassiere. I had never seen her wear anything but simple shirt-waist cotton dresses, in small floral patterns. The same thing she might have worn fifty years earlier. A woman frozen in time.

It was always a challenge to find stores that still carried the kind of dresses she liked, long after they went out of style, so she wore the few dresses she had until they were threadbare. Now, at least, she had a place to hang them: a large east-facing bedroom in the rear of the house, with an ample double-door closet.

My brother Jerry, not much for words, was quietly taking it all in. He was thirty-four years old, two years my senior, a soft-spoken man whose shoulders were rounded like soft clay, the hunched posture of a man who lifts boxes in a warehouse every day. He had been working thirteen years in the shipping department of the Milford Shoe Company. I can't remember a time he wasn't working, ever since he was a boy delivering newspapers. When our father died many years earlier, someone told Jerry he was now the man of the family—a thoughtless thing to tell a twelve-year-old boy—and my brother took that pronouncement to heart. From that day on, there was never a time when he wasn't there to provide for our mother.

Tall and olive-skinned, Jerry wore a much-too-thin windbreaker jacket for this frigid day, well-worn jeans, and thick-soled white sneakers that he wore year-round, through sun and snow. He paused for a moment in the doorway of his very first private bedroom, a large corner room that faced the street. I could see his eyes assessing where his prized record collection would go—Rolling Stones, Jefferson Airplane, Beatles—arranging the album crates in his mind on the carpeted floor. He could already hear his new room filling with music.

Meanwhile, in the kitchen, Ma was stepping tentatively onto the impossibly shiny linoleum floor, as if afraid of spoiling it. She tested the kitchen faucets, turning the lever up and down and side to side, from hot to cold. The water wasn't turned on yet, but she instinctively held her hands under the spigot, imagining the soothing warmth running over her labor-scarred fingers.

"Look over here, Ma," I said, pointing to a phone jack by the kitchen doorway. "Here's where you plug in the wall phone. I'll get you one with nice big numbers, so it's easy for you to read."

"Oh, for goodness' sake." Ma stared at the metal mounting plate, running her thick fingers over it. "Our very first telephone. I wonder what our number will be? Greenleaf three…"

I smiled. "They don't use words and letters in phone numbers any more, Ma. In Milford it's 4-7-3, not Greenleaf-3."

I suddenly had another thought. "You know, Ma, whatever number it is, we'd better make sure it's listed. Remember all the times people tried calling us and ended up calling Uncle Albert instead? He was the only Marenghi that was ever in the phone book!"

I remembered, with a sudden sharp flinch of pain, the schoolyard taunts I used to hear. "You don't have a phone? Why not? Everyone has a phone!" And now here it was, a virgin metal plate on a bare wall. Our long-awaited private line to the outside world.

As my mother and brother continued to test cabinet doors and knobs and fixtures, one by one, as if they were all part of a futuristic theme park, I stepped quietly toward a rear-facing kitchen window, looking out to the old house where all of us once lived. I could barely see it now, with its tarpaper roof and weathered cedar shingles, never painted, camouflaged behind the winter-plucked trees. It seemed small and distant now, as if it had never even mattered.

A feeling of lightness washed over me. An unbearable weight had finally been lifted. That terrible old house would hold no power over us anymore.

℘)℘

Prairie Street was a dead-end road on the eastern edge of Milford. It was miles from the noisy shoe factories and sprawling mills on the opposite end of town that once attracted legions of Italian immigrants, including my grandparents, around the turn of the twentieth century.

Few people had any reason to go to this part of town. Long before Prairie Street even had a name, it was the site of a pig farm, its pungent odors a discreet distance from the more populous neighborhoods. When the farm's owners, an elderly Italian couple, faced foreclosure for failure to pay taxes, a young man named Gerolamo Marenghi stepped in. He was my father.

He snapped up the land for just three hundred dollars, the amount of back taxes owed. There was no house on the property, just a small tarpaper shed and a spring-fed well. But my father must have seen possibilities no one else could in that rich, black, well-manured earth.

It was 1945. The year the war ended. The year my parents were married. A time of new beginnings.

My father was thirty-eight years old, and my mother, twenty-five. The newlyweds had set up housekeeping in a small apartment closer to town, while my father set to work building a house on Prairie Street. By day he was a factory worker, one of 3,000 men building textile machinery at the Draper Corporation. On nights and weekends, he was a solitary carpenter, slowly assembling a tiny one-room structure with his own hands.

I had always heard stories, just snippets here and there, about how my father did all the work himself—clearing the land with a hatchet and scythe, pouring a shallow cement foundation, running the crude electrical wiring, even laying an underground pipe from the well to supply fresh water to the house. He really had no business doing any of this work. By training, he was neither a carpenter nor a plumber nor an electrician. But he *was* a poor man. And a poor man must assume many professions that are not his own.

Three years after he started, in 1948, he declared his work complete and moved in with his wife and now two young daughters—Marcia, two years old, and Celia, one.

It was never meant to be more than a temporary dwelling. It couldn't have been. Made from scraps of cheap lumber, some of it salvaged one stick at a time from demolished buildings, the house was a patchwork of mismatched cedar shingles, ill-fitting windows, and crumbling sheetrock, all stitched together to form an out-building of sorts, a passable barn perhaps, but never a house. Surely, this was never meant to be a permanent house.

And yet, for my parents, this unlikely starter home was a place to call their own, to be free from the watchful gaze of landlords and disapproving families. What were they thinking when they moved into this makeshift structure? Maybe they thought it would be fun, a kind of adventure even—and once they were on their feet, a real house could be built, something closer to the road and in public view, and not hidden behind the trees at the end of a long dirt driveway, a ribbon of wild grass between two golden brown tire tracks.

The house was as far back from the street as it could go without pushing its face against the tall pine forest that bordered the land. The house had a single door with a square glass window that looked toward the woods, as if it were turning its back on Prairie Street and anybody who might pass there.

A stack of cinderblocks formed a narrow chimney on the outside wall to accommodate a massive wood-burning stove on clawed feet. That stove was the biggest thing in the house, a good six feet wide and over five feet tall with all its extensions and shelves, coated all over with pale yellow enamel trimmed in green. It would occupy an entire wall on the left side of the door, a source of coal- and wood-fired heat in winter, and a place to cook year-round.

A deep double-basin utility sink, the only water source in the house, was on the other side of the door. That left a third corner for a large iron bed, and the fourth corner for the rough, ladder-like steps to the upper loft. The steps terminated abruptly against the wall on the lower level, forcing anyone descending them to step sideways down to the floor.

Surely, this strange architecture was never intended as a permanent place to live. How else would you explain the lack of forethought to delineating space into rooms, or the absence of central heating, an indoor toilet, cabinets, closets, or a telephone? No one would ever approve this space as fit for human habitation. But forty years later, this temporary structure would still be the only place a family with five children would call home.

I was the fourth of those five children, all of us huddled together, sharing beds, washing each morning in a dishpan filled with hot water from the kettle, with never a moment of privacy, living this primitive existence every day as if it were normal. There were times when I wished we lived in an urban ghetto, side by side with other families who shared the same circumstances. Instead, the house on 13 Prairie Street enjoyed no such camaraderie. Ours was a house unlike anyone else's, a blip, a freak, an aberration, on the outskirts of an otherwise average blue-collar town.

Cramped and cluttered, the house was littered with useless objects and broken things. How it escaped being condemned by the Board of Health, I will never know. Sometimes there were mysterious, unannounced visits from social workers, all fresh-faced and earnest with clipboards in hand, and we'd all hold our breath and hope they wouldn't board the place up, mark it condemned, and ship all of us kids to separate foster homes. Perhaps because they had more serious cases on their hands, like drunks, wife-beaters, or felons—and we seemed to be hurting no one—the social workers always just walked away and left us alone.

The most ordinary things in other people's houses amazed me. Radiators—we didn't have those. Flowered wallpaper. Kitchen cabinets. Windows that were properly caulked and sealed, that opened and shut, and didn't crust over with white winter frost, inside and out. Ceilings with swirls of plaster, and not planks with rusty nails poking through.

There would be no birthday parties, no sleepovers, no dinner guests, no boys to come calling on a Saturday night. Instead, that house kept every possible friend at arm's length. I became expert at spinning excuses to keep people away. "No, let's meet at your house, not mine." "I'll wait for you at the corner of the street." "No need to drive me home—just drop me off here." And on and on. I was a fortress, ringed round and round with a protective moat of excuses.

I couldn't wait to leave home. In 1972, at the age of seventeen, I moved away to go to college, and I never lived in that house again. I was always a very good student, and that was my ticket to escape. I was high school valedictorian. I got scholarships and work-study grants and summer jobs, enough to get me through four years of a fine liberal arts college. I squeezed a graduate program into my undergraduate years, earning a combined bachelor's and master's degree *summa cum laude* from Tufts University, all without taking a penny from my family.

I worked. I traveled. I had a career and a car and a condo and a life in Boston, my own private little universe. I lived in a sunny Queen Anne Victorian, with turrets and bay windows and fine architectural details, furnished abundantly with beautiful objects and friends of my own choosing. But I never talked about my roots with anyone, not even my most intimate friends. Not even the man who shared my bed. I had even suppressed my Boston accent, so no one would ever guess where I came from.

It's not that I forgot my family. Far from it. I thought if I worked hard enough, invested, saved smartly, and planned ahead, I'd be able to set aside enough money to get my family out of that awful house. But then, in 1984, my plan got an unexpected boost. My mother received an insurance settlement—$40,000. It was an unheard-of sum. My mother had never seen that many zeroes in her bank balance. By then I was in a position to chip in a matching amount from my own savings, and that would be all that was needed to break ground on a new home.

Now the long-awaited house was here, and I had the great joy of knowing I had a hand in its making. The past that had always haunted us could now be put to rest. The old shack, once emptied of its few useful possessions, could be knocked down and carted away. We could declare victory.

My story should have ended here. But how could I have thought that forty years could be undone in a single stroke? There was so much I didn't know. The tale of the old house and the untold chapters written in its rotting timbers were only just beginning to be told.

2

In the Company of Men

"Time to get up, Catrina!"

It was a frigid Sunday morning in late February, and my mother was rousing me early from a deep winter sleep so I could join my dad on an ice fishing trip. I was six years old, still sharing a bed with my nine-year-old brother Jerry, which had the practical purpose of keeping us both warm. Our simple bed, just a cotton-batting mattress on a metal frame, was a covered with several layers of blankets and old winter coats. There was no heat on the upper loft of our little house, so you could see your breath indoors on mornings like this. My two sisters shared another bed nearby. Marcia and Celia, fourteen and thirteen years old, were likewise buried under a stack of heavy quilts, covers, and coats.

The first thing I saw on winter mornings as I awoke in the dim lamplight, looking straight up as I lay on my back, was the unfinished ceiling, with menacing rusty nails piercing through the knotted planks. The ceiling was just a thin layer of wood separating us from the pile of snow on the roof. On mornings like this, a ring of frost formed a perfect white circle around the base of each nail, creating a constellation of glittering snowy stars in uneven rows between the rafters.

My mother had no bed, only a dusty quilt on the floor between her children's beds. She who worked harder than anyone, who deserved a bed most, had none, always giving up what she had for her children. She was always up before everyone else to stoke the coal-burning stove downstairs. She coaxed me out of bed, helping me into my clothes, one shivering limb at a time, buttoning up my flannel shirt and my favorite aqua-blue corduroy pants, and tying my well-worn brown oxford shoes.

Stepping down from the bed onto the floor, I had to be careful not to tip the pee-can under the bed. That's what we called the makeshift chamber pot my mother had fashioned from a large cylindrical tin can, the 48-ounce size, its top lid removed with a lever-type manual can opener, leaving a jagged edge of torn metal around the top rim. It was a handy thing to have if you needed to pee in the middle of the night, and just couldn't get to the outhouse in time. It took some skill, though, to hover over it and never sit down, with its sharp edges perilously close to one's delicate bottom.

Later I would discover there was an edible nut called a pecan. I pronounced the word the same way as my chamber pot—pee-can. I couldn't understand why anyone would name a food after something you would pee in.

I followed my mother down the rough creaking steps to the lower level. A cloud of cigarette smoke laced with the smell of burned coffee permeated the room. My father sat alone at the table wearing his winter jacket, a scratchy woolen in a dull red-and-gray plaid. The stove never threw off quite enough heat to warm even the downstairs space, a single open room with drafty windows on the southern and western walls, so we all wore coats indoors in the winter.

My father was a tall, ruggedly built man in his early fifties, with angular Italian features, but his hair was already well grizzled and nearly white. As far back as I can remember, he always seemed very old to me, with short white bristles poking through his pointed chin.

He had lost quite a few teeth and could never afford dentures, so he rarely smiled, and he had a shy tendency to keep his head down.

"Toots, can you top me off again?" he asked, extending his milk-glass coffee cup to his wife, a cigarette dangling from the edge of his mouth.

My mother dutifully filled his cup from the stove-top percolator, which he lightened with a touch of Carnation evaporated milk in the red-and-white can, with two triangular holes punched out on top. The tabletop radio was on with the volume turned down low, tuned to the local WMRC radio station in Milford, and Anita Bryant was crooning the mawkish chorus of her latest song:

> *Paper roses, paper roses, oh, how real those roses seem to be.*
> *But they are just imitation, like your imitation love for me.*

My mother was softly humming along. She was thirteen years younger than her husband and seemed, unlike my father, always very young. The way she wore her hair, short and straight and tucked behind her ears, gave her a girlish appearance. She did nothing to alter her natural features—a face with nothing to hide. Her eyebrows were unplucked, her full mouth was unpainted, and her fine bisque-colored skin and dark hair had a natural oily sheen, setting off the startling hazel green of her eyes.

Perpetually in motion, adding wood to the fire, scraping the blackened toast before smearing it with margarine, she whirled between stove and utility sink and the small Coldspot refrigerator, somehow finding a spare moment to help me with my rubber boots, the kind that fit over my shoes, before shooing me outside to use the outhouse.

A rush of icy air flooded the house and flakes of loose snow blew in, so I quickly shut the door behind me. The outhouse was discreetly set back and out of sight, framed by two tall pines on the edge of the woods. The narrow path was neatly shoveled through a foot of snow; and my mother had sprinkled the path with cinders from the stove to make it less slippery. As the wind whipped through my hair, I dreaded the prospect of sitting on that cold linoleum-covered two-seater, my bare bottom shivering over the open pit of human waste below.

I always tore off exactly four sheets of toilet paper—folded once, then folded again—just as my mother taught me. Fifty years later, I would still be tearing off no more than four sheets at a time.

I was finished quickly and ran back to the house, breathless and pink-cheeked. My mother was waiting with a rank gray washcloth to scrub my face and hands before I sat at the table. Still wearing my coat and boots, I bit into my crisp black toast and gulped my milk while my mother did my hair, first unraveling my long red braids. The braids made my otherwise straight hair form tightly undulating waves down my back. My mother combed out the knots and carefully braided my hair afresh for the day, in a complex style with two braids close to the crown of my head that pulled the hair up and away from my face. Those two tight braids were then woven into thick longer braids that trailed down my back.

She was snapping the elastic bands around the ends of my braids when we heard my father's friend Rocky honking his horn outside. Rocky was a pleasant, soft-spoken man, with a face so bony, it was millimeters away from being a bare skull. My mother tugged on my scratchy wool hat and mittens and wrapped a scarf around my mouth and neck before sending me running out the door and through the white plumes of exhaust smoke from Rocky's car. I climbed into the back seat, slamming the heavy door shut; Dad and his friend were already settled in the front.

Dad often took me along with him to places that were the province of men, sometimes with my brother Jerry, but just as often I was the lone girl child tagging along. As soon as I was old enough to keep up with my father without tiring, often trekking hours at a time through rough, wooded terrain, I happily joined him on his hunting and fishing trips with his friends, mostly men like Rocky, old friends from his factory days. Dad had a more solitary job now, working as a cemetery caretaker and handyman for the St. Mary's Parish, but somehow he remained connected to a community of men whose bonds were forged like molten steel decades before I was born.

Dad never spoke to me very much on these outings. I think that was his way of raising me—no words, no explanations. I was simply expected to watch, listen and learn.

As Rocky drove off over the frozen dirt driveway, I made a point of being so quiet in the back seat, the two men could easily forget I was there. It was a kind of game. I practiced intense silence, crafting it to a fine art. You could almost hear the ringing of my silence. Meanwhile I was wide-eyed and open-eared, taking in everything.

A large gathering of men had already assembled when we arrived at the lake, at least two dozen, all of them sons of Italian immigrants, solid broad-shouldered men who made their living by the sweat of their necks. I was amazed by the sight of the huge bonfire they had built in the middle of the frozen lake. I couldn't figure out why it didn't melt the ice. And I was the only girl among them, playfully sliding on the ice in my rubber boots. As they boiled pots of coffee in speckled enamel coffeepots and roasted sweet Italian sausages on sticks over the fire, laughing and talking among themselves, I skidded on the ice around them in wide circles, around and around, trying to pick out phrases from the clatter, which I snatched like brass rings from a merry-go-round:

"It wasn't like that in the Old Country" … "Man, was she built. I mean, *built*."…"Nobody can sing like Mario Lanza. Am I right? Am I right?"

My father's usual contribution to these conversations was simply to shrug and punctuate everyone else's sentences with an "eh" and a knowing expression.

While some tended the fire, singing "Oj Marí, oj Marí," that old Neapolitan song that sounded to my ears like "Weigh Marie, Weigh Marie," others were busy cutting a massive hole in the ice with an impressive-looking drill that was taller than I was. These men knew the value of good tools, handling them with great reverence. I watched as they hoisted a disk of ice from the lake's surface, like a thick manhole cover, revealing the water below looking black and almost oily under a steel gray sky.

"Oj Marí, oj Marí, Quanta suonno ca perdo pe' te..."

My mother had no comparable gatherings with women; she seemed tethered to the house and her chores, isolated, with only her children to talk to. But somehow my father, silent and reclusive in so many ways, remained connected to the outside world and welcome in the company of male friends. Why they accepted me, the lone girl among them, I really don't know.

The men didn't seem to pay much attention to me, but I was observing them with a watchful eye. I loved the way men moved, so free in the world, so comfortable in their own bodies. I wanted to be like that. I liked the way men stood solidly on the ground, with their feet planted wide apart, while women in those days seemed to stand and sit with their knees pressed tightly together, making small minimal gestures, as if they were trying to take up as little space as possible.

I loved the way the men smelled, an honest smell, a mixture of motor oil and cigarettes. Their strong, heavy hands were at my eye level, and I could detect the woody aroma of tobacco on their fingers, drawing my eyes upward to the perpetual halo of cigarette smoke around their heads. I was fascinated by how smoking created an instant bond among men. My father could always approach any man on any street, even men of color—surprising to me, in that era—and casually ask for a match for his cigarette.

"Hey, Mack, gotta light?" my father would say, barking like a tough guy from a 1940s movie. And then suddenly, two strangers would be standing impossibly close to one another in an intimate ritual, their faces both lit dramatically by the fire passing between their cupped hands.

I wanted to be like that, and do everything men did. I learned by watching how to bait a fishhook, threading it through a fat night crawler or a wiggling crayfish, without flinching or making a face, and how to attach a red-and-white plastic bobber at the right place on a fishing line. I fearlessly handled daddy-longlegs spiders and green grasshoppers and Japanese beetles that exuded brown sap onto my fingers, and furry-legged creatures of all kinds, and I knew how to run and climb and jump like a boy, without the slightest hint of self-consciousness or any attempt at feminine grace. But I wanted to know more. I wanted to be conversant in tools and gears, things that moved and made noise and changed the world around them, not curtains and doilies and things that stood still.

I think I always wanted to *be* a man, if truth be told. I don't mean I wanted to take the physical form of a man. I just wanted to live a man's life. To be free to move and stretch and yawn and scratch my belly, and never be told to sit like a lady. To walk down any street as if I owned it. To be admired for strength, never praised for softness and delicacy. Never to be told to smile and look pretty, for no apparent reason at all.

It was perhaps a bad beginning for me, to be circulating in the world of men, spending more time with brothers than sisters, father than mother. To my detriment, no one ever taught me how to use femininity as a weapon, or to practice the fine art of helpless charm, which might have served me well in later years. Instead, I was simply convinced I could, and should, do anything my male counterparts did. More often than not, it only got me into confusing confrontations. Because I was always forgetful of the fact that I was carrying around with me the body of a little red-haired girl in freckles and braids, or later, that of a blossoming young woman—all very poor advertising for the thoughts and ambitions percolating within.

3

THE NEWS

1961

"If it's a boy, we'll call him Stephen—after my fathuh."

Dad was at the head of the table, grinning sheepishly and looking quite pleased with himself, as my sisters and brother sat in stunned silence, taking in the surprising news. We had just finished supper. I was only six years old, and I was not entirely clear on what was happening. Did they say Ma was expecting? Expecting what?

Ma was quietly clearing the table, wearing the faintest smile on the corner of her lips, as she scraped the remains of each plate into the compost can in the sink. She paused behind me as she reached over my shoulder for my plate, bending down until her face was close to my ear, and said softly, "Catrina—you're not going to be the baby of the family anymore!"

My mouth fell open and my eyes grew wide. Breaking the silence, I blurted out, "I'm going to be a big sister!" The family erupted in laughter.

There was a rare celebratory feeling in the air. Ma handed her husband a new box of Oreos, and he ripped off the top and tore open a fresh stack of cookies, spilling them out onto the table, reserving one to pop whole into his mouth, while his children greedily snapped up the rest. Ma refilled our glasses with a rare second serving of milk, but for her husband, she poured a jigger of his own homemade chokecherry wine from a glass gallon jug, a sweet opaque purple liquid, and left the open jug on the table, while she finished attending to the dishes.

It was an unseasonably warm evening in April, and the door was left open, allowing the fresh night air to rattle the loose-fitting wooden screen door. My head was rattling, too, with dozens of questions.

I hopped off my chair and began tugging my mother's hand, pulling her away to the door. "I have to pee! Come with me, Ma! Come with me!"

I always pretended I was afraid of the dark and didn't want to venture out alone to the outhouse at night, but I really just wanted my mother's company. Some of my favorite childhood moments were late-night talks with my mother in the outhouse. They were wonderfully intimate times. I had her all to myself, sitting beside her in the unlit privy, feeling her warm bare thigh touching mine. In a house that had no private spaces, this was my one quiet place to talk with my mother.

"But where is the baby now?"

"In my tummy, darling."

"But *how* did the baby get in your tummy? *How?*"

"Well…when two people get married, they can make babies."

"But *how?* Can you have a baby the same day you get married? Can you have a baby the next day? The day after?"

"It's usually, oh, about a year after you get married."

"But why does it take so long? Can anyone make babies? Can boys make babies? Can Grandma make babies?"

I could hear her gently sigh at my endless questions. I was too young to understand how bone-tired she always was, but even in the dim moonlight that poured through the tiny outhouse window, I could see she was closing her eyes.

In the evenings, she often closed her eyes and appeared to be sleeping in a wooden kitchen chair by the table until I tugged at her arm and asked, "Are you awake? Are you awake?"

Her answer was always the same.

"Just resting my eyes, dear. Just resting my eyes."

In the months before Stephen was born, I suddenly found a new calling in life. I was a little mother in training, fulfilling a self-imposed regimen of daily caregiving rituals, using my rubber baby doll—one of the few toys I owned—as my surrogate baby brother. When the real baby arrived, I would be ready.

I named the doll Stephen. Its molded head had thin grooves and a wash of light brown paint where its hair would be. Its blue eyes with stiff nylon lashes opened and shut. It had a yellow flannel diaper with blue scalloped edges, and a matching hooded jacket. I became expert at joining the three points of the triangular diaper and fastening them with a safety pin at the belly. How confusing it would be to see the rectangular gauzy diapers my mother would later use on baby Stephen, with safety pins on the sides instead of in the front.

Every day I fed water to my doll with a plastic baby bottle, which fit in an opening in between the doll's lips, and the liquid flowed out through a tiny hole in its pink bottom. I then dutifully hung the wet diaper with a wooden pin on the clothesline outside, just as my mother had done with all the diapers she had washed by hand for each of her five children. The tiny diaper hung between the ragged towels and bed sheets my mother had pinned on the clothesline, a cotton rope strung between two trees, which she propped up with a long forked stick to keep it from sagging. I used to love walking inside the folds of the hanging bed sheets, a white cotton cathedral, smelling their sweet wind-washed fragrance.

Stephen was born on October 31, 1961. A Halloween baby.

The day he came home, I was playing outside with Jerry, kicking the fallen leaves into piles and taking turns jumping on them, when we saw Dad pull into the driveway. He was driving a borrowed car, a shiny black Plymouth with voluptuous curves and chrome. Ma was sitting in the front seat, wearing a woolen coat and a flowered kerchief tied under her chin, and holding a pale flannel bundle in her arms.

I thought it was *my* baby Stephen that had come home—the one I was practicing for. I honestly had no idea my mother figured into this more than I did.

How tiny Stephen was when I first held him. His fingers sprouted like daisy petals from the ends of his flannel sleeves.

4

SUMMER

1963

A barefoot girl, eight years old, ties her long red braids in a knot on top of her head. The sun beats down.

Wearing only her cotton slip, and her little brother his cotton briefs, dressed in their favorite sun suits, they go sliding down a shallow ditch that straddles the foot-worn path to the house. The drought-hardened earth is gently sloped, and the dust is slicker than silk—all the makings of a perfect slide! Dust rises in golden clouds amid squeals of bright laughter.

Looking back on those two children through the flattering, softening veils of years, it's hard to believe I was once that skinny, sunburnt girl. Is it she? Is it I? It's hard to know what voice to use to tell my own story.

&ONLINE;

"Again!" cried Stephen, the gleeful toddler, covered with pale dust from head to toe like a gilded statue. There was no stopping him from scrambling back to the top of the ditch, over and over, and skidding down the slope on his bottom. "Again! Again!"

It was late August, a blazing summer day. Our hair and faces were tinted from the sun, and our makeshift playground was ours alone.

These were the last precious days to savor before school started; I would soon be going into the fourth grade. My big brother Jerry would be entering the sixth grade. Jerry was off somewhere for the day, no doubt getting in some serious fishing before the school bells rang, hooking horned pout and kivers along the Charles River.

My sisters Marcia and Celia, when they weren't quarreling over something ridiculous and yanking each other's banana curls, spent hours seeking cool shade in the woods that bordered our home. There were lovely beaten paths to the old granite quarries, lined with ferns and moss, lady's slippers, and milky Indian pipes. Hard to believe these quiet woods were once teeming with thousands of stone cutters, mining the prized pink granite that Milford was once famous for. The quarries had all gone dormant now, silent and overgrown with tall pines, although if you dug into the soft mossy earth near the quarry holes, you might still find a rusted gear or a railroad spike.

My sisters liked to gather wild flowers and later press them flat between sheets of waxed paper, tucked in the pages of a heavy book. Other times they gathered sassafras bark, which made a lovely sweet tea, or picked little white mushrooms with red caps that were delicate and delicious. They even snapped tree mushrooms from the bark of the tall pines, and my mother would slice them and dry them in the sun on a great wooden breadboard.

Ma spent these late summer days tending the vegetable gardens and putting up everything she could in Ball jars for the winter. She had a small potbelly stove that she kept outdoors, stoking it red-hot to boil the canning jars in a large blue-and-white speckled lobster pot. That kind of work was too hot to do indoors in summer.

Dad was at work at St. Mary's Cemetery, a lonely caretaker, tending acres of sunburnt lawn all day, often coming home with his arms loaded with flowerpots, vases and baskets he salvaged from grave sites after mourners had thrown them away. We had towering stacks of clay flower pots in every conceivable size, hundreds of them, piled up neatly in a corner of our yard, more than we could ever possibly use in a lifetime. Each one a remembrance once left on a grave.

Sometimes he came home with small animals and birds, too, wild creatures we adopted as pets. The cemetery where he worked was bordered by woods, and my father had an eerie ability to coax wild things out from the safety of the undergrowth. A pair of chipmunks once stepped right into his hands, and he brought them home in his deep jacket pockets. We kept them outdoors in a pair of threshing crates, fastened together to form a cage, and returned them to the wild just before the winter came.

Another time he brought home a small brown sparrow perched on his finger. The bird was allowed to fly around freely inside the house, resting on the indoor clothesline my mother had strung from the ceiling near the stove. Whatever happened to its droppings, I never knew or asked. There was even a friendly raccoon that roamed around the yard outside the house, scratching around on the roof at night, and happily taking his daily meals from my father's hands.

One never knew what to expect from my father when he came home. Like the animals he felt so at home with, he had a wild, unpredictable quality—calm and docile one minute, ferocious the next. That's why there was always an easy, weekday lightness, a playfulness in the air that didn't exist when Dad was around. There was no one to boss us, or tell us we couldn't play in the dirt in our underwear.

I loved being outdoors in the summer. Our square acre of land was surrounded by skunk cabbage and swampland, a magnet for croaking frogs, snapping turtles, pheasants, and foxes, and, in the evenings, fluttering bats. As a child, I thought it was a place of abundance, crammed with natural beauty in every corner. A place to make mud-pies from the most lovely ingredients—hard green grapes clustered in broad leaves with curly tendrils; delicate Queen Anne's lace to form doilies around the edges; milkweed pods shaped like paisleys, with silky feathers inside; velvety mosses, the most beautiful shade of green; and jewel-like purple-black elderberries. Our house was not much to look at, but I thought the land around it was a Garden of Eden.

On this lazy August day, when the sun got too hot and the dust kicked up from our slide had turned to muddy grit on my neck, I said, "Stevie, let's get out of the sun for a while. I'll make Kool-Aid!"

His face brightened. I took his hand and led him down to the spring-fed well, a round cluster of mossy stones topped with a cast-iron pump. It took all my strength to crank water into a galvanized metal pail. I splashed some onto my face and neck, and then pressed my chilled wet hands around my brother's face to cool him. My hands around his face formed the shape of a heart, and I held them there for a moment, as he smiled up at me. How I loved that boy.

After helping him rinse his own face and hands from the pail, I dumped the dirty water on the wild asparagus patch, already gone to seed and towering over my head with delicate feathery branches. After a few quick splashes of water to rinse out the pail, I pumped some more of that deliciously cold, mineral-laden water to bring to the house.

We didn't have running water in the house any more. An underground pipe once carried water from the well to the old utility sink in the house, but one deep freeze was all it took for the pipe to burst and crack. My father, who had laid the pipe when he built the house, never got around to fixing it, so now water had to be carried to the house by hand.

Carrying water in pails was just something you got used to after a while. A person can get used to almost anything.

Walking up the dirt path, I squinted in the sun and saw Ma out in the vegetable gardens, bent over from the waist, weeding the tomatoes. Her pale cotton dress was bleached nearly white from the sun. She was born and raised on a farm, and she had a special talent for making things grow. It was in her blood. My father did, too. Between the two of them, the yard was ablaze in flowers—roses, lupines, day lilies, daffodils, jonquils, tulips, and my favorite, the delicate bearded irises, not to mention all the blossoming fruit trees—plum, peach, apple, cherry, quince, and pear. Even in the winter, our drafty windows bloomed with red geraniums, surrounded by shallow wooden boxes of tomato seedlings with their tiny yellow blossoms, ready to plant in the spring.

I was already in the house, swirling a packet of purple Kool-Aid powder in a water-filled jelly jar, when Ma burst in through the ragged screen door, her bounty wrapped in her kitchen apron—huge tomatoes with deep brown scars, the last of the Swiss chard, wax beans, crooked carrots, a few parched ears of corn, and zucchini squash that were left to grow to gargantuan proportions.

In summer, we ate.

I loved my mother's summer perfume, a heady aroma of pungent tomato plants, earth, and sweat. Her thick body was hardened from years of wielding shovels, axes and hoes, and her large sagging breasts hung low in her shirtwaist dress. I loved her sensual girth, and the secure feeling of perching on her ample lap, as solid as sitting on oak. How proud I felt the first time I was big enough to reach all the way around my mother's wide waist so that my fingertips touched together behind her back.

Ma wiped the sweat from her face with her crumpled apron and set to work making tomato and mayonnaise sandwiches on coarse Italian bread. I loved to watch her hands as she worked, strong, thick, and leathery, more like a man's than a woman's hands, with dark earth permanently etched under her fingernails no matter how hard she scrubbed them. She was worn and weathered all over, like the old apple tree, bearing all the marks of too many harvests, too many children, too much caring and tending for others, but never for herself—always saving the best for her husband and children, while sopping her bread with gravy from the frying pan for her supper.

ℰℛ

Every day at noon, Ma stopped to make her husband a thermos of hot coffee, sandwiches wrapped in Cut-Rite waxed paper, and a slice of her homemade gingerbread cake. She put them in a brown paper bag, and delivered the fresh lunch to her husband at the small garage where he took his midday break at St. Mary's Cemetery. I never knew why he didn't just bring his own lunch with him in the morning. Was it a labor of love for my mother to deliver lunch to my father, or was it a forced march, dictated by a demanding husband? I was too little to know.

When I was younger, before Stephen was born, I used to take the daily lunch-walk with her. She never talked much on those walks, but I loved to hear the clicking of her thick heels on the pavement as we walked. It was one of my favorite sounds. She had small metal caps, shaped like eyebrows, nailed to the heels of her shoes, to make them last longer, and the effect was like castanets.

The cemetery was remarkably beautiful in summer, full of shady walking paths and tranquil ponds studded with water lilies. My mother would point out the painted turtles poking their heads out of the water, or sunning themselves on the lily pads, while silver-gray squirrels darted among the gravestones. So much teeming life in a place reserved for death.

Nowadays Ma took the cemetery walk alone and left little Stephen in my capable hands. I liked taking my mother's place, washing and feeding and changing my baby brother, presenting my mother with a sparkling clean boy with wet, neatly parted hair when she returned from her walk.

I was at a halfway age, wanting to be a very grownup big sister for my little brother, but still wanting to be my mother's little girl, relishing the rare moments of her attention when she wasn't absorbed in the daily, incessant, backbreaking labor of a farmer.

5

THE NEW NEIGHBORS

There was a small vacant patch of land on one of the four corners of our property that, for some reason, did not belong to us. As if someone had snipped away a corner of our land to make a random patch for a quilt, it was a tiny square lot that fronted on Prairie Street, and had always been an insignificant tangle of brambles and weeds that blended into the abundant raspberry bushes my father had planted all around its edges.

One warm summer day, we saw a clearing where the overgrown brambles had been, and shortly after that, a pair of house trailers miraculously appeared, still sitting on their tiny wheels propped up on cinder blocks. I had never seen anything like them before; I thought they were quite beautiful. I certainly had no idea that mobile homes were modest dwellings. Compared to my drab little house, these trailers were gleaming, sleek and modern, with two-toned aluminum exteriors: one of them half pink and half white, and the other red and white.

"Oh, those trailers are mah-vels of modern engineering," Marcia informed her younger siblings. "They have compact little kitchens and bathrooms, and ingenious storage spaces. They're like the house of the future!"

To me, they were simply mysterious and new.

We saw a woman had moved into the pink trailer with her daughters, one of them about my age—maybe six or seven years old. The other two daughters were taller, in their teens or possibly older. We started to see them working outside together, turning the long-vacant lot into a pretty suburban lawn.

It never occurred to my parents to greet their new neighbors with a friendly cup of coffee or a bouquet of flowers from our yard. Instead they seemed to eye the newcomers suspiciously, seeing them as invaders, threatening their long-cherished privacy. They were touching our sacred perimeter, the land my parents so lovingly planted and tended. The land was, in fact, where my family actually lived, the place they considered home. The house was almost incidental. The land was where my parents decorated and redecorated year after year, carpeted the ground with soft flower beds, furnished and draped it with lovely growing things. On the rare occasions when relatives came to visit, my father proudly showed them his gardens, never his house. The land was our one and most precious holding.

And now strangers were molesting it. What were these people doing here?

Curious to know more, I crawled on my stomach to the edge of the new neighbors' yard, making my way through a natural tunnel formed at the base of the mature raspberry bushes, and peered through the weeds at the new neighbors. I saw a woman I guessed to be about my mother's age, probably in her early forties, pushing with all her strength against a heavy garden roller to flatten the bare earth, making it ready for planting grass seed. Her hair was an unnatural shade of blond, but she looked very trim and tanned, wearing a one-piece red bathing suit as she labored in the sun. I had never seen anyone wear a bathing suit, and the concept of deliberately encouraging a suntan was beyond the realm of my experience.

It soon became a daily habit for me to spy on our new neighbors this way; it was my secret window on the outside world. The tunnel I had blazed grew wider and flatter with every passing, and the area that became my observation deck grew big enough to accommodate two children. Over time I collected clumps of velvety green moss from the nearby woods, and used it to carpet the bare ground in my hiding place, making it softer to lie upon. I left a border of tall grass to shield me from the neighbors' view, which I could draw aside like drapes at will. It was more than a secret hiding place; it was a room of my own.

It wasn't long before the little girl next door noticed me, and I instinctively held my finger up to my lips as if to say, "Shh! Don't give me away!" She looked over her shoulder, and then scurried over to my hiding place.

"Whatcha' doing?" she asked, eagerly crawling toward me.

"I'm making a secret house!" I replied. "Don't tell anyone!"

The little girl seemed to enjoy visiting my hiding place as much as I did. I was happy to have a new friend my own age—and a place to which I could invite a friend for the first time. We met there frequently as mid-summer melded into August, and we occasionally brought dolls to play with, or simply lay on our backs gorging ourselves on sweet raspberries that were ripening over our heads. But I urged her not to tell anyone about our friendship. My father wouldn't have liked it, I told her, but I couldn't say why.

Meanwhile my father's animosity toward the new neighbors was simmering like a cast-iron kettle, slowly gathering heat. That's because the tiny trailer park seemed to be quietly expanding, as the neighbors gradually cleared more and more brush each day. The new neighbors were pushing beyond their legal border, claiming bits of our land as theirs—or so my father believed.

I don't know if my father ever talked with the neighbors to present his grievances, or if he ever verified his claim at the Town Hall. But he had made up his mind. As far as he was concerned, the neighbors were nothing but land thieves, and he was not going to let them get away with it.

Dad came home from work one evening and saw his neighbors noisily mowing down yet another row of tall grass at the border between our properties, even cutting into our abundant raspberry bushes. That was it. The simmering pot had boiled over.

Dad burst in the door, just as Ma was laying food on the table, and he was fuming.

"Son of a bitch of a bastard! Son of a bitch of a bastard!"

His eyes were wild. He pulled down his shotgun from the highest shelf, along with the cardboard box of Remington buckshot shells. He snatched the last handful of the red paper-wrapped shells and stuffed them in his pants pocket, tossing the empty box aside.

"Jerry—no!" my mother said, but she quickly covered her mouth and held her tongue after that. There was no reasoning with him at a time like this. Dad tucked the rifle under his arm, grabbed a wooden chair from the kitchen table, and headed out to the sprawling vegetable gardens that bordered the neighbors' property.

Ma and I watched anxiously through an upstairs window as my father strode quickly and deliberately through the tall rows of tomato plants. He slapped his chair down in the middle of the garden, where the squash and cucumber vines were low and afforded a clear view. He sat down, facing the trailers, with his gun plainly visible in his hands. The stock was resting on his lap, and the barrel was pointed directly at the trailers. He just remained there, unmoving, in a field the size of a parking lot, a lone man staring down his neighbors, as if challenging them to a showdown.

"Oh no. Oh no. Oh no," I muttered repeatedly, to the rhythm of my pounding heart. "Please don't shoot anyone," I said to myself, as my mother peered over my shoulder. I was terrified to see my father out there, an angry man with a gun. What if someone reported him to the police? Would he take aim at them, too? And what if the neighbors came out of their trailers and called his bluff? What if they had guns? Would he have dared to pull the trigger?

Thankfully I never had to find out. No one ever emerged from the trailers to confront him. No one ever tested his will. He eventually tired and returned to the house, but he took the same position day after day in the late afternoon, poised with his loaded shotgun in hand, guarding his property until darkness fell.

My father eventually gave up his daily sentinel when he saw no further encroachments on our property.

"I showed them who's who!" he boasted, practically thumping his chest, certain his actions were successful. He had done the right thing. He was being a man, holding his ground, protecting his vital interests.

As if to confirm his assessment, the neighbors erected a tall stockade fence around their land, as if to declare the demarcation permanent. We couldn't see them. They couldn't see us.

I never went back to my secret crawl space, and when school started, the little girl and I never spoke. Not that year, or the next, or all the years after that. Even as children, she and I had quietly taken sides, each of us branding the other an enemy, carrying on our parents' silent feud as a poison inheritance. Even though we walked the same path to school each day, often just a few steps ahead or behind each other, we never exchanged a word.

ℰℭ

Decades later, I would see the girl again at a fortieth high school reunion party. It was at one of those typical roadside family restaurants, close enough to our home town of Milford and affordable enough to accommodate a range of income levels.

Surveying the dining tables for an empty seat, I saw an empty spot next to my former neighbor, and I caught her eye.

"Have a seat," she said without hesitation.

The ice was broken quickly. We traded notes on marriages, children, careers. She was a registered nurse, I learned between forkfuls of lukewarm pasta. We commiserated on the high cost of college tuition, and made small talk until our plates were cleared. And then I asked her.

"Do you remember—how we used to meet on the borderline between our yards?"

"I do," she said. "We were best buddies for a while."

"Did you know, I used to be so jealous of your pink trailer. I thought it was adorable. I really wanted to come inside."

She looked down. "Do you know why we moved there?"

"No...." I said, somewhat puzzled by the question.

"Before we moved there, we used to live in a big beautiful house. My father was a musician—very brilliant. He trained at Juilliard. But...."

She paused to take a gulp of wine. "He had a problem. He'd get into these moods. And when he drank, he was ugly. Really abusive.

"My mother decided she'd had enough. Late one night, as she was packing to leave, he pulled a gun on her. She was afraid he was going to kill her, kill all of us. She called the police, who tried to defuse the situation. The police stood by as she moved her things to the waiting truck, and the next thing I know, they're waking me up and carrying me out the door. That's how we ended up in that little trailer. It was all my mother could afford. Quite a let-down, considering where we came from."

"I'm stunned," I said. "I had no idea."

I was numb. All those years, I thought of my neighbors as the privileged ones. The people in the pretty pink trailer. The glamourous mother with the suntan and the red bathing suit. But despite my family's circumstances, I had never suffered what they did. I was never torn from my home. I was never threatened or abused by either of my parents. I was never anything but loved.

And what did her mother think, so many years ago, when she saw my father with a shotgun? Here was a woman already threatened with one man's gun, now staring down the barrel of another.

6

THE PLAYING FIELD

November 1963

It didn't take me long to realize I was not Miss Casey's favorite student. Her fourth-grade class at the old Plains Elementary School was arranged in a perfect square grid of six rows of six desks, arranged according to what she thought was the child's IQ. The one she anointed as the smartest kid sat in row one, seat one. And those sitting in the sixth row had a constant cruel reminder that Miss Casey didn't expect very much of them.

I sat in the first row, fifth seat, and if Miss Casey had her way, I would probably have been sitting out in the hall. She didn't like me one bit. The reasons for her distaste were never entirely clear. Was it my family, and how we lived? Did she know?

Was it because we were Italian? Few today can appreciate the simmering tension that once existed between Irish and Italians, one wave of immigrants on the heels of the other, all vying for the same low-paying jobs. Milford was like an artist's study for a larger canvas, a miniature portrait of immigration in America, with each group unsympathetic to the shared plight of the next, only to end up in an orgy of intermarriage, sealed and sanctioned by a common religion.

Or was it that I never smiled appreciatively at Miss Casey's jokes? She made pitiful attempts to endear herself to her class by telling tired old jokes, but her delivery was so flat, I honestly could never tell when she was delivering the punch line. Singling me out for my blank expression, she sneered, "You could at least *smile*, Catherine!"

For whatever reason, Miss Casey took every opportunity to belittle me in front of my classmates. Every morning she went up and down the aisles like a drill sergeant, inspecting each child, expecting us to have a fresh handkerchief and clean fingernails every morning. It was hard for me to keep my hands clean, living in a house without running water, and to make it worse, I loved throwing my whole body into outdoor games. I played rough, like a boy, running and jumping and kicking balls and swinging baseball bats with abandon, never thinking twice about sliding into first base. My hands and fingernails were never clean, and Miss Casey let everyone know it.

"Filthy again!" she snarled, pointing at the dirt on my hands with her perfectly manicured fingers. "Here, here, and here!" Miss Casey kept her own fingernails polished with a blood-red lacquer, but only painted her nails as far as the quick, so the clean white nail tips would show. She was a paragon of clean fingernails.

Did she know that I was a girl who never had the luxury of a hot bath or a shower? If she did, it was certainly not kind of her to call me out that way.

It was not kind.

My classmates seemed much more forgiving. They never seemed to comment on my dirty fingernails, and never made me feel I was a lesser person than they. It was a small town; the parents knew which families were better off than others, and if their children knew the extent of my family's poverty, most were good enough to keep it to themselves. The one exception was Barry, an older boy in my sister Marcia's high school class. He lived near the corner of my street, and enjoyed sitting on his brick steps and taunting me when I passed. "M'enghi, M'enghi, mangy Marenghi," he jeered. "You don't even have a bah-h-hth-room!"

Somehow Barry was easy to ignore. Even as a little girl, I knew Barry was a bully and a thug, someone not to be given a second thought. My sisters told me he had once taken a chain saw to one of the ancient twin pine trees that stood as gateposts in front of the old high school, just for the sake of destroying something. What kind of person does that—cuts down a century-old tree—for fun? That's just the way he was. Even then, I would not have been surprised if you'd told me his life would end badly—and it did. He would be gruesomely murdered thirty years later, cut down by men of his own kind.

For the most part, school was a safe haven, a great equalizer, a place where I could be like everyone else. I could occupy the same kind of desk everyone else had, play in the same schoolyard, and read all the same textbooks.

Of course, my very first days of school were something of a culture shock. When I entered kindergarten in 1959, I quickly learned I did not have the same vocabulary other kids had. I didn't know the names of different rooms in a house—kitchen, living room, bedroom, den—because our house was not divided into rooms. I had never heard of fairy tales, like *Snow White* or *Jack and the Beanstalk*, stories other kids knew by heart, because my exhausted mother could barely keep her eyes open at the end of the day, let alone regale her children with bedtime stories.

I had never been to a movie, a restaurant, or a show of any kind. I didn't know what Chinese food was. I didn't know what was on TV, since we didn't have one that actually worked. After the annual airing of *The Wizard of Oz*, all the kids would come to school chattering about flying monkeys. I didn't know what they were talking about. I didn't know about Santa Claus or how he came down a chimney. I didn't have any Christmas presents to brag about. I didn't know about vacations, or beaches, or swimming pools; no one in my family had ever learned how to swim.

I didn't understand half the conversations I heard around me. It was as if I were from another planet, trying to circulate unnoticed among an alien race known as "everyone else." But I quickly picked up a valuable life skill—how to listen to conversations I didn't understand, never letting on what I did or didn't know, and if I listened long enough and hard enough, I would decipher just what I needed to get by.

I once saw a line of Canada geese, a mother followed by her fuzzy brown goslings, and at the end of the line was a full-grown mallard duck, about the same size as the goslings, trying to blend in as if it were part of the family. My childhood was like that. I did my best to blend in—to "pass"—all the while certain I was a different sort of creature that didn't belong. When girls came to school every Tuesday dressed in their "Bluebird" uniforms—the Bluebirds were the first step to becoming Camp Fire Girls—I found a way to get my hands on a used Bluebird costume and wore it to school on the same day as the others did, as if I were part of their troop. But I was never a Camp Fire Girl or a Girl Scout or part of any other group that required hosting meetings in my house. No one was ever allowed to see my house.

By the time I was in fourth grade, I had several friends in my class, although our friendships were confined to the schoolyard. I looked forward to reuniting with my friends at school each day.

Hopscotch was my favorite game, and my friends and I took great care to draw the most perfectly symmetrical hopscotch grid, laying out exquisitely straight lines with a stick in the dirt. For markers to toss into the squares, we used pieces of broken glass from old bottles, which were surprisingly easy to find in the schoolyard or on the walk to school. I saved the prettiest pieces of glass—emerald green, deep blue, amber, even lavender—and hoarded them in my school desk. My teacher was astonished one day to open my desk and find it overflowing with my glittering treasure. She quickly summoned the school janitor to dispose of the hazardous collection.

Sometimes, during our recess periods, I noticed an outline of a tall man, standing in the shade of the trees that surrounded the schoolyard, looking at us through the six-foot chain-link fence. His outline was familiar. I drew closer one day and saw that it was my father, watching me and my friends as we played. What was he doing there? Was he out on a work-related errand? There was a concrete company bordering the school; maybe he was picking up something he needed to lay a monument or a grave marker. I didn't know. When he realized I recognized him, he withdrew into the shadows, and I never saw him at the schoolyard fence again.

If I were any other child, I might have yelled to my friends, "Hey, look, it's my dad!" If he were any other father, he might have waved us over to greet him. Instead we seemed to share the same unspoken understanding. My life in the outside world and our private family life were two different countries, and the two should never be allowed to meet. I looked away and said nothing to my friends.

Our school days were punctuated with morning and afternoon recess periods, in addition to long lunch hours. I'm sure we spent more time outdoors than in. When we weren't playing hopscotch, or jacks, there was always double-Dutch jump rope; two girls skillfully swung two ropes simultaneously in opposite directions. As the ropes cracked rhythmically against the pavement, girls hopped to the rope-swingers' singing:

Two, four, six-eight-ten,
Two, four, six-eight-twenty,
Two, (pause, pause),
Thirty-two, (pause, pause),
Forty-two....

There was time to linger on the monkey bars, swinging on the metal pipes that left a distinctive iron smell on my hands, or just sitting on the upper rungs and daydreaming out loud. With one of my friends, Susan, I imagined fantastic inventions we would create together. I was particularly obsessed with the idea of building a time machine, something that could carry me off to a dazzling future where everything was easy, everything perfect, everything working the way it was supposed to.

I clamped onto the idea with a fervor. Thinking about time travel was my one precious luxury. I could imagine the future any way I wanted it to be.

I was convinced we could do it, we could figure out how to make a time machine, if we just concentrated hard enough. I drew pictures of elaborate contraptions with tangled masses of belts, pulleys, and gears. Susan and I even dreamed of starting a company to manufacture time machines, spitting them out on mass assembly lines, like the ones where so many of our parents worked, and she designed a corporate logo that fused the initials of our last names— P and M. Years later I would learn that Susan and I had both started companies around the same time, although our enterprises never crossed paths.

On a late-November Friday afternoon, Miss Casey asked everyone in her class to clean out our desks for the weekend. Arthur Martin, one of the new kids in the class, raised his hand to be excused to go to the boys' room. Not long after he left the classroom, descending the long wooden staircase to the basement, he must have quickly forgotten his reason for being there when he overheard the news come over the radio, blaring in the janitor's basement office.

Arthur came running back and burst into the classroom, breathlessly announcing the news:

"President Kennedy has been shot!"

Teachers soon were huddling in the hallway, while the classroom buzzed with excitement. The decision came quickly to send us all home. All over town, children began spilling into the streets, sent home early by bewildered teachers who didn't seem to know what to say.

My brother Jerry, whose sixth-grade class was two doors down the hall from mine, walked home with me, and we speculated on what happened to Kennedy on the way.

"I'll bet it's a Communist plot," I theorized, feeling very pleased with myself for sounding so serious and grown-up.

"I think Castro has something to do with this," Jerry suggested, not knowing he would soon not be alone in that theory.

"Or Khrushchev!" I countered. "It's the Iron Curtain!" I never quite understood what the Iron Curtain was, but it was a phrase I heard frequently in radio broadcasts, in public service announcements for Radio Free Europe. "The Iron Curtain isn't soundproof," the ads declared, a slogan that became as permanently embedded in my memory as "ring around the collar," or "things go better with Coke."

Our sisters Celia and Marcia, both students at Milford High School, would already be on their way home at this time of day. Dad had been home that week to work on the roof. He had recently elevated the roof on both sides, creating full shed dormers, to give us more headroom on the second level. Now he was laying a new sheet of tarpaper on the roof, folding it at the corners like bed sheets and nailing it down tightly, to seal it before winter. As Ma later told us, she went running outside, with Stephen in her arms, and called up frantically to her husband at the top of the ladder: "I just heard on the radio—JFK was killed!"

Rarely had any event brought our family together, but we now found ourselves all huddled around the TV set, hoping Dad could arrange the rabbit-ear antennas just right to make the picture emerge. Dad had a habit of tinkering with cast-off TVs that no one wanted, just to see if he could make them work, and usually we found ourselves staring at crackly salt-and-pepper patterns on dusty TV screens, saying hopefully, "Well, you can *almost* make out what the people look like!" Now we stared at the newest in a long line of second-hand TVs, mounted atop the large console of an earlier model, not getting much more than the sound of the news. The images would have to come later.

I knew my parents were no fans of John Kennedy, and I was curious to hear what they would say. Neither of my parents had voted for him. Mistrustful of wealthy men, my father had always voted for the socialist candidate, and his parents' generation leaned toward the anarchist party for similar reasons, the same party as one of Milford's more famous townsmen—Nicola Sacco, of Sacco and Vanzetti fame.

Even worse, the Kennedys were Irish, and nothing could be worse in my father's mind. I was too young to understand what my father had against the Irish. For the longest time, I honestly thought the word *Irish* was a profanity, just because of the way my father said it. And any time someone assumed I was Irish, just because

I had red hair, I quickly corrected them: "I'm the opposite of Irish. I'm Italian!"

For whatever reason, I had never heard a kind word said about a Kennedy.

But now something had changed. All the words were different, as if they were all talking about someone else. "Such a good man ... So handsome ... Poor Jackie ... How terrible to die so young ... Such a tragic loss ... A great man." I was surrounded by voices of genuine sorrow and grief.

Now my eight-year-old mind was completely confused. *What's this?* I wondered. *They never liked Kennedy. Shouldn't that mean they'd be pleased to hear he was dead?*

It was my first lesson in death: People speak differently of the dead than they do of the living.

7

THE HOUSE ON HAYWARD STREET

The first time I saw a clear image of JFK's funeral service was at Aunt Lizzie and Uncle Emilio's house. Lizzie, who had been christened Elisabetta, was my father's oldest sister, and she had used a home movie camera to record the JFK funeral as it first unfolded on TV. My whole family had come to watch a grainy movie of a TV program.

Going to that grand old Victorian house at 7 Hayward Street was always a special occasion, and we dressed up for it in our best clothes, as if we were going to church. It was, after all, the hallowed former home of my deceased Italian grandparents, Stefano and Celesta Marenghi, the place where they raised my father and his seven siblings. The house demanded respect.

Built in the late 1800s, the house was a massive three-story structure, sitting on a triple lot of land along with a detached double garage, a guest cottage, and a large barn. The house and all the out-buildings were a matching chocolate brown with white trim. The handsomely landscaped property, lush with vegetable gardens, grape arbors, and fruit trees, was contained within an imposing fieldstone wall, topped with rough spikes of white marble, protruding upward like a row of jagged teeth.

Grandpa Stefano had expanded the original house over the years: what started as a classic Victorian, with many small parlors on the first floor, was extended in the back to frame an enormous kitchen the entire width of the house. Everything happened in that kitchen. No one ever came in through the front door, with its classic columned porch and grand oak doors facing Hayward Street. You entered from the side of the house, from the immaculate concrete driveway, with its strip of neatly mowed grass down the middle, and then you stepped into the narrow side portico that fed directly into the kitchen.

That kitchen was the most important room of the house, the place where all visitors were received, where everyone ate great quantities of food, drank homemade wine, and watched the huge television set, always from the vantage point of the heavy oak kitchen table.

The table was always covered with clear plastic over a white linen tablecloth, edged with hand-tatted lace that my aunt had made. Nearby stood an old-fashioned wooden cupboard, painted white, with tiny flowered decals, a relic from the 1920s. There was a large, double-basin sink with a gingham skirt, and a giant gas stove with an exquisite glass coffee pot on the back burner, all surrounded by darkly varnished bead-board cabinets. It was really somewhat plain, but to me it was grand and elegant. I especially loved the expansive linoleum floor, with gleaming red and white checkerboard squares. How I would have loved to live in a house with a clean open floor like that, a place to move, to dance, to play—not like the cramped and cluttered quarters where I lived.

That house on Hayward Street was the heart of our social lives, a favorite destination on Saturday nights, when my older siblings and I made the half-mile walk in our awkwardly stiff and dressy clothes. I sometimes dabbed my face with my sister's face powder, making my pale skin even paler, and pilfered a few drops of her Evening in Paris perfume, a cheap dime-store variety sold in sapphire blue bottles.

All this primping and ill-fitting hand-me-down finery was to celebrate nothing more than a weekly family gathering at my aunt's and uncle's home, where we sipped hot tea and habitually watched my aunt's favorite television program, the *Lawrence Welk Show*.

So many times when I was sitting at my aunt's table, being shushed to silence whenever Lawrence Welk's Champagne Lady, Norma Zimmer, came on for her soprano solo, I wondered why my grandparents had bequeathed this grand house and property to Lizzie and Emilio, a childless couple, instead of giving it to my family, whose tiny house was bursting at the seams with children. Did they like their daughter Lizzie so much more than my father?

Aunt Lizzie was a heavy woman in her late fifties. Her luxuriant white hair, naturally streaked with faded blond, was pulled back from her dark square face in loose undulating waves and pinned neatly into a French twist in the back of her head. She had the face of a lioness. She always wore a brightly flowered cotton apron, the kind that covered the whole front of her dress, with large pockets at her hips.

Lizzie was a lifelong factory worker, starting at the age of nine, a little girl at a sewing machine, stitching together pieces of leather for men's shoes. Like my mother, she had the thick limbs and coarse hands of a manual laborer. Somehow her meager wages were enough to support her simple but comfortable life in her enormous home, which she presided over as the reigning family matriarch, with her frail and now retired husband Emilio at her side.

On this particular Saturday evening, we watched the home movie of JFK's funeral. A whirring projector on the kitchen table was trained toward a white screen hung in front of the TV cabinet. As always, we eagerly consumed cups of Red Rose tea with lots of milk and sugar, along with graham crackers, mint jelly, and cream cheese. While that was going on, Lizzie went shuffling through a coat closet for some clothes she could send home with us. She rarely let us go home empty-handed, and my family was long accustomed to accepting cast-offs.

Lizzie came back to the table with a dusty old pair of short black leather boots, possibly made by her own hands at the Milford Shoe Company.

"Look Jerry," she said to my father. "You could use these. They're *pahtly new!*"

My brother, across the table from me, caught my eye as we both wondered what word Lizzie meant to say. I was thinking, "Practically new. She meant to say 'practically new,' not 'partly new.'" And I knew my brother was thinking the same thing. It certainly wasn't Lizzie's fault she never went past fourth grade, entering the work force as a child to help support her family. It would be very mean to laugh at her for misspeaking. But that's exactly what Jerry and I always struggled not to do at Lizzie's strange word choices.

I could see the crack of a smile form dangerously at the corner of Jerry's mouth, as I tried mightily to suppress my own smile, in the face of a simple act of kindness, a gift of boots, while flashing on the projector screen was the blurry image from Kennedy's funeral procession—the riderless horse, with tall leather riding boots wedged backward in the stirrups—and history itself passing before my family's eyes.

8

THE GRADUATION PARTY

June 1964

Most of my father's generation had quit school at an early age, never finishing elementary school, let alone high school. Long before the passage of child labor laws, it was not unusual for the very young children of immigrants to help support their families with their wages, in factories or in fields. Now my father's first-born, my sister Marcia, was graduating from high school, and it was a proud and glorious occasion.

Her graduation day demanded a great celebration. Aunt Lizzie and Uncle Emilio had graciously offered the use of their house on Hayward Street for the party. My great-aunt Mary Speroni, my grandmother's younger sister, owner of the popular Speroni's restaurant in town, provided most of the food, including great aluminum trays of lasagna, and antipasto plates laden with provolone, salami, mortadella, sweet cherry peppers, and olives. Mary also furnished an astonishing rum custard cake with white frosting.

Both sides of my family were invited to Marcia's graduation party, and it was a new experience for my mother's side, the Thomases, to enter this house. It was no secret that my mother's parents never approved of her marrying an Italian. Now, for the first time, they were entering the Marenghi ancestral homestead.

I saw their cars line up, one by one, outside the great stone wall on Hayward Street. Not one of them dared to go into the house alone. Only after all of the Thomas-family cars had assembled, they entered together as a united front and stayed clustered together the entire evening.

The Thomases were certainly outnumbered. Throngs of Italian relatives poured in and spilled from the house into the yard. It was impossible to keep their names straight. At the bright center of it all was my sister Marcia, and she never looked prettier, blushing and smiling as cards and envelopes were pressed into her hands. Aunt Lizzie had bought us all new clothes for the occasion. Marcia was radiant in a black silk shantung dress, fitted closely at the waist with a softly pleated skirt, and a scoop neckline that attractively set off her curly reddish blonde hair.

I was very pleased with my own new dress, a frothy yellow dotted Swiss with a flower and grosgrain ribbon at the waist, and white patent-leather T-strap shoes. My proud father was wearing a gray suit and dress shoes—an amazing sight. I had never seen him in anything but his standard work clothes: a blue chambray shirt, black twill pants, and dark leather work boots. Even my mother shed her cotton shirtdress for a pretty flowered outfit, probably borrowed from one of her sisters.

The party ran well into the early hours of Saturday morning. I was just nine years old, and I had never stayed up so late. It seemed the entire town was there to celebrate, many of them men who smelled like cigars, grabbing my little hand and pressing coins or a crumpled dollar bill onto my palm and folding my fingers around it before dashing away. Others pinched my nose and then showed me their thumb protruding from their index and middle fingers—"Look, I got your nose!" I always thought that was a silly trick. Did anyone ever fall for that?

Even Uncle Albert, my father's only brother, made an unexpected appearance, to everyone's great surprise. He was not on speaking terms with my father. It had been that way as long as anyone could remember, and I never knew why. I don't recall ever seeing his face before or since that day, but he was instantly recognizable, tall and dark like my father, with the same elongated face, the same thick crop of wavy hair combed back from the face, and the same classic Roman nose.

Albert was surely there out of respect for his sister Lizzie and his Aunt Mary Speroni, not from any sense of obligation to my father. He sat apart, quietly smoking a cigarette by himself, sitting in near darkness in the front parlor, while the party raged and swelled in rooms all around him.

I would later learn that my family had hosted wakes in that front parlor, where coffins displayed the dead bodies of the dearly departed while neighbors poured in to offer condolences, long before funeral homes came into vogue. It was there that Albert would have paid his last respects to his father, Stefano, in 1940. And in 1952, it was where he last saw the body of his younger sister, my eponymous aunt Catherine, who died two years before I was born.

If Albert was quietly contemplating those sad events, I wouldn't have known. For my part, I was delighting in what I thought was surely the party of the century. I couldn't wait to come to another great gathering in this house.

In just five short months, I would have my wish.

November 1964

Everything seemed to be going downhill since that memorable graduation party. Dad was staying home quite a bit. I wasn't sure if he was still working at all, but money seemed tighter than ever. I noticed we were getting more handouts, including strange boxes shipped to us marked "US Government Surplus." The boxes contained large cans of mysterious cooked ground meat with a layer of white fat on top, looking more like dog food than something for human consumption. My mother heated it and served it on toast, making a soggy open-faced sandwich. It tasted horrible.

Somehow, though, there was always enough money for my father's daily packs of Camel cigarettes, and the ever-present quart-sized brown bottles of Narragansett beer—"to settle his stomach."

Months after her celebrated graduation, Marcia was still living at home, idle, and not looking very hard for work. There were offers, including one for a full-time secretarial job at the old Quartermaster, a US Army research center in Natick, Massachusetts. They had actively recruited young women fresh out of high school for clerical jobs, and Marcia was an excellent typist.

Secretarial work was thought to be quite glamorous in those days. We had grown up with the image of Della Street, confidential secretary to TV's Perry Mason, the pretty brunette with her cashmere sweaters and pencil skirts, who made an entire generation of girls want to grow up to be secretaries. To everyone's surprise, my sister turned the job down.

My father was furious.

"Whassa madda with you, Marcia? It's a nice clean job. A *clean* job!" That was just the kind of work my father wanted for his children, sitting behind a desk, not like the gritty factory labor his generation had known.

"I don't have transportation," Marcia protested, her nose in the air and arms folded tightly against her chest. She had the stubborn, imperious look of a duchess.

"It's just two towns away! The bus is cheap! Aw, you're just making excuses!"

Marcia only dug in. "I don't have the right clothes."

"Son of a bitch of a bastard. My whole life I spend, waiting for my ship to come in, and you—you get everything handed to you on a silvuh plattuh. And you just spit on it!"

My mother quietly shook her head on the sidelines, in solidarity with her husband. But Marcia was unmovable. My guess is that Marcia was simply afraid. The prospect of being out in the world, starting a career, mingling among other people as if she were just another ordinary middle-class young woman, was too big and ambitious for her to contemplate.

For a while Marcia pondered becoming a nun, which would have been perfect, I thought. She was so prim in appearance, always wearing a plain black raincoat, even on the warmest days, and a black lace mantilla covering her pretty red hair. She already looked like a nun. She had even sent away for brochures from the Trappists, a strict local order of Roman Catholic monks and nuns. The brochures described a rigid schedule of prayers and duties starting at 4:00 a.m. each day. Life as a nun would have given her structure and purpose, something she craved.

Instead, she lingered aimlessly, paralyzed by indecision, at a time when Dad was spending too much time at home, and close quarters created a swirling cauldron of emotions. Dad could quickly turn explosive, with my mother getting the worst of it. It was not unusual for him to slap her face hard with the back of his hand, making a sound like a cracking whip, sending her tumbling backwards onto the floor.

It was horrible to watch. I instinctively shut my eyes tight and covered my ears. My father also turned his rage against Marcia, who gave him back as good as she got. She called him ugly names like a "prick" and a "farce." Sometimes it became a taunt—"Farcy! Farcy!" I didn't know what the words meant, but I knew they weren't good. I once saw Marcia bring a garden spade into the house and hurl it toward my father, although it was clear she deliberately missed. It was all for show, a dramatic operatic gesture, aimed only to drive tempers to a fever pitch. And it did.

It was a time of frayed nerves and sickening tension. All of us were craving an outlet, some momentary relief. One day Ma decided to lighten things up by splurging on some mail-order dolls for me. I hadn't had a new toy in years, and had learned not to expect any, but I had been captivated by a magazine ad for a series of international dolls, each in the native garb of her country. I had shown my mother the ad.

"Look, Ma. The Spanish doll has black hair and a red dress— she's a flamenco dancer! And the Hungarian doll is blond, just like

Zsa Zsa Gabor! There's an Indian squaw—there's even a Japanese girl with a kimono!"

They were little eight-inch plastic dolls, cheaply made, and sold for just a dollar each.

"Go ahead, Catrina," my mother said. "You deserve it. You never get anything new. Pick out six of them."

Six dolls! I was elated! My mind had wandered hundreds of times to the places I would travel someday, and now I could choose six dolls to match my fantasy travels. But the day the postman knocked on our door with a COD order of $6 in hand, Dad flew into a rage.

"Six dollars! Whaddaya think, I'm made of money?" He slammed the box against the wall.

Ma quietly paid the startled postman, but I took no joy in the new dolls, and the whole episode cast a pall over the family for weeks. My brother Jerry and I were afraid to speak at the dinner table, for fear of another outburst. Jerry seemed to take it harder than I did, visibly shaken and often sickened by the frequent violent arguments. I remember simply being annoyed at the pointless bickering. *Grownups are stupid,* I thought, scooping up little Stephen and taking him outside to play—and to keep him out of the path of flying objects.

Ma was now different, too. She didn't seem to have the same energy she once had. She didn't can any fruits and vegetables this year, the way she used to, so meals were scant. Only a few dusty Ball jars remained on the pantry shelves underneath the stairs, left over from my mother's work the previous year: sliced pears, pickled cucumbers, and stewed tomatoes, and some paraffin-sealed quince jelly were all that was left. The sparse pickings on the dinner table, coupled with the ever-increasing appetites of his growing children, only seemed to fuel my father's rage. He criticized every meal my mother prepared, while the rest of us held our breaths and hoped to get through a meal without a fight.

Every night, I looked forward to bedtime, the only peaceful time of the day, withdrawing with my mother, sisters, and Stephen to the second floor loft of our house, leaving my father and Jerry downstairs. Now twelve years old, Jerry slept in a folding cot near Dad's big bed, while everyone else slept upstairs. Marcia and Celia, seventeen and eighteen, still slept together in the large bed that dominated the upstairs space; I had a little cot of my own, and Stephen was still in a crib. Ma, as always, slept on the floor between her children's beds.

I loved watching my mother step out of her dress at night to emerge in her full slip, the kind with satin straps and lacy hem. I thought she looked elegant. It would be the closest she would ever come to wearing an evening dress. One night as I watched her undress, I imagined her dancing in her ivory slip with a handsome tuxedoed movie star, someone like Clark Gable, gliding across a marble ballroom floor in her perpetually bare feet.

"What are you staring at, you ugly moron? Can't your mother have some privacy?"

It was Marcia, shouting at me from her bed.

"Why don't you pick on someone your own size?" Celia piped in.

"Why don't you mind your own business?" Marcia shot back at Celia. The next thing I knew, the two sisters were engaged in full hand-to-hand combat, pulling each other's hair, biting, punching, and rolling onto the floor in a thud, shaking the whole house. Meanwhile my mother was silently ignoring the fray and pulling her blanket up over her shoulders.

Dad yelled, "What the hell's going on? Go to bed! Don't make me come up they-uh!"

I don't recall my father ever coming up to the second-floor loft. It was solely the domain of mother and children. The prospect of his coming up there was a terrifying threat, and it stopped my sisters' bickering cold.

Marcia glared at me and hissed, "It's all your fault! I'm going to wait until you fall asleep and cut off both your braids in the middle of the night!" I pulled the blankets up over my head, tucking it in all around my body in a tight cocoon, leaving only a small opening to breathe, hoping my quilted armor would protect me until morning.

Early the next day, a chilly late-November Monday, a little after seven thirty, I stepped down the crude stairs, dressed for school, ready to wash my face and hands in the sink.

Surprisingly, Dad was still sleeping. Usually he rose before dawn and was already at work before we got up. He was fully clothed, the way he always slept, lying on his side, facing the wall, as his wife and children quietly tip-toed around him in the dimly lit open room.

"Sh-h-h," Ma whispered. "Dad's not feeling well today. Heartburn. Keep your voices down."

It was getting late, and I needed to leave for school. Ma quietly offered me a plate of cold toast as I washed and dried my face, while Jerry nervously fussed, "Hurry up! We'll be late!" Jerry still walked me to school, although he was now at Stacy Junior High, which was about a mile farther away than the Plains Elementary School where I went. I wolfed down the toast and ran out the door, calling after Jerry, "Hey, wait for me!"

I was in Miss Realini's fifth-grade class. Miss Realini was a thin, older woman with her hair dyed a burnt dark reddish color. She was strict and severe, spending her lunch hours reading the Bible at her desk, and she was known for reducing her defenseless young students to tears with her withering rebukes.

"Wee-e-e-e-p, wee-e-e-e-p," she would say almost gleefully, sounding eerily like the Wicked Witch of the West, as she taunted one of her wayward pupils for crying through one of her tirades.

Miss Realini was not popular. But she was a demanding teacher, much more disciplined than Miss Casey, and under her iron will, her students would learn a thing or two. We learned, and never forgot, that Balboa was the first European to reach the Pacific Ocean via the New World, in 1513, the same year Ponce de Leon explored Florida in search of the fountain of youth. She made us memorize names and dates, drilling the timeline of history into our heads. I respected her for that.

It was late morning when I noticed Marcia had appeared unexpectedly at the classroom door. Miss Realini stepped out to the hall to speak with my sister, and she returned to the class looking like an entirely different woman, wearing the softest expression I had ever seen. She walked directly to my desk and put her hand gently on my shoulder.

"Close the book, Catherine. Just leave everything. You need to go home."

When Marcia and I arrived at the house, a small group was standing outside, including a few neighbors and relatives. My mother's younger brother—Uncle David—was there, along with his pretty dark-haired wife, my Aunt Kay. They lived in a neighboring town. What were they doing here? Something very strange was going on. Now Jerry and Celia were arriving, and Marcia gathered all her younger siblings together in a small circle just outside the house to make an announcement:

"It's Dad. He's gone. He passed away this morning."

Dad was just fifty-six, although at the time I didn't understand how young that was. I imagined he had died of old age. He had passed away in his sleep, an apparent heart attack, and had just been taken away an hour earlier. I wondered if he might have been dead when we left for school that morning.

Jerry turned around and walked off alone, with his head down and his back to us, so no one could see him crying. The rest of us were just stunned and silent. I didn't know what to say—or even what to feel. Strangely, I wasn't immediately saddened by the news; I was simply trying to absorb it. Dad was an enigma, always detached and distant, never showing affection toward me or anyone else in the family as far as I could see. A figure of authority, but not of fatherly affection or love. I never saw him kiss or embrace my mother, or any of his children. What should one feel when a stone statue topples over? Regret, surprise perhaps—but not sorrow. I could not muster any sorrow.

We were never a religious family, but I somehow felt I should pray, silently, to myself. I closed my eyes and filled my head with the words of the Lord's Prayer, the same prayer that schoolchildren in our town recited aloud each morning, right before the Pledge of Allegiance. The opening words to the prayer seemed to fit the moment. "Our Father, who art in heaven. Our Father, who art in heaven."

Ma was sitting alone inside the house; she would allow no one to come near until her own mother arrived. That's when all of us understood, perhaps for the first time, the depth of her feeling for her husband. When Grandma Bertha Thomas burst in and asked, with a pained expression, "What happened, honey?" Ma gave out a plaintive wail, a chilling animal-like sound, and sobbed on Grandma's shoulder.

"He's gone, Mama, he's gone!" She was inconsolable. Despite all the hardship of her married life, she was utterly inconsolable.

In the days that followed, no one knew what to expect, but each day a new surprise unfurled. Sympathy cards, money, casserole dishes filled with lasagna or manicotti, tins of cookies, fruit baskets, and offerings of all kinds began appearing at our doorstep. A family that lived in isolation from society had a surprising number of friends.

Ma primped for her new public role as widow, first by going to the hairdresser—something we had never seen her do before— and she had her dark hair set and sprayed in the bouffant style of Jackie Kennedy. Now in her early forties, she looked striking in a black dress and matching hat with black netting over her hazel eyes.

The DePasquale Funeral Home hosted two wakes a day, morning and evening, Tuesday through Thursday, and the funeral was scheduled for Friday. It was my first experience with a funeral home, and the bizarre ritual of embalming a human body for public display. The coffin was lined with shirred white silk, and an elegantly dressed man I barely recognized was reposing in this white luxuriance. Surrounded by tall bouquets of white gladiolus, Dad was impeccably groomed and dressed, with black rosary beads looking ill-placed in his clutched hands.

I sat with Ma, Marcia, Celia, and Jerry, all of us arranged in a row of stiff chairs, oldest to youngest, next to my father's open casket, while little Stephen stayed with Grandma. We sat quietly and shook hands as hundreds of people filed in and paid their respects. Who would have known that our quiet loner of a father knew so many people? Some were relatives, but many others were men he had worked with in the course of his life.

In between shaking the hands of total strangers, I studied the abundant gladiolus arrangements. Such strange flowers, so tall and exotic, with thick green spears and clusters of trumpet-shaped blooms running their entire length. I had never seen them anywhere but in funeral bouquets. My mother used to point them out to me in the baskets adorning gravestones in St. Mary's Cemetery, where I first learned the flower's name. I remember her telling me once that she and my dad used to grow them—glads, as she called them—but I never saw them growing anywhere. It must have been long before I was born.

To me, they were always arranged in funeral baskets. Flowers of death.

As my mind wandered, which happened often that week, the crisp white gladiolus blooms drew me into their funnels, into their mysterious reproductive depths. I imagined myself shrinking and hiding among the powdery stamens, their fragrant orange powder dusting my head.

Day after day, the funeral home was overflowing with mourners. The most startling mourner was Aunt Lizzie. She threw herself on her knees in front of her brother's body, clutching the casket, and wailed out loud, between gulping sobs, "Jerry, Jerry! Please don't leave me!" No one ever had ever seen such emotion— a torrent of appreciation, of a kind that is never expressed for the living.

After the funeral at Sacred Heart Cemetery, where my father was laid to rest in the large Marenghi family plot next to his parents and sister Catherine, we all gathered at 7 Hayward Street. Aunt Lizzie and her sisters from Vermont—Tillie and Chezz, short for Cotilda and Cesarina—were busily preparing tuna sandwiches on finger rolls for the huge crowd. Tillie and Chezz ran a restaurant in Vermont, and their trained hands quickly turned out platter after platter of sandwiches—"sangwiches," as they called them. Just as it was five months earlier on Marcia's graduation day, the house was swelling with relatives, breaking bread together once again.

All through the week of mourning, I wondered, *What will happen to us now? Who will take care of us? Ma hasn't had a paying job in decades. Marcia still hasn't found a job. How will we get by?*

As Christmas approached, we expected lean and somber times and little cause for celebration. Most years we never had much in the way of presents, except the group gifts given to my whole family. There might be a box of Florida oranges and pink grapefruit from my mother's sister, a *Reader's Digest* subscription from another, some homemade Italian cookies or Torrone candies from an aunt on my father's side, and a smattering of cards. We never received gifts from our parents on Christmas; there just wasn't any money for them. This year we didn't know what to expect.

We were all startled to see a Salvation Army truck pulling up to our house on Christmas Eve. I don't know what triggered their arrival, but they knocked on the door, deposited a shopping bag in my mother's hands, and quickly stole away.

My baffled mother brought the bag inside and spilled the contents onto the table. Along with assorted canned goods and boxed food items, there were two wrapped gifts. One was labeled, "For a little boy." Another, "For a little girl."

Jerry and I stared at each other. Could these gifts be for us? These were for children who didn't have names, other families' children, who somehow landed on the Salvation Army's list. Not for us. We weren't poor and needy children—were we?

Our hearts sank as we gingerly tore back the paper. Jerry got a jigsaw puzzle in a worn cardboard box, which we would soon discover had several pieces missing. I got a plastic doll, faded and dirty, with ballpoint-pen scribble on its face and most of its body. Used and battered toys, discarded and unwanted by other children.

I've never forgotten, or forgiven, what the Salvation Army gave us that day. Their gift to the poor was the gift of poverty itself, a wrapped-up secret that, once revealed, could never be undone.

9

RELIGION

If my mother struggled with grief and loneliness in the wake of her husband's death, she never let her children know. Like so many of her generation, children of the Great Depression years, she quietly shouldered her losses and moved on. It would be unseemly to make a show of grief. And she had to be strong for her children.

When I think about it now, it amazes me that my parents produced a houseful of children without ever displaying the slightest hint of physical affection. How and where were all these children conceived? Did my mother tiptoe downstairs in the night, while her children slept upstairs? Did my parents have late-night liaisons outdoors? I'll never know. But a woman who conceived her first child in 1945, and her last in 1961, had a physical relationship with her husband for at least sixteen years. The arithmetic of their love was undeniable.

She never had another man in her life again. She remained a single mother, although that was certainly not a term anyone used at the time. She was known only as a widow, one whose life was delineated by the tenure of years spent with her husband. Yet another word, *relic*, was once used to describe widows, carved on old New England gravestones, as in "Hannah Smith, Relick of Josiah Smith." Relic, relick, relict—all variants of the same archaic word—

meaning the woman who was left behind, the pitiful artifact that remained after a man died. It sounds so much better now to call a widow a single mother, giving her a proud and active role in her children's lives.

For me, a ten-year-old girl, I had no sense of how young my mother was, just forty-four years old, with as many years still ahead of her. From then on, it seemed to me, she lived only for her children. She was the most selfless of souls, and not entirely in a positive way. She had no self, it seemed, no voice that said, "*I am here. This is who I am. This is what I want. Pay attention to me.*" Instead, she simply blended into her children's lives, as if her own life no longer mattered.

She never changed her hair, or the simple cotton dresses she wore. Never wore pants. Perhaps her husband liked her to wear dresses? Did she wear them for him? Did he once tell her she looked pretty in that kind of dress? She never explained.

For me, my father's death was not so much a source of sadness, but confusion and anxiety. I didn't know how a family was supposed to live with just one parent instead of two, especially when the departed had been the breadwinner. I didn't know what we would do next. For all my family's quirks, it had a veneer of normalcy, anchored by two hard-working parents and a healthy brood of kids, all behaving like good citizens, working hard, and keeping out of trouble. Now the veneer was shattered.

And I didn't understand this strange new concept of poverty, so bluntly delivered to us in gift-wrapped packages by the Salvation Army. I thought poverty was something in stories I'd read, like *The Little Match Girl*, about a waif standing on a city street corner, selling matches to survive. I never had to stand on a street corner, never had to beg, never even went hungry. I might have eaten things that were odd, like the mysterious stews my mother made from whatever animal my father brought home from hunting, anything from deer to mallard ducks to rabbits and even squirrels. Or inexpensive filler food, like those large yellow cakes of polenta my mother made from boiled cornmeal—about as flavorful as sawdust—that she allowed to congeal in the pot, sliced and fried, and covered with tomato sauce. Not the most appetizing fare, but nonetheless, I never, ever went hungry.

The images of poverty I saw on TV were even more confusing. There was a Lana Turner movie, *Imitation of Life*, about a struggling young widow who somehow managed to support herself and her child, as well as her housemaid, a black woman with a child of her own. So many poor people in old movies had servants, or people who came into their homes to wash their clothes. And they had beautiful hair and telephones and bathrooms. And they looked like Lana Turner.

I remember my mother's receiving a mailer from a Christian charity. It showed pictures of an Appalachian Mountain family, described as desperately poor, sitting on the front porch of their log cabin. The caption under the picture read, "Won't you help?"

My brother and I were fascinated by the picture.

"Look at their house," he said. "They have a porch! We don't have a porch."

"Yeah," I said. "Their house is way nicer than ours. They should send *us* money!" We both laughed ourselves silly.

Whatever *poverty* meant, the worst of it was being different. I didn't want to have money. I just wanted to be like other people, to feel normal—even ordinary. As I rapidly began to realize, there was no one in town who lived the way we did. No one.

෨෬

The recent experience of attending my father's Roman Catholic funeral mass had made me acutely aware of religion once again. It suggested the possibility of belonging to something.

The Catholic religion was an unlikely place for me to look for comfort. Although I was christened in the Catholic faith when I was a baby, I had been non-practicing since the tender age of seven, when I was abruptly expelled from Catholic Catechism class.

Catechism class was the Roman Catholic equivalent of Sunday school, except the classes took place on Wednesday afternoons. In a decisively Catholic town, the public elementary schools closed early every Wednesday to allow all the Catholic children to walk two-by-two to attend these religious classes, which took place at the local parochial schools.

There were two Catholic churches in town, and for the better part of a century, they were split along ethnic lines. Most of the Italians went to the Sacred Heart of Jesus Church, a solid Romanesque structure of yellow brick with a clay-red tile roof, and an altar adorned with gold and splendid Italian marbles. The Irish attended St. Mary's, an appropriately northern European gothic cathedral with soaring spires of gray granite and narrow stained-glass windows.

From the age of six to seven, I had attended Catechism class at Sacred Heart—and I hated every minute of it. I did not yet have the vocabulary to express what I felt. I couldn't vocalize the words, *"I sense the inauthenticity of your language, and I find your motives suspect."* But I instinctively knew the nuns were being dishonest with me. They forced us to memorize prayers that sounded like gibberish: "Hail-Mary-full-of-grace-the-Lord-is-with-thee-blessed-art-thou-amongst-women-and-blessed-is the-fruit-of-thy-womb-Jesus." What does "fruit of thy womb" mean, I would ask? My curiosity, however, was punished. Questions of any kind were not tolerated. That alone made me suspicious.

But when the nuns talked about heaven, that's when my young brain shut down completely. They said heaven was a place with gumdrop trees and roads paved with candy canes. This was, to me, such a blatant attempt to deceive, to paint a picture of heaven they *assumed* any child would love—but this would be no heaven for me. I was one of those odd children who lacked a sweet tooth. I never ate gumdrops or candy canes. They were just saying that to seduce me, to win me over. From that point forward, I simply refused to memorize prayers or do anything I was told. The

Catechism instructors didn't know what to do with me. My stubbornness got me ejected from the class.

To my surprise, my parents weren't angry. They didn't attend church themselves, and my father's job as cemetery caretaker for St. Mary's had removed from him any fear or awe of the Church. The priests were just ordinary men to him, and he habitually addressed them by their first names, like "Joe" or "Frank," instead of as "Father." In fact, he half suspected my expulsion from Sacred Heart was motivated by his own connection with a competing church.

There were no consequences for me, and the message was clear: Religion didn't matter. We could live without it. Even when I fell into the odd limbo of non-Catholic kids who were left behind at school on Wednesday afternoons, along with a handful of Protestant or Jewish children, I was free to while away the time reading books or drawing pictures. It was much more fun than Catechism.

Now here I was, three years later, staring the Catholic Church in the face once again. I remembered my father's funeral mass, sitting in the front pew reserved for the deceased's immediate family; I was nearer to the altar than I had ever been, getting a very close look at the gold chalice and the priest's elaborate liturgical vestments, all white satin with golden embroidery. The soaring majesty and opulence of a Catholic cathedral can inspire awe in anyone, and it certainly gripped my young imagination.

With the taste of the Church's grandeur still fresh in my mind, it suddenly struck me that the Church might have a purpose. It was a kind of template that told us what to do at critical points in our lives, like birth, marriage, and death. It provided a narrative to follow. For that alone, I thought it was worth another try.

I signed up for Catechism classes at St. Mary's—I didn't think Sacred Heart would take me back—and I studiously prepared for my First Holy Communion. Most of my friends received their First Communion at the age of seven. As a ten-year-old, I was quickly playing catch-up to receive Communion the following spring. Aunt Lizzie had pitched in to buy my Communion dress; it was hard to find one for a girl my age. When the day arrived, I stood several inches taller than the other girls, but I didn't mind, all of us clad in white lace and veils, walking down the aisle like little virgin brides about to receive the body of Christ.

This renewed focus on the church left me imbued with a feeling of holiness, which I wore like a somber mantle. After First Communion, I continued Catechism classes, went to confession on Saturdays, and attended church every Sunday. I imagined my soul looking like dirty laundry, stained with my imagined sins, washed weekly by confession and penance, then coming out clean and white as the fresh sheets on my mother's clothesline. And on Sunday mornings, the thick mingled smells of incense, ladies' perfume, and cigar smoke on the clothes of older men were enough to inspire hallucinations, especially on an empty stomach—since fasting was a requirement before receiving Communion. The stained glass windows pulled my eyes upward toward the heavens, where a God with flowing white hair looked down on us, and his stern face was that of my own father.

In the months that followed, the loud, brash, rough-edged tomboy child was suddenly quiet, serious, and upstanding. My classmates seemed to see a change in me. They treated me with new gentleness and curiosity. I was special and different, the first among them to have lost a parent, and this status made me feel much older than my peers. When I played house with other young girls, I always played the role of the parent—usually the father.

I conformed to religion's strictures with the hope that it would make everything better. Things would start making sense. I would be good, and I would be eternally rewarded for it. That's what gods were for.

10

ALLOWANCE

For a time, my theory seemed to be working. My family's circumstances actually improved after my father's death. God was easing up on us.

The house was calmer. The violent arguments that had crackled around my father like sparks to a lightning rod had now subsided. We still bickered and quarreled and pulled each other's hair and kicked each other's shins as siblings do. In such close quarters, it was hard not to. But we were also united, a kind of exclusive club. We were isolated from the world, but also tightly bound to each other.

My mother started receiving widow's benefits from Social Security—some for her, and some for each of her minor children. It wasn't much, but it was more than my father had ever earned, and it was enough to fund small weekly allowances for Celia, Jerry, and me. There wasn't enough money for a new house, and my mother didn't have the means to do the massive reconstruction the house needed to make it truly livable. But we all fell into a new state of normalcy—not normal by any conventional measure, but more normal than we had ever known.

Even if it was just a few dimes and nickels a week, I could sense what a difference it made to have a little money. Schoolmates gathered around me when I arrived at school in the morning, to see what treat I had purchased from the candy store, and most of the time, I just gave it away. I wasn't much of a candy eater any way, and it seemed to make the other children happy. So I resolved to save half my money for the future and spend the rest on things that either filled an immediate practical need or made the people around me happy. Everything else, I thought, was a waste of money, and I hated to see money wasted.

My ideas about money were further solidified when Celia had the idea to form a kind of social club, with the Marenghi siblings as its only members. Jerry had been anointed president from the very beginning—"Because presidents are always boys. Everyone knows that," Celia declared.

"Why can't a girl be president?" I asked, predictably.

"Oh, shut up. I'll be vice president, because it was my idea. Marcia will be secretary, because she knows how to type. And that means you'll be treasurer, little smarty-pants," she added, glaring down at me.

We had our first meeting in a rickety lean-to shed that was once used as a coal bin. We dubbed it The Clubhouse. At first we really didn't know what to do with our newfound alliance, but now that we were getting weekly allowances, I had an idea.

"We should have membership dues! And since I'm treasurer, I'll collect them," I said. "Ten cents a week from each of us. Before you know it, we'll have ten dollars. Then twenty dollars. Then we can all do something fun together."

"Like what?" Jerry asked.

"Oh, I don't know. We can decide later, when we get enough money!"

I ran off to collect an old Sucrets cough-drop tin that I had been using to store small coins. The word *Sucrets* looked pleasingly like the word "secrets." Then I dutifully collected membership fees from everyone, adding them to the existing pennies, nickels, and dimes already in the kitty.

"We already have sixty-five cents!" I exclaimed, watching the coins jingle around in the tin, then snapping the lid shut with a click. I felt infinitely wealthy, with the promise of even more riches to come.

"This will be our secret treasure," I said, looking around The Clubhouse for a hiding spot. "Here. I'll hide it here."

I slid the box into an opening in the floor in the corner of The Clubhouse, and turned to my siblings, in a conspiratorial whisper, "Don't tell anyone about our secret!"

A week later, I retrieved the Sucrets tin to begin my rounds and collect the second week's dues. To my horror, the tin was empty. The thief had to have been one of my own siblings. More than an act of treachery, of stealing money from one's own family, it was also a failure to work together for a shared goal. A failure to value the future. The disappointment was soon forgotten, but the lesson was not. I had a very different view of money than some of my siblings did.

Marcia, now nineteen, was earning wages of her own at a local commercial laundry, the Home Laundry Company, just a short walk from our house. She quickly saved enough to buy a used car, a pretty pink-and-black 1958 Rambler with rear tail fins. Its bobby-socks-era exuberance seemed utterly out of character for the gloomy girl in the black raincoat, but the car was a bargain. It cost only two hundred dollars, and it was the first family car I can remember.

Swept up in this wave of consumer confidence, I bought some wheels of my own. I counted all the birthday money I'd saved over the years, a dollar here and a dollar there from aunts and uncles, and bought a sapphire-blue bicycle from a Sears catalog. It cost about thirty dollars, and it was nothing like the beat-up, paint-splattered bike my father had salvaged from the town dump, which drew sarcastic jeers from boys whenever I rode it into town. No, this bike was exquisitely, deliciously new. When my brother started delivering newspapers and asked to use my new bike to make his rounds, I actually had the nerve to charge him a rental fee to use it! All of us were taking in a little money, our own little economic miracle.

My sisters Marcia and Celia quickly started splurging their newfound cash on junk food—Fritos and Cheese Curls and onion dip and Coca-Cola—something my father never approved of, even if he could have afforded it. We always thought Dad was hopelessly old-fashioned, always reading the labels on food packages and shunning any foods with added chemicals. He never allowed his children to drink Coca-Cola. The only soft drink he ever allowed, when he had the money for it, was locally bottled Miscoe Springs Orange Soda made from spring water and pulpy orange juice. He just didn't understand modern eating—frozen TV dinners, condensed soup, instant mashed potatoes, and other processed packaged foods—which we now consumed with a vengeance. We didn't appreciate it then, but my father believed in natural whole foods well ahead of his time.

He would have been horrified to see my sisters guzzling a new concoction, the radioactive green color of antifreeze fluid, called Mountain Dew, and devouring Chef Boy-R-Dee ravioli, that god-awful starchy pasta with sugar-laced sauce, which they ate straight from the can. The notion of eating cold canned pasta never appealed to me, but for my sisters, it seemed to satisfy a pent-up desire for luxury, for special treats. Or maybe it was just a way to be more like other people.

A family that never had anything now seemed to be buying things and clinging to everything it acquired, throwing nothing away. We bought cheap TVs with rabbit-ear antennas, and plastic transistor radios that quickly stopped working, and we never threw out the old things when we got new ones. Even old newspapers piled up, as if there might be some valuable information hidden in their pages that no one could afford to miss. My sister Celia was the worst offender, acquiring the most, and allowing nothing to be discarded without a fight.

When Celia started working after school at the Atlas discount department store, she spent the entirety of her small paychecks the minute she cashed them. Most of her purchases seemed pointless to me. She was seduced by every collectible craze from figurines to commemorative coins. Perhaps it was a distraction from her chronic health problems. She had trouble hearing, and had serious ear infections and occasional surgeries throughout her life. Her acquisitions caressed her in ever-expanding piles around her bed, like a shrine to prosperity. She made it worse with frequent trips to the town dump, bringing home all manner of junk that no one else wanted.

"Look at this lamp, everyone," she would say, showing off her latest find. "It would be nice if it wasn't broken, wouldn't it?"

While I hoarded my allowance money like a tight-fisted little banker, saving it for an occasional new blouse or dress, Jerry used most of his to buy records. He loved rock-and-roll, starting with The Beatles. We had both seen their American debut on The Ed Sullivan Show in February 1964. From the very first line of their opening song—*"Close your eyes and I'll kiss you, tomorrow I'll miss you"*—their harmonies and energy filled Jerry with ecstasy.

Jerry started buying Beatles singles on 45 RPMs, playing them on an old Victrola that must have come from my grandmother's house, a tall wooden cabinet with a wind-up crank on the side. Designed for 78 RPMs, the Victrola made the Beatles sound like Alvin and the singing chipmunks. With the earnings from his paper route—minus my cut of the profits, of course—he eventually got a proper electric record player, a portable in a latched case, and he bought as many records as he could get his hands on.

My mother seemed to exercise no authority over this rampant consumerism. We were each allowed to do as we pleased with our money. Accustomed to being silent beside a domineering husband, she continued her passive muteness long after his death, as her children went about aimlessly spending their pocket money. I had always hated my father's strict rules, but this wantonness troubled me even more.

Our waistlines expanded with our fortunes. The ceiling above the first floor of our poorly built house started to sag dangerously under the weight of more belongings, more clutter, and heavier inhabitants. My mother and sisters propped up the ceiling downstairs with a pair of two-by-fours in the center, the crude pillars standing about a foot and a half apart, and they wrapped them together with sticky plastic contact paper with a faux-wood pattern, a half-hearted attempt at making them more decorative. The resulting misshapen pillar looked awful. The exterior roof was visibly sagging as well, and it leaked through to the upper level and into a complex system of plastic sheets that steered the leaks into a series of pails. Nothing in the house was safe from mold, rust or rot.

For my part, I could not understand the lack of forethought, the utter disregard for the future, in this new life of ours. I was sickened by the aimless spending of our meager incomes, the temporary-fix mentality, with never a thought of what would come next. Maybe it's why I was always obsessed with time machines that would carry me into the future. If I saved my allowance, my savings would grow and I could buy something special one day. If I worked hard in school, I could go to college and have a better life. If I kept going to church every Sunday, I could save my eternal soul.

It seemed so simple to me. Every action has a consequence. Every step has a destination. But every day, I found myself more and more at odds with my family's shortsighted choices, especially those of my sisters. I didn't understand them. Why did they continue living in that house, well into their adult years? Why didn't they break away? Maybe they were more damaged by their longer exposure to my father's influence. I didn't know. Or maybe it was the malevolence of the house itself. I was sure that living in that house, and all the shame and isolation that came with it, had a poisonous effect on their minds.

Both were painfully shy and quiet in the outside world, but unleashed their demons when they entered that house. Like my father, they could each erupt into fury without warning.

Marcia never missed an opportunity to find fault with me. Glancing in the mirror one day to fix my hair, I saw Marcia looking over my shoulder, darting a contemptuous look at me.

"You're *not* pretty, you know!"

I turned and looked at her.

"You're an ugly, buck-toothed witch!" she added, her lips curled like a growling dog.

I don't know why I never responded in kind. Most of the time I just stared at her, with a genuinely puzzled look. Why would anyone say something like that, deliberately to hurt a person's feelings? I honestly didn't understand it. Did she look at me and see a younger version of herself, with the same strawberry blond hair and coloring? If she did, she seemed to despise what she saw.

Celia expressed her feelings in more physical language. Her typical way of greeting me, starting when I was about five, was to grab my hands, hold them over my head, and kick my feet out from under me, leaving me spilling to the ground. I did have a response—picking myself up and kicking her shin bone as hard as I could, and then racing away like hell while she roared expletives at me.

One day I saw her coming up the path after school, and I didn't want her to see me. I wasn't in the mood for being tripped or abused, and so I tried to slip behind a tree. She saw me and pulled me toward her, but to my surprise, it wasn't to hurt me. She looked as if she had been crying, and she spoke to me in an unusually soft and gentle voice.

"I want to tell you something, Cath." Pointing her finger at my face, she said, "Your mother is the best mother in the world. Don't you ever let anyone tell you different. Ma is the best mother in the whole wide world."

"*What brought that on?*" I wondered to myself. I watched Celia slouch toward the house, her head down, and I quietly followed, sidling up to the window to hear what she was saying to my mother inside.

"Everyone was laughing at me!" she was sobbing. "They said, 'Oh-h-h, nice skirt. Did your mommy make that for you?'"

I peeked through the window, and looked down at Celia's skirt. I remembered now. It was a recent project of hers, an attempt to follow a popular fad at the time: girls were making skirts from men's old neckties. The idea was to stitch them together vertically into colorful stripes, with their pointed ends forming a zigzag hem.

I don't know where Celia got the neckties, but she somehow took it upon herself to participate in this fad. Celia, unfortunately, was a very poor seamstress, and my mother was even worse. We didn't have a sewing machine, so it was all done by hand. One side of the skirt was visibly longer than the other, and the ties buckled and bulged where the stitches were wildly uneven. The idea was very poorly executed.

Her one attempt to fit in, and do something all the popular kids did, was met with disaster. The insults were especially cutting, because they were aimed at our mother as well. I heard Celia stomp up the creaking steps to the upstairs and retreat into her corner.

My sisters were so much older than I, and never spoke to me as a peer. I had no way of knowing what difficulties they faced in the outside world every day, just trying to be accepted and to belong. There was always something that held them back, something that thwarted every attempt at normalcy. I thought it always came back to the same thing: living in that house.

Like a controlling lover, that house seemed to hold an unwholesome power over my sisters. It said, "Stay with me. You belong to me. You can do no better. You should ask no more."

My brothers and I were younger. There was more hope for us. We could get along better in the world. I was sure of it.

Especially little Stephen, the youngest—he would outshine us all.

11

SNAPSHOTS

"Hold still! Let me shoot you!"

That was my mother's way of saying, "Let me take your picture." She had a 1930s-era Eastman Kodak folding camera with extendable black leather bellows. She held it low on her waist and looked down into the viewfinder. She used that old camera with its heavy brushed steel and textured leather case for well over twenty-five years.

The first picture my mother took of Stephen and me together was always my favorite. It was black-and-white, but it has always blazed with color in my memory. It was late August. I was eight years old, wearing a short-sleeved blouse under a dark green pinwale corduroy jumper—a new outfit for school, probably purchased by my Aunt Lizzie.

My brother and I posed on a wooden chair in front of the old shed, surrounded by orange dahlias that towered over our heads, and I held Stephen on my lap. His blonde hair was cropped unevenly and bleached nearly white from the late summer sun. Both of us had eyebrows and eyelashes that were also sun-bleached and invisible against our faces. My golden red braids trailed down to my waist.

My mother loved taking pictures of her children. She always said she had the most beautiful, the most talented, the most gifted children. I could be wearing anything—a hand-me-down dress, a pair of used sneakers clearly two inches longer than my foot—and my other would exclaim, "Princess! Let me shoot you!"

For the longest time, the photos were only shot outdoors; the house didn't offer a very pretty backdrop, but outdoors there was always a blooming peach tree or a fresh snowfall to pose in front of. And we were always smiling. So many smiling pictures. You would think there was never a happier family.

We had piles of black-and-white pictures from my sisters' younger years, when they were girls with long banana curls. The photos dwindled in number when my brother Jerry and I came along, and they soared again with Stephen. Most of the photos came bound in little four-by-six booklets, with glossy red covers and a white plastic spiral binding.

In the 1960s, my mother put aside her heavy Kodak for a Polaroid instant camera, including one called the Polaroid Swinger, her first of many instant cameras. It was a time when everything we touched was suddenly lightweight and plastic, from soda bottles to transistor radios. It was the dawn of the throwaway world. Nothing was built to last twenty-five years any more.

The advent of instant photos meant we no longer had to take rolls of film to the local drugstore to have them developed; we didn't have to be careful about what other eyes might see. Now it was safe to take pictures inside the house, because we alone would see them. And Stephen was the rising star of my mother's new instant-film era. Stephen was a photogenic toddler, with peach-colored skin, a heart-shaped face, blond hair, and soft golden-brown eyes. There were pictures of Stephen in his pajamas, pictures eating sugary Lucky Charms cereal, pictures of him opening presents under a Christmas tree, wearing the forced toothy smile of a child saying "cheese."

The pictures also captured the things we didn't want to reveal. The piles of clutter under and around the Christmas tree. The dirty, broken patches of linoleum on the floor, showing the bare wood underneath. The shabby rust-stained curtains over cracked windows, held together with dirty masking tape. The teetering piles of brown paper grocery bags, stuffed with newspapers. The pictures did not lie.

My mother never seemed to see anything amiss in these photos, or in anything else, for that matter. Her children were all beautiful and talented in her eyes, and she never uttered a disparaging word or complaint about the house her husband built.

"This place could be a dream house," she often used to say, as if a vase of flowers and a few throw pillows were all that was needed. She would say this while staring lovingly at the battered walls, the way an old married couple might stare into each other's eyes, seeing only the beautiful creatures they once were. It was as if she saw only the dream, the promise of that house when she was first married.

Had she taken a harder look at her own Polaroids, and viewed things more critically and clearly, would she have done things differently? Could she have taken some decisive action, perhaps pursued a job after my father died, to improve our standard of living? After all, she was still relatively young, and I knew she had once worked as a typist and stenographer. She was working in an office when she met my father, or so I was told. But the question of employment is perhaps unfair to ask. Her business skills were stale from disuse, and her fingers were so thick and hardened from manual labor, it's hard to imagine them tapping the keys of a typewriter. And she was certainly not idle, always chopping wood and hauling coal for a wood-burning stove, washing clothes by hand, and cooking for a house full of children. If her worst crime was seeing the best in everything, it was hard to fault her for it.

My sister Marcia was a dreamer, too, one who imagined a better life to come, but did absolutely nothing to make it happen. She dreamed of being married and having a lovely home, like the ones she would see in women's magazines. I often accompanied her to department stores, like the iconic Jordan Marsh store in downtown Boston, and Marcia went straight to what was then called the Domestics Department—curtains, bed linens and the like. She pointed to things she wanted for her hope chest, carefully fingering the material of soft hand towels and linen tablecloths, but never buying a thing—just wishing for them.

I was bored to tears, tagging along behind her, itching to see something besides frilly café curtains in the big city of Boston, but I was too young to wander off on my own. Sales clerks often looked at me and commented to my sister that she had such a pretty daughter.

Traveling to and from Boston with me by Greyhound bus, she loved flipping through *Good Housekeeping*, looking at dream homes with exquisite furnishings, studying floor plans, and pointing out to me the ones she liked best.

One day she seemed transfixed by a particular floor plan with a sunken living room, a cocktail bar, and a floor-to-ceiling brick fireplace. "This one is just perfect for entertaining," she said authoritatively.

Exasperated, I asked, "Why do you keep talking about houses? Why don't you do something to make it happen? Save your money, make a plan, get married. Just do something!"

Marcia gave me a cold, hard look. "Not everyone can be like you, Catherine. You're the smartest kid in your class. You can do whatever you want."

I was stunned. I had no idea my siblings and I weren't all cut from the same cloth, capable of the same things. Weren't we all smart and gifted and beautiful? My mother certainly made me think so. And was I really the smartest in my class? I knew I was a good student, but I hadn't thought of myself as exceptional.

I thought we would all grow up and be whatever we wanted to be. Marcia, I thought, was going to be a glamorous secretary, with high-heeled pumps and matching purses and pastel suits that were called ensembles. I didn't know why Marcia was working at an industrial laundry, sorting out loads of dirty linens from hotel and restaurant customers, working alongside much older and less educated women, all daughters of Italian immigrants. Surely that was only temporary—she would do better than that, eventually.

And Celia, it seemed to me, was the budding artist. My mother encouraged her to paint and draw, and I thought she was going to be a brilliant artist after she graduated from high school. Or at least, she would go to art school. She was pretty, too, with long dark hair and high cheekbones. I pictured her in an artist smock, holding a painter's palette in one hand, sweeping her long hair from her face with the other, standing before a virgin canvas in an artist's loft apartment.

Oddly, after she graduated from high school, Celia didn't pursue any creative work at all. She seemed to have no ambitions, no plans, no friends. As a child, I found it so sad, such a let-down after the idealistic speeches of high school graduation ceremonies, to know that sometimes, the things you say you will do when you grow up may never happen at all.

Celia lingered at home, as her weight swelled to well over 250 pounds on her five-foot-four frame. She dabbled in a series of dead-end jobs like retail sales clerk, temporary typist, and factory assistant, never lasting very long at any of them. She had some health issues, to be sure, but none that would keep her from working.

Like Marcia, Celia often spoke of wanting to be married and having children one day, and she had plenty of crushes on men she worked with. Celia had a particular interest in one of her managers at a local factory. Because her boss had a hobby of collecting toy trains, suddenly Celia was obsessed with collecting toy trains. It made me sad to see her go from one foolish craze to another, spending her money on nonsense, never on a shared activity with the object of her affection.

And it puzzled me that neither sister did anything to improve their appearance. While Marcia was prim and nun-like, Celia had cropped her beautiful long hair into a short, mannish cut, parted down the middle, and she dressed her heavy frame in plain, ill-fitting, gender-neutral clothes. Rather than attracting future husbands, it seemed both sisters were doing everything possible to avoid attention.

While Marcia was usually soft-spoken and subdued, Celia was volatile and quick-tempered. One day I invoked her rage over a bag of newspapers. I found I couldn't sit down at the kitchen table because every chair was covered with junk, including bags of old newspapers, and I couldn't even pull out the chairs because of so much tangled clutter on the floor.

"Damn it!" I said. "*Things* are more important than people around here. *Things* have a place to sit, and I don't!"

I grabbed a bag of newspapers and headed for the door.

"Where are you going with that?" Celia bellowed.

"You just watch me!" I shot back. I headed outside toward a large metal oil drum we used as an outdoor incinerator. Plumes of smoke were drifting up from a dwindling fire.

Celia grabbed my arm, dragged me back into the house, threw me across her knees, and started whacking my bottom as hard as she could.

"*I'll* decide what goes in the trash, you friggin' little brat!"

I had never been spanked before, and at the age of twelve, it was humiliating. What right did my sister have to do this to me? I looked pleadingly at my mother and at Marcia, who shrugged and did nothing to stop the beating. My mother seemed paralyzed, as if struggling with divided loyalties.

There was always a gulf of years between my older sisters and me, but the gulf widened considerably that day. I was convinced neither of them would ever have anything in common with me. And my mother's passive silence, forever standing in the background, never speaking up when it was time to take a stand, made me pull farther away from her as well.

I was angry with my mother for a very long time. Why didn't she ever say anything?

ഗ്രര

As I moved into my teen years—never a harmonious time between parents and children—I became downright mean to my mother. I knew it. I was dismissive and distant, and treated her as if she knew nothing. She patiently tried different tactics to get through to me. She clipped newspaper articles that she thought would interest me, and laid them out on the table for me to find when I got home from school. She was hoping they would spark a conversation with me. But I brushed them aside dismissively.

"Well, that's what you call a 'TT'—a typical teenager!" My mother said it of me in an affectionate tone, but the label became just one more thing she did that completely irritated me.

Even when I began menstruating, there was so little conversation between us; I didn't know what was happening. No one had ever told me what to expect. I knew from my classmates that I'd start getting periods soon, but I was expecting to see something that looked like blood. No one told me it would start out as a sticky brownish effluent. My mother found the stains on my underwear, and finally pointed out, uncomfortably, "You're having a period, hon." But she didn't mention it until it had gone on for days, as if she were uneasy talking about it and hoping I'd figure it out for myself.

My sisters smirked and taunted me, "Oh, Catherine has her 'friend' now!" Code words like that disgusted me. I hated the whole rite of womanhood, from sanitary napkins to training bras, and my mother didn't offer much consolation. She seemed embarrassed to talk about any of the changes I was going through. I just wanted to be free and comfortable in my own body, the way boys and men always seemed to be. Not pinned and strapped and girdled.

At odds with my emerging womanhood, I found comfort in the company of my brothers. Jerry was the quintessential big brother, teasing me mercilessly one minute, protecting and defending me the next. We were the closest to each other in age, just two years apart. He was my first playmate and friend, the one who taught me to play baseball with just the two of us and a team of invisible men. Every time I hit the ball and ran to first base, I would leave an invisible man and go back to bat, and my next hit would move all the runners on base forward.

Sometimes to spice things up, he would tempt me with opportunities to steal another base by tossing a ball in the air and giving me time to run before he caught it. A silver opportunity was a ball tossed a couple feet in the air. A golden opportunity was a ball thrown several feet in the air. If I was lucky, he dropped the ball, and I would run like crazy all the way home.

We still walked to school together, listened to the radio together, and shared the same acne creams as our faces erupted into puberty. We did laundry together, loading our embarrassingly tattered towels and frayed clothes into paper grocery bags and lugging them to the nearest laundromat.

As soon as Jerry learned how to drive, we would go out in my sister's car in the evening, just the two of us, listening to the radio cranked up loud as it would go. While other kids were listening to Jimi Hendrix and Jefferson Starship in their bedrooms and rec rooms, we were in our musical home on wheels.

And then there was Stephen. As he grew from baby to toddler, he joined the circle of playmates and coconspirators with Jerry and me. One of our favorite games was playing pretend taxi, using an old abandoned Plymouth sedan that once belonged to my father. The car hadn't worked for decades, and it was left to rust in a corner of the yard. But for the three of us, it was a terrific plaything.

Jerry would get behind the wheel, and bark, "Where to, lady?" while Stephen and I hopped into the back seat and pretended to be passengers.

"Downtown Milford, please. And driver, could we listen to the radio?"

Jerry would punch the old radio buttons, supplying his own extemporaneous sound effects by singing verses from current songs, interspersed with mock static, as he went rapid-fire from one station to another. Stephen and I rolled with laughter in the back seat as Jerry crooned the Top Ten hit songs.

Stephen and Jerry were my best friends, closer to me than any friend I would have in school. With them, I could be myself. It's not that I didn't have any friends from school, but there was always a limit to how close those friends could get. Not once, in the entire time I lived in Milford, the first seventeen years of my life, did I ever invite a friend from school to visit my house. Even if I could get over the embarrassment of their seeing how I lived, what would I do if they needed to use the bathroom? If anyone knew we had an outhouse, I'd be mortified. I'd never live it down.

And so my brothers were my refuge from the world. Listening to the radio late in the evening with Jerry, I could be the ordinary girl who loved Mick Jagger and Grace Slick, not the geeky smart girl that no one ever invited to their beer-drinking parties. And with Stephen, I could be the fun big sister who made him laugh by singing silly songs like "Molly Malone." He would giggle warily whenever I started singing, *"In Dublin fair city, where girls are so pretty…,"* because he knew what was coming. I would tickle his sides mercilessly as soon as I got to the chorus, *"Cockles and mussels, alive, alive-oh!"* He always thought the words were "tickles in the muscles."

I loved having Stephen all to myself. Just to get out of the house, we often stole away to downtown Milford, a good two-mile walk. We wandered around the old W.T. Grant department store, the biggest store in town, a place that reeked with stale popcorn from the greasy popping machine by the soda fountain; we'd take the wide dusty stairs to the lower level to see the children's books, records, and toys, or peer at the tropical fish and parakeets in the pet department.

On the way home we liked stopping at the town library, a lovely old granite castle of a building with a Civil War cannon outside. Stephen already had his own library card to check out books, and I loved reading aloud to him on the library steps. I think he was interested in everything, from fairy tales to astronomy, from comic strips to cars, and he remembered *everything*. It was clear to me that he was very bright, definitely the brightest person in the family.

Stephen also had a soft spot for pets. With his insistence, we took in every feral cat that wandered through our yard, and they happily multiplied and grew fat with the abundance of field mice and birds in the summer, and table scraps year round. We had one store-bought pet, a lumbering tortoise that feasted on grass and dandelion leaves in the summer, and salad greens in the winter. Stephen wrote a charming letter about the tortoise to his Uncle Bruce, my mother's youngest brother, who was an Air Force lieutenant stationed in Vietnam at the time.

He wrote, "Dear Uncle Bruce, why don't you come and visit my tortoise? You can bring ten of your men, too. Love, Stephen.

"P. S. And tell them to bring lettuce!"

My favorite part of every school day was coming home and seeing Stephen. No matter how weary I was from the long walk home or the weight of my schoolbooks, my spirits quickly lifted when Stephen came running down the path to greet me. Tugging me into the house, he'd say, "Tell me a story! Tell me a story you learned in school today!"

It didn't matter what it was. Even when the subject was my high school Latin class, he seemed to want to know everything. I read him my translations of classic stories we read in Latin, like the adventures of Jason and the Argonauts in search of the Golden Fleece. Even my translations of Julius Caesar's *De Bello Gallico* intrigued my little brother, and he loved to announce dramatically, "All Gaul is divided into three parts!"

It was as if he wanted to turn me upside down and shake everything out of my head and into his. But he knew plenty of things I didn't know, too. I remember walking him out to the outhouse one cold night, both of us with our heavy coats on over pajamas, and he wanted to linger outside to look at the stars. Shivering in my rubber boots, which thinly protected by bare feet, I said, "Stephen, please, not tonight. It's cold out here! And besides, the stars will be here at least until next summer!"

But no, he insisted, he had to see them *now*. Only eight years old, and he pointed out constellations I'd never heard of: Aquila, the Eagle. Auriga, the Charioteer. Cannis Major. Cassiopeia, the Queen.

Whom could I tell about this? Could I tell my friends at school that I learned about constellations from my little brother—on our way back from the outhouse?

I was like an accountant who "cooks the books," with one set of records for public view and another kept private. Or like my mother's two kinds of photos, the ones on rolls of Kodak film that were sent out for developing, and the candid Polaroids that captured life as it was, the private collection that no one outside the family would ever see.

12

GUIDANCE

"I used to buy gladiolus bouquets from your parents. Every Saturday, I got a great big bunch of red gladiolus for my sweetheart."

This unexpected declaration from Mr. Harold Moran, my high school guidance counselor, startled me. I didn't know he knew my parents, and I didn't know they ever sold gladiolus to anyone. I had heard they grew glads at one time, along with a lot of other flowers, but I never knew anyone ever bought them. And why would anyone give a gladiolus bouquet to a girlfriend? That seemed ridiculous. The only place I had ever seen the flower was in a funeral arrangement.

It was just one more idiotic thing that grownups did.

It was 1970, my junior year of high school, and Mr. Moran had already taken a special interest in me. My name was on every Honor Roll. I had won regional spelling bees and essay contests. There were photos of me accepting medals and trophies in the *Milford Daily News*. I had poems and essays in the school newspaper. It had not gone unnoticed.

Mr. Moran had invited me to his office to talk, the first of many such talks, while he nibbled on a delicate sandwich cut into quarters with the crusts trimmed off. He was an elegantly dressed man in his sixties, but he looked much older, a heavy man with hunched shoulders. He had a bad leg and walked with a cane, and he made horrible guttural noises clearing his throat before he spoke. As a fifteen-year-old, it was hard for me to imagine him a young man with a sweetheart, standing hopefully on her doorstep with an armful of flaming red gladiolus spears.

"You need to start thinking about where you'll be going to college. Think big. Harvard. Yale. Wellesley. You can go anywhere you want." He pulled thick college brochures off his shelf while he spoke and slid them across his desk toward me.

"But won't that be expensive?" I asked.

"Don't worry about it. There are scholarships. Financial aid. Plenty of time for that. What I want you to do is to start preparing now. Get a folder. Put your poems in it, your drawings, anything you can think of. You need to start building a *portfolio*."

All of this was so foreign to me. Other than my teachers, I had never known anyone who went to college, let alone an Ivy League school. So many of my peers were like me, the grandchildren of Italian immigrants who came to this country with nothing in their pockets, all of them poor and illiterate. Their children, our parents, were mostly factory workers. Each generation did a little better than the one before, the great wheels of progress moving us all forward, but a college education was never a foregone conclusion.

But now there it was, my future course laid out for me by an elderly man who once bought flowers from my parents.

I had encouragement from teachers, too. There was the free-spirited Mrs. Robbins, a young English teacher who actually invited her whole class to her house for a party. Teachers never did things like that. Mrs. Robbins encouraged her students to write poems about the Vietnam War, and she made me think my childish singsong rhymes were brilliant. When she read my first poem, she slapped her forehead and said, "Wow!" Because of her influence, I considered myself a poet from then on.

And there was Miss Burns, my French teacher, a tiny wisp of a woman who was pale and pink and elderly. You could barely hear her voice when she spoke. A gust of wind could knock her over. But she adored *Cyrano de Bergerac*, and Moliere's *Tartuffe*, and under her passionate teaching, those two books became forever embedded in my imagination. There was Nello Allegrezza, David Hayes, Philomena Colavita, Tony Villani. In a school system that had very poor rankings overall, there was a handful of exceptional life-long teachers, and as my great good luck would have it, they all took an interest in me.

These high expectations also created pressure. I felt all eyes were upon me, and I didn't want to let anyone down. As the last weekend in October approached, I had two things on my mind: studying for the mid-term exams that started the following week and buying a gift for my brother Stephen. Halloween 1970 would mark his ninth birthday.

13

HALLOWEEN

1970

On Saturday, October 31, I was up and out of the house early before anyone else was awake. I had a part-time job on Saturday mornings as well as weekdays after school, working at the Central Mass. Travel Agency in downtown Milford. My boss, Mr. Sweeney, was also my high school Latin teacher, and he ran the business when he wasn't teaching. He had offered me a job starting the previous summer, and it was there that I actually learned how to use the telephone for the first time. My family never had one in the house.

"Really, it's okay to hang up the phone after you transfer the call to me," Mr. Sweeney repeatedly explained. I found it hard to believe, always wary the phone might blow up if I did the wrong thing.

I worked at the travel agency until noon that Saturday, and on the way home, I stopped to buy a special birthday gift for Stephen. It was a small mechanical helicopter, bright orange—a perfect Halloween color—and something I knew he had been eyeing.

By the time I got home, it was about three in the afternoon. I had already mapped out a schedule in my head. Study a couple hours, break for supper and birthday cake, and then back to studying all evening. Study all day Sunday. Study, study, study.

When I walked into the house, my first thought was to wish Stephen a happy birthday. Everyone was home, anticipating a birthday celebration. Stephen was sitting on the big iron bed downstairs, the one my father used to sleep in. The sagging old bed was now my brother Jerry's, but it served as a couch by day.

Stephen was still in his pajamas, sitting up on the edge of the bed with a knitted afghan wrapped around him. I had noticed he was coming down with a cold late in the week, and now it appeared he was still not feeling better.

"Happy birthday, Stevie-pie! How's my birthday boy?"

If he answered me, I have no memory of what he said. All I knew was there was something strange about the sound of his breathing. I dropped the bag I was carrying on the floor. My chest seized up as if it were being pierced by sharp icicles from within. I couldn't breathe. I was overcome with a full-body shudder, a deep chill that I can only describe as terror.

I turned around to my mother, who was calmly stirring a pot on the stove, and I unleashed a fury on her the likes of which had never had been heard in that house before or since. I had never raised my voice at my mother before. She was a quiet woman, and there was never any need to holler in a small house. But today I was lashing out at her with all the force I could muster.

"Why haven't you taken him to a doctor? What is wrong with you?! Stephen is sick, he's sick, he's sick, and if you don't take him to a doctor right now, *you're* sick! You're *sick*!"

This violent outburst caught everyone by surprise. My mother just stared at me, wide-eyed, looking shocked and hurt. And all around me, the voices of my sisters were lashing back at me in return.

"How dare you talk to your mother that way! Shame on you! What the hell is wrong with you?!"

All at once, I was feeling the triple assault of something terrible happening to my brother, the pain and disappointment of my mother, and the censure of my siblings. I stormed outside and paced around the yard, trying to calm myself down and make sense of what had come over me. My face was hot and sweating, and I was sobbing so violently, I thought I was going to vomit.

What made me think something was wrong with Stephen? Was I tired, overstressed, not thinking clearly? Just my emotions getting the better of me? I wasn't a doctor. How could I be so sure something was wrong?

And why was I so enraged at my mother? I didn't know where all that intensity came from. Like a storm that was years in the making, it came out roaring out of me with hurricane force. I never knew how much anger had been welling up in me. Anger over how we lived. Anger at a drafty house that seemed to breed pestilence. Anger that a sick child wouldn't just be taken automatically to a pediatrician, the way normal families did things. Anger that nothing ever changed. And so much anger at my mother for just letting things happen and never speaking up, never stepping up. Never doing or saying anything. Always the same acquiescence, the same animal-like silence.

When I finally calmed down and summoned the courage to come back into the house, my face reddened and hot with tears, my mother looked at me with an expression that was more concerned than angry.

"Stephen's got a bad cold, honey, that's all. Just a cold. He'll be all right."

I couldn't look at her. Instead I went to give Stephen a kiss and whispered in his ear, "I'm sorry for yelling like that on your birthday." I silently withdrew up the stairs, retreated to my corner, and curled up on my cot. I felt sick and hollow. I had no appetite for supper. The rest of the weekend, I kept to myself and tried as best I could to concentrate on my schoolwork.

On Sunday night, I had difficulty sleeping. My cot was only a few feet away from Stephen's, and the sound of his heavy snoring and coughing kept me awake all night. By Monday morning, I was red-eyed and weary and wracked with worry. I was worried about

Stephen, and worried that I was in no shape to be taking an important mid-term exam that day.

My head pounding, I made my way down the stairs in my nightgown. My mother was already up, making me a Plumrose ham and American cheese sandwich on white bread for lunch—the same sandwich she made every day except on Fridays, when she switched to peanut butter. That was her remaining homage to the old Catholic custom of eating no meat on Fridays.

I pulled the kettle from the stove, poured hot water into the dishpan in the sink, and started bathing myself while still in my nightgown. By now I had perfected a system of demurely sponging myself every morning, including my underarms and between my legs, without exposing myself to anyone.

The next thing I knew, Stephen was bounding down the stairs and cheerfully asking, "Hey, what's for breakfast?"

My mother smiled broadly. "Hooray, he's hungry! Now I *know* he's feeling better." I joined my mother in a sigh of relief. Stephen has an appetite. All is well. As every mother knows, nothing can be wrong with a child who has a good appetite.

I went back upstairs to finish dressing. By now Jerry was waking up. He was taking some classes at a local junior college, and they didn't start until later in the day. Marcia and Celia were both already at work. Just another day.

I waved good-bye to my mother and two brothers, and plodded off to school.

ഔ

Later that morning, I was sitting in study hall and my stomach was growling. I was starting to think about the ham sandwich in my bag when I heard my name announced in a robotic voice over the school intercom: "Catherine Marenghi, please come to the principal's office. Catherine Marenghi, please."

"*Uh-oh,*" I thought. Maybe Stephen had a relapse? Maybe he was in the hospital? Just in case, I instinctively stopped by my locker to grab my coat and bag before heading to the principal's office. As I hurried down the hall, I could see my sister Marcia standing outside the principal's office. That wasn't a good sign.

Without saying anything, she firmly took my arm and ushered me out to her car. Descending the granite steps, I asked, "Is it Stephen? Is it Stephen?"

She nodded.

"How is he?" Marcia got into the car without answering and turned on the ignition. I got into the passenger seat and asked her again, more insistently. *"How is he?"*

Without looking at me, she said, "He…. he isn't."

I quickly put my hand over my mouth so I wouldn't unleash a shriek of horror.

"No, no, not Stephen. No." My voice was shaking, pleading, but Marcia said no more, keeping her eyes trained on the road. The pain was unbearable, something screaming to escape my body. It came flooding out of my eyes while constricting my throat. I felt as if I was suffocating, my internal organs collapsing as I sunk into the seat.

Marcia silently drove me home, as I sobbed loudly all the way. When we got to the house, everyone was there, Ma, Celia, and Jerry, all choking with grief. I don't think any of us stopped crying for days.

From what I could piece together in the days that followed—no one was capable of talking coherently—I gathered that Stephen had started having trouble breathing some time mid-morning, not long after I had left for school. My mother had told Jerry to run to the nearest neighbor to call an ambulance.

When the ambulance arrived, Jerry was waiting, carrying Stephen in his arms and running down the dirt path toward the ambulance. Stephen had been gasping and his lips were turning blue before his body went limp in Jerry's arms. Ma and Jerry rode with him in the ambulance.

Stephen was pronounced dead on arrival at Milford Hospital.

I didn't know the cause of Stephen's death until I read about it in *The Milford Daily News*. It said Stephen had died from septic shock, resulting from fulminating pneumonia.

Fulminating. From the Latin word for lightning, meaning very fast. In a flash. Flash pneumonia.

The word evoked a memory of a late summer day, when Stephen was just a baby. He was playing in the dirt, just outside the house, when a sudden summer storm blew in. Deafening bolts of lightning were cracking the sky apart. Without thinking twice, my mother ran toward her baby and draped her body over him like a tent, to shield him from lightning. She would have laid down her life for him. But she couldn't save him from *this* lightning.

Why did it have to be Stephen? The youngest, most beautiful, most beloved of boys. Why did it have to be him?

The morning after Stephen's death, Reverend and Mrs. Washburn from the local Baptist church dropped by to offer their condolences. They had never come to our house before, and the visit was awkward and unexpected.

"I'm very sorry for your loss, Mrs. Marenghi," we heard him say from outside the door. "May we come in?"

We were unaccustomed to visitors, and the thin, pink man in a navy-blue topcoat and his gray-clad wife looked wrong and out of place as they walked in. All of us had been sitting together all morning, not saying a word, swallowing our own tears, and we looked warily at the couple who interrupted our grief. Without asking for permission, the minister assumed it would comfort us to lead us in prayer. I remember him standing just inside the door, bowing his head, folding his hands, and saying words he must have said a thousand times before:

"Let us pray. The Lord giveth and the Lord hath taken away; blessed be the name of the Lord."

The words made my heart sick. What did they mean? The Lord giveth, the Lord taketh, the Lord can do whatever He wants, anything at all, and get a free pass? What kind of a God is that? Surely, no good, benevolent God would end my brother's life in such an utterly pointless, arbitrary way. And if there is no good, benevolent God, no God who watches over us and cares about what happens to us, I wanted no part of that God.

The day my brother died, so did God.

But if not God, what then? What else was there to make sense of this death? What was the point of living if a cherished life could end at any moment? What was the point of loving someone if the one you love could be suddenly taken away?

In the days that followed Stephen's death, I could feel the weight of my love for him bear down on me, an impossible burden. It was a palpable heaviness. I didn't know what to do with it, who to give it to, this massive love that I once reserved for a little boy.

As I sat at Stephen's wake that week, for hours on end, the nightmarish vision of a young boy in an open casket, looking waxen and doll-like, was almost too gruesome to bear. Stephen's unnaturally small coffin was surrounded by sprays of white gladiolus, just as my father's had been some six years earlier. Again, they were flowers of death.

One of my former grade-school teachers, Miss Seaver, stopped by at the wake to pay her respects, and the sight of her reminded me of a childhood that Stephen would never have. My face began wrinkling up into a sob, and she squeezed my hands, fighting back tears of her own. And later, at the funeral mass, the sight of another young teacher, Mrs. Sarkisian, Stephen's fourth-grade teacher, followed by her entire class of thirty-five children filing into the church, made me almost collapse in grief.

I remember the day of the funeral being unusually warm and bright. I remember a cloudless sky, the particular dazzling shade of blue that seems unique to New England autumns. I remember the hearse driving into the Sacred Heart Cemetery, past the large family gravestone where my grandparents and father were buried, and on to the small, tree-shaded headstone that also said Marenghi, but it was small and sized for a young child. I remember the face of a young apprentice from the funeral home, with an expression of horror on his face as the small box was lowered into the earth. Was this the first child he had ever embalmed?

And then it was over. There were no more arrangements to be made, no more ceremonies to attend. Nothing more to be done.

I didn't know what else to do but go back to school, back to work, and schedule my make-up exams for the week I missed. The mid-term exams I was so dreading a few weeks before were actually a welcome relief, a return to normal, something to get my mind off Stephen.

But in every quiet moment, whenever I allowed myself to think of Stephen, the words to a song that just came out that year, "Fire and Rain," would echo in a continuous loop in my head: "*But I always thought that I'd see you again.*" I've never been able to hear that song without being overcome with an unbearable ache. For me, those words will never be about anyone but Stephen.

It's not as if the pain ever went away. Decades later, I can tell you it never does. But at some point, a stillness came over me. Not an acceptance, but a steadiness. I don't know when it happened, but a realization came to me like another kind of lightning.

It occurred to me that, even though life can be lost, it can also be created. It was such a simple but profoundly comforting idea. New life can be created. In fact, I held the seeds of new life in my own imperfect body. It's not that any newborn child could ever replace Stephen, as if it were a one-to-one trade. But the possibility of new life, I decided, was enough. It was the one and only thing I could think of to make up for the fact that people can die.

I was like a bird, aware of its wings for the first time, and now confident of their purpose. Life wins in the end. Life wins over death. This was the religion I was looking for. This is what I believed in.

14

FLOWER CHILDREN

"Everything all squared away at home now?" Mr. Sweeney asked.

It was my first day back at work at the travel agency since Stephen had died. I was mechanically and silently restocking the travel brochures on the wall display near the front counter, neatly arranging the pictures of beach umbrellas on the Cote D'Azur and lavish cruise ships, and Mr. Sweeney had noticed my silence.

"Mr. Sweeney," I said, looking at him directly, "I don't think things will ever be squared away."

"Give it time," he said. "Give it time. The Lord moves in mysterious ways."

He meant well, but I was growing weary of hearing about the Lord's mysterious ways, what the Lord giveth, what the Lord taketh, as if a child's sudden death could possibly be part of some divine plan. It was not in any plan. It just happened, and there was no good reason for it on heaven or earth.

I was trying hard to get back into a routine. Walk to school every day. Go to classes. Walk to work after school. Walk home. Study. Go to bed. It was a deliberate effort to get into a mindless rut. I would have welcomed a rut. I was tired of aberrations.

As I left work that mid-November evening, it was already getting dark, and Main Street was filling up with people, just "hanging out." It had become something of a public nuisance in Milford:

hundreds of young people, night after night, just standing around on downtown streets, or milling about by the low wall near the high school. Any stranger passing through town would think a parade was about to begin, with so many apparent spectators on the sidewalks.

And where there were aimless loiterers, there was something else: drugs. A thriving drug trade had taken root in our little town. President Nixon had declared his war on drugs, but coming from such a reviled character, it had the opposite effect in the trenches. Pot, acid, even heroin were making their way into the hands of children. Milford, tiny Milford, had attained the unfortunate distinction of having the third highest drug usage rate per capita in the country, after New York and San Francisco. It was even mentioned on the *Tonight Show*, causing Johnny Carson to exclaim, "Where the hell is Milford, Massachusetts?"

As I started my two-mile walk home, my arms loaded with school books, I heard a familiar voice call out, "Hey, Cath!"

I turned and saw a young man known locally as "Tiger," but I could never bring myself to call him that. I called him Dave. He was standing in the recessed doorway of a storefront, as if waiting for someone. Dark and husky, wearing a bomber jacket, he looked intimidating, like a bouncer in a bar.

"Hey, I'm sorry to hear about your bruthuh, Cath."

"Thanks, Dave." I thought it was decent of him to say that. I didn't exactly know why he had a bad reputation. I could only guess. But he was always nice to me. Respectful even.

"Hey, Cath, can I ask you somethin'? How much money you make in that travel agency?"

"Enough, I guess. Maybe $30 a week?"

"I feel so bad for you," he said, with an expression of genuine concern. "I see you work so hahd, every day. And for what?"

He stopped to pull his collar up against the cold, and put his hands back in his pockets.

"You know what I got in my pockets?" he asked.

"No….what?"

"Ten thousand bucks, cash. That's what I make in a day."

I just smiled and shrugged and walked on. I didn't doubt him, and I didn't want to ask for details. It just reminded me how easy it would have been for me, for anyone, to stray just two steps to the right, or two steps to the left, and fall into the wrong crowd.

So many of my classmates did. More than a few died of drug overdoses while still in their teens. Several more would be found dead in hotel rooms, with needles in their arms, in the coming years. My family never dabbled in drugs, alcohol, or illegal activity of any kind. At least we had that much going for us.

Dave might have been in the thick of the drug trade, for all I knew, but his consistent presence on Main Street always comforted me. I felt somehow he was watching over me. Nothing would happen to me as I walked through downtown Milford.

On my long walks home, leaving the brightly lit town center and heading down Main Street, and then turning onto East Main at Sacred Heart Church, I often felt exposed and vulnerable. It wasn't just the drugs that made the town scary. Men often stopped to offer me rides. By then I was tall and longhaired and fair-skinned, and probably prettier than I realized. I didn't dress in a provocative way, and I wore no makeup, but I was young and obviously a schoolgirl with my armload of books.

And I was always alone. I would hear male voices yelling from car windows, "Hey, red!" "Hey, carrot-top, look ova hee-ya!" Sometimes men drove slowly alongside me as I walked, trying to get my attention, asking, "Hey, what's your name?" I would veer quickly toward the nearest house and pretend to turn the handle of the front door, as if I lived there, until the car drove on.

Those long walks gave me my first lessons in pick-up lines from men. "I used to know your fathuh," was a typical line from older men, standing in doorways, looking to start a conversation with me and probably any other girl who walked by. Most everyone in my father's generation would have worked in the same factories at one time or another, so it was a believable ploy.

Until I heard the same line from two or three different men.

And there were younger men trying to get my attention, too. The drug traffic brought so many strangers to town, you never knew who you might come across. I was naive enough to think I could tell the right people from the wrong people. A young man in a pickup truck pulled up to me one day as I was walking home, initially to ask for directions. He was soft-spoken, long-haired and bearded, telling me he was from Vermont, where he "lived off the land"—speaking the language of flower children, language I had heard from popular songs. He used words like "mellow" and "laid-back," and referred to people as "chicks" or "dudes." His easy smile caught my attention, and I lingered a bit to chat with him through his car window. At that moment, my brother Jerry and cousin Richard just happened to be driving by in Richard's car, and I heard it screech to a stop.

"Hey, Cath, get ova hee-ya!"

I got into the car as the pickup truck quickly sped away, and my protective brother gave me a good scolding for talking to strangers.

If truth be told, the attention of boys and men made me feel better about myself, even if it scared me half the time. It also made me feel human. It was a way to be anonymous, to be seen just as a girl—not the poor girl, the smart girl, the tragic girl, or any other kind of girl. Just a girl.

When I got home at night, my mother seemed to be mindless and distant, robotically preparing dinner, trying not to notice one less person at the table. I couldn't help but feel a little less angry, a little more sympathetic toward her. Somehow her loss of a child seemed even bigger than my loss of a brother. It softened how I felt about her.

During the week, she frequently made simple meals, like Mama Celeste frozen pizzas, heated in an old toaster oven that was missing its glass door. She had an odd practice of sticking the large frozen pizza onto the toaster oven rack, even though it was too big, and half the pizza would stick out, stiff and frozen. When the half that was inside the oven cooked through, it would cause the frozen half on the outside to flop downward. That was her signal to spin the frozen half to the inside, and somehow prop up the cooked side that now stuck out. Why she simply didn't cut the pizza in half in the first place, I didn't know. I didn't say anything, not wanting to be critical at a time like that. And she seemed so pleased with the system she devised, I didn't want to spoil it for her.

It made me wonder how this could be the same woman who could cook nearly anything my father brought home from hunting trips, from rabbits to ducks to deer, so many years ago. Back then she could skin, gut, pluck, debone, scale, and dress nearly anything. She could even turn a squirrel into a passable stew, her personal interpretation of *cacciatore*. Now she seemed befuddled by a frozen pizza.

৪৩

For my remaining time at Milford High, I just wanted to get through it as quickly as possible. I was focused on college like a guided missile. I thought about little else. I wanted to leave home at the first opportunity, and college was my escape hatch. I wanted to live, to see the world, to have a home and a life I could share with others, without hiding anything from anyone.

Everything I did was aimed at building my portfolio for college, just as Mr. Moran had advised. I took part in every extracurricular activity I could, the school newspaper, the chorus, the yearbook, anything to step outside of my life and myself.

I didn't have much social interaction, beyond writing letters to my school friends—my only way of communicating with them outside of school. Occasionally a friend or two might invite me to her house, but I was never able to reciprocate the invitation, and so every friendship had an unspoken limitation, As for boys, I didn't think much about them. Not much hope for that. Being one of the smart girls in the class was not conducive to a social life.

The one exception was a late winter night my senior year when I went to see a local rock band playing at the Hopedale Town Hall—the tiniest of venues in the tiniest of towns. It was an unknown group called Aerosmith, a band I was certain would never amount to anything, seeing as how they were clearly no more than a tribute band, with its lead singer Steven Tyler desperately imitating Mick Jagger. I remember him opening his bright silk shirt, exposing his boyish hairless chest, and then rolling his eyes petulantly when the security guard made him button back up again.

A boy on the dance floor with long black hair and pale skin, an unintended goth look, approached me as if he knew me.

Yelling to be heard above the music, he said, "I know your sister!"

"What? I can't hear you."

"I KNOW YOUR SISTER—MARCIA—I WORK AT THE HOME LAUNDRY AFTER SCHOOL."

"How do you know she's my sister?"

"I've seen you with her. You look just like her."

Well, I didn't believe that for a minute. But it was as good an opening line as any. I soon learned he lived and went to school in another town, and luckily he had no way of knowing I was a smart girl. That bit of knowledge would have taken the starch out of him in a hurry. I certainly wasn't going to tell him.

On the dimly lit dance floor, in a sea of young bodies pressed close to each other, he wasted no time stealing a kiss, my first French kiss—and I found it appalling. What was he doing with his tongue? He was getting saliva in my mouth. Horrible. I really had no idea what was going on. Meanwhile I felt my body getting heavy and moist, like an orange segment left on a radiator to warm and plump until it burst.

I didn't have a phone number to give him, but I promised I'd call him soon from a pay phone not far from my house. I knew of a pay phone with a marvelous kind of diarrhea—it had no ability to retain any coins you fed it. The dimes and quarters would jingle down and pass through to the refund slot, even though the call went through. And so began a telephone affair with the boy who would one day take me to the senior prom—but he was never ever invited into my house.

With the rest of my free time, I busied myself sewing clothes, almost fanatically, turning inexpensive cuts of cloth into dresses, skirts, and even a winter coat. It became a kind of game for me to see how far I could stretch a dollar. Even my mother's grocery shopping became a challenge; given a shopping list and a $20 bill, I would find a way to buy everything on the list and still come home with change.

I spent hours writing poetry and stories and essays, even music reviews, for publication in the school newspaper, and I typeset everything myself at the offices of the *Milford Daily News*. Through an arrangement between the town newspaper and the high school, students could use the newspaper's facilities and equipment on weekends, when the office was silent and almost empty.

There was a ghastly typesetting machine that required typing everything twice to make evenly justified columns; the first time you typed a line, it calculated the extra picas of space you would need to add or subtract to make the column the correct width, and then you would retype the same line with the manual insertion or deletion of imperceptible picas of space between words.

So it went, line after line, and once the column was finished, you would cut out the perfectly rectangular text with an X-Acto knife on a cutting board, run the column through the rollers of a hot wax machine, and then carefully press the sticky waxed column onto a page template. If you misspelled anything, you could run all those extra words you typed through the wax machine, cut out the correct text, and paste it over the mistake.

The finished page would be mounted on a board and submitted for printing. This is what passed for automated typesetting at the time, but it was oddly irresistible to me. Hour after hour on weekends, I worked alone in that newsroom. It made me feel I was creating something. It was my first taste of publishing.

I wish, at that point in my budding career, I could have learned more than the mechanics of publishing. I wish I had learned the skills I would later learn as a journalist: how to do an interview, how to ask questions, persistently, rephrasing the same question over and over, until you arrive at an answer. There were so many questions I would later wish I had asked my mother, but I had been frustrated in the past by her incomplete or indirect responses.

When I was a girl, I once asked my mother, "Why did Dad build the stairs this way, so they force you to walk into a wall?"

"Oh, well, back then, times were hard. We didn't have much. But we always had our good name…."

"But that's not what I asked. Why did he build the stairs this way?"

And so I would get frustrated and impatient, and usually gave up on conversations like this. My mind always worked in a linear path, from point A to point B, where point A had a clear and logical conclusion at point B. My mother never seemed to think that way.

I never knew if she was deliberately evasive or just didn't want to talk about anything. I wish I had known how to ask better questions. I wanted so much to know why my family was so different, so poor, so isolated, so ridiculously out of step with everyone else. Did my mother know? If she did, why wouldn't she tell me?

I wasn't any better, never sharing anything I was thinking or doing with my mother. I coexisted with her, each of us in our own separate universes. I gave my mother my report cards to sign, without which she would never have known what I was studying. Meanwhile I was applying for college admission, for financial aid and scholarships, producing endless documents that I pushed in front of her, without explanation.

"Just sign it!" I would say, rolling my eyes and tapping my fingers impatiently with every document I presented.

"But I want to read it before I sign it!"

"I've already read it, so you don't have to. Just sign it!"

I was so unkind to her. I wouldn't allow her to help me with anything. With all the certainty and self-importance of youth, I thought no one could help me but myself.

By a narrow margin, my grades were the highest in my class. I would be valedictorian. In the spring of my senior year, just as the long dirt path to the house was melting into mud, and Ma was laying down long wooden planks to form crude stepping stones over the mud, I began to receive my college acceptances one by one, along with generous scholarship offers, from Harvard, Wellesley, and Tufts.

Perhaps because I was so focused on my escape plan, I didn't stop and think about what a big deal this was. Harvard? Me? Some of my relatives had been surprised I had the audacity even to apply to Harvard. They were even more were surprised when I turned Harvard down.

My reasons were very practical: Harvard, it seemed, frowned upon taking a junior year abroad, and I was aching to study Renaissance art in Italy and explore the mysteries of my Italian ancestry. And Harvard's application form had so many questions about family lineage, asking if I was related to long-dead alumni with upper-crust Anglo-Saxon names—not an Italian name in the bunch. The snobbery of it turned me cold.

Wellesley too, felt just as patronizing. Its admission officer assured me I'd "feel right at home there" because they had lots of poor girls like me, from inner-city slums and Iowa farms, as if I would immediately see something in common with them. As if poor people were all card-carrying members of the same exclusive club.

Tufts alone was small, friendly and welcoming. It encouraged study abroad, and it offered an Experimental College to try new approaches. In an era of revolution and protest, Tufts went against the grain. That won me over completely.

I was headed to the light on the hill, as Tufts was known, in the town of Medford, Massachusetts, just north of Boston. The campus was situated on Route 16, the same road that cut through the center of Milford, connecting my past and my future like an umbilical cord. In my heart I was already cutting the cord, and I wouldn't be turning back.

15

RITES OF PASSAGE

Barely a week into my freshman year, I arrived at my dorm room after morning classes to find my roommate standing on her bed.

"There's an ant! An ant! Over there!" She pointed nervously. "Get it! Step on it!"

"An ant?" I thought. *"Seriously? This young woman can't handle an ant?"* I once saw a snake slither across the floor of my family's house, probably from some hole in the rotting floorboards, which were only inches above the bare earth. What would she have said if she saw that?

"It's just a carpenter ant," I said, showing little concern as I picked up the shiny black creature with my bare fingers and flicked it out the open window.

"Why didn't you kill it?"

"It's not hurting anything."

"Where do you come from anyway?" she asked. Coincidentally I was wondering the same thing about her. What pristine place did she come from that had none of the ants, spiders, moths, beetles, silverfish, woodlice, praying mantis, or any number of other creeping crawling creatures that I had known as constant bedside companions?

I had already told her the town I came from in our first meeting. This time I elaborated, saying I came from a somewhat rural part of the town, where living with insects in summer was pretty common, and I hoped to leave it at that.

"Were you very poor?" she asked me, looking wide-eyed and sympathetic.

I hated the question. I had spent my first days of college trying to avoid conversations with well-heeled classmates on topics like household help, horseback riding, equestrian attire, and high-end stereo equipment. This was a young woman from what I guessed to be a comfortably affluent family, nothing like the people I knew in a town just forty-five miles away. She ate strange foods I had never seen before, like lox and bagels, and celebrated holidays I had never heard of. I must have seemed equally alien to her. I was a pale-skinned ghost of a girl with crooked teeth, no makeup, and hand-sewn clothes.

"You might say that," I said warily, not wanting to explain. Her wide eyes expanded further.

"You must be full of hatred and hostility," she said with a serious expression and concerned tone. Was that something she had read in an article somewhere? That the poor are boiling over with hatred and hostility? The fact is, just the opposite was true. I felt very grateful. And very lucky.

I couldn't have this conversation any more. I sensed I was in danger of becoming her pet project, a social sciences experiment in dealing with the exotic species known as the very poor. I excused myself to use the large communal restroom across the hall.

Safe behind the locked bathroom stall, I tried to collect myself. I noticed my face getting hot and beading lightly with sweat. I felt disoriented, even a little dizzy. For so many years I had worked for this, to get away from home, to be in college, but now I was wondering if I would ever belong here.

Where on earth was I? What month was it? You couldn't even tell it was harvest season. It had been years since my family actually farmed in earnest, but you could always sense the season by what you saw growing around you. Goldenrod would be blooming, the wild white grapes would be ready to pick now, plump and sweet, and my mother would be stoking the stove with coal on the lengthening nights. And I remembered that rush of panic every fall when the first frost was forecast, compelling the whole family to rush out and harvest whatever was still growing before nightfall. There would be no such seasonal urgency here.

Here at school, I felt so uprooted and disconnected. Was I actually missing home?

Looking down at the underpants rolled down to my ankles, I noticed they were drenched in blood. I was menstruating. Again.

Maybe that's why I felt so woozy. My body was always a little haywire, menstruating uncontrollably for months without interruption, and then stopping for unpredictable lengths of time. I made my way back to the dorm room, holding on to the wall for fear of fainting, and bent forward as if I were punched in the gut. When I got back to my room, I gave my roommate a shock.

"Catherine, what's wrong with you? You look terrible! You're white as a sheet!"

"It's nothing. Just my period. It's always been this way."

"Not any more. You need a doctor. You're going to health services right now!"

I hadn't been to a doctor in years. And I had never sought any medical advice for the wildly erratic menstrual periods I endured. I didn't know any better. I just thought it was something I was supposed to live with.

The campus physician gave me a cure to regulate my body that I would never have expected. Estrogen tablets. Birth control. The fabled Pill.

It was beyond my wildest dreams. The Pill would regulate my periods like clockwork, making them utterly predictable, and they would be shorter and lighter. And as a little side benefit, I was also protected from getting pregnant.

I wouldn't get pregnant? Oh. Oh! Now that changed everything, didn't it?

Now I could really be as free as a man, as free as all the men who once gathered with my father to roast sausages over an open fire on my childhood ice-fishing trips. Never again would I have to worry my body would sneak up on me with some unpleasant surprise. Now I could be as free as my father and all the men through history who have ever gathered around bonfires, while women stayed home with the children. I could be as wild and promiscuous as I wanted. It was years before anyone had ever heard of AIDS, and the era of free love was still reigning supreme.

හිഇ

College was a time to experiment, to push limits. So when I joined my first drinking party on a Friday evening in the crowded lounge of our co-ed dorm, I said yes to every drink that was handed me. I never drank in high school, so I had never learned what my limit was.

Whatever that limit might have been, I exceeded it that night. I have no recollection of what happened. I only know I was carried to my room and deposited safely onto my bed, where I woke up the next morning feeling remarkably refreshed. At some point in the night I had vomited the contents of my stomach, at some unknown location, leaving some trace evidence on my hair and sleeves, but I remembered nothing about it.

I was later told I was surprisingly entertaining the evening before, standing up and regaling my classmates with speeches like, "I came to college with the *express purpose* of losing my…. my *dignity!*" I don't know if anyone knew what I was talking about, but they found me hilarious. The whole episode left me wondering what I might be capable of if I weren't always so self-conscious and upstanding, if I just allowed myself to let go.

My initial awkwardness as a newly matriculated freshman softened after a while. I found it easiest to make friends with those who didn't flaunt their Scarsdale-Long-Island wealth, and I found a few who shared my lack of means. I met a young Italian American student, Lou, who was raised not far from my hometown. It was he who asked me out on my first college date. We went to a Harvard Square restaurant called 33 Dunster Street, where I had my first experience with the art of ordering a bottle of wine. I wore a sundress that I fashioned out of a colorful bed sheet, and I thought the evening went well. Not a romantic date, but a date nonetheless, and the beginning of a long friendship.

Lou and I soon became "food friends," bound together by the pleasure we took in eating. Lou seemed to know a lot about fine cuisine and gave me my first cooking lessons, showing me how to mince garlic very fine and how to sauté spinach in olive oil until it barely wilted. Many years later, he would work at the top-rated restaurant in Boston as its chief "fromagier," an expert on fine cheeses. Quite possibly the best job title I have ever heard.

Some time into my sophomore year, I overheard him one night in his dorm room, in the early hours of the morning, with a young male friend of his, listening to loud music that I hadn't heard before, the two of them screaming the singer's name as if in a delirious rapture: "David Bowie! David Bowie! David Bowie!"

I stood outside the door looking a bit puzzled, until another friend of ours took me aside and explained.

"Lou is gay."

"He's what?"

"Gay. He's gay. Isn't it obvious? David Bowie? Come on."

Having no prior experience with anyone who had openly professed to be gay, I was bewildered. I wondered if it was somehow my fault, if something I had said or done had thrown him over the edge.

Making friends with outsiders, minorities, and the full-scholarship kids seemed to be my niche at college. More than a few of my friends were black—the preferred term at the time for African American. James Brown sang it, "Say it loud, I'm black and I'm proud." It wasn't too long ago that all people of color were called "negroes," a word I once used myself and had to deliberately unlearn.

I met a number of black women when I signed up for beginner swimming classes my freshman year. Learning to swim was a requirement of graduation, and I was the only girl in the class who was *not* black. It was such a stunning statement of economic class: only the students from low-income families had never learned how to swim.

One of my best friends was a poet and folk singer of Jamaican descent. He had café au lait skin, small almond eyes, and large soft lips that I wanted to rest my face on, like a sweet pillow. I loved the fact that he wrote poetry and turned his words into songs. I felt a powerful attraction to him, but he made it clear I was not his physical type. No matter. We spent many evenings sitting in the stairwell of our dormitory, where his guitar chords echoed magnificently against the cinderblock walls, and there he introduced me to my first sip of Jack Daniels—surprisingly delicious for a whiskey, I thought, and one that has remained my preferred drink.

I often wondered what my father would have thought if he were still alive. On the ladder of his prejudices, the Irish were quite low, and Sicilians were lower. Anyone of color had to have been competing with them both for the bottom rung. And anyone who was gay would not even have existed in his universe. What would he have thought if I brought my young Jamaican poet home to meet him? I wasn't sure he would even have approved of my going away to college.

I was living in a new world, populated with Jews, blacks, gays, lesbians, Communists, women's libbers, Muslims, Puerto Ricans, Christian fundamentalists, and foreign students from every country imaginable. All of this was new to me. And yet, I felt at home. All of these people were there because they were good students. I blossomed among smart, politically active, poetic, passionate, argumentative young people. For the first time in my life, it was okay to be smart, to be different, and not have it held against me in my social life. Everyone was smart, so it didn't matter. I wasn't a freak any more.

A new book had come out in 1971 called *Our Bodies, Ourselves.* It was a feminist manifesto on women's health and sexuality. It was a groundbreaking book, written by twelve Boston feminist-activists. Well before the Internet era, it was next to impossible for women to get straight talk on things like sex and the workings of our own bodies. It was one of the first books I bought my freshman year, using my savings from my job at the travel agency. I hoped it would explain what was always a mystery to me: What on earth is virginity? And how could I get rid of it?

I hated the way virginity was always spoken of, as a precious gift you save for your wedding night, an honor bestowed on a man. That gave it far too much significance, and ceded too much ownership to the male of the species. This was my body, no one else's. I wanted to be rid of this impediment to my liberation as expeditiously as possible, the way I would brush aside a spider web that stood in my path. I just wanted to know what it was, how to get rid of it, and how much it would hurt.

The book, as it turned out, was a disappointment. It said, "Virginity is a state of mind." That wasn't very helpful. I wanted more basic information than this book was able to give me. I would have to find out for myself. I devised a plan to be rid of my virginity without ever giving any man the satisfaction of saying, "I am the one who took her virginity."

My plan was simple. The next time a young man lingered too long at my bedroom door before saying goodnight, got a little too close to my face, and put his hand on the curve of my hip, I would invite him into my room and lock the door behind me. We would lie on my twin bed with the Indian bedspread, which was mostly a cranberry red pattern, perfect to hide any stains. And if I bled on that bedspread, I would brush it off as an unexpected early onset of my menstrual cycle. No one but I would ever know what had just happened.

And that's exactly what I did.

Because I had grown up in the late 1960s and early 1970s, an era of social ferment and equal rights for all, I was always trying to prove I could do anything a man could do. If a man could wield power tools and make things with his hands, so could I. If a man could lift a heavy suitcase and carry it up four flights of stairs, so could I. Any job a man could do, any hard liquor a man could swallow, so could I. And if a man could be free to sow his wild oats, then so could I.

Now I was, in my mind, completely and totally liberated. Poverty was my chastity belt in high school, keeping every boy at bay. College unlocked it. I welcomed men into my bed as easily as a mind entertains a whim. And if someone rolled a joint and passed it around, I didn't refuse that, either. No longer did I have to be the good girl, the paragon of my high school class, the one everyone had such high hopes for. I was living my own life, by my own rules.

There was always a limit, though, to how far I would go. Smoking a joint seemed harmless enough, but I never bought any pot with my own money, never smoked pot or drank alcohol alone, and never moved to anything more serious, like LSD, which was plentiful on campus back then. I had learned my drinking limit, once, and stayed well below that threshold after that. Having lost a father and a brother, I placed too high a value on my life to ever do anything to harm myself. And I didn't think my family could handle another casualty.

My mother sent frequent letters, usually once a week, from the very beginning of my college years. She was a prolific letter writer; lacking a phone all her life, and it was her only way of staying in touch with anyone. Like my father, she had beautiful handwriting, and her grammar was flawless. She often wrote that she missed me terribly, noting sadly that she was sitting on my cot in what was formerly "my corner" while she wrote to me.

"This corner of the house is so empty without you," one of her letters began. I was the first of her children to leave the fold. But I think she was happy for me, too, always eager to hear of some small achievement I had to report.

When I wrote and told her I won a coveted spot in the famous poet Denise Levertov's writing class, she wrote back her beaming approval, and she asked if I had ever heard of the poet Edgar Guest. From the little I knew, he seemed old-fashioned and stilted, someone who might have been popular fifty years earlier, so the only conversation we ever had about poetry ended there. If I had been more persistent, I might have asked my mother many more questions about poetry. I might have learned she kept a box of poetry books from her school days, including some of my favorites, like Emily Dickinson, and that she sometimes wrote poems herself.

Except occasional visits on school breaks and holidays, I never lived with my family again. Even over the summers, I found ways to stay on campus, mowing lawns for the Tufts Facilities and Maintenance Department in return for a free dorm room, and working as a waitress to earn my bread. Whenever I did visit my family, I felt like a stranger, worried that anything I said might be misunderstood or perceived as showing off. I was acutely and guiltily aware of my unique privilege of going to a fine college.

On one of my visits during the Christmas holidays, I joined my family in watching a made-for-TV version of *Gulliver's Travels*. It was truly awful. Without thinking, I said, "Jonathan Swift must be rolling in his grave."

Celia shot back a look at me, her lips curled in contempt, "You think you're so *smaht*, don't you?" I felt ashamed for saying out loud the name of the story's famous author, which I thought was common knowledge, and even more ashamed for noticing my sister's thick Boston accent—something I had so carefully excised and trimmed from my own speech.

Despite my eagerness to get away from Milford, I was always connected to the town and my family. I never missed a family birthday gathering, never discarded the old skeleton key that unlocked the front door, and never ceased to call the place "home." I would rent many apartments and own many houses in my life, but not one of them was ever more than a fifty-mile radius from Milford.

16

FOREIGN

In nessuna
parte
di terra
mi posso
accasare.

(From *"Girovago,"* by Giuseppe Ungaretti.
Translation: *"There is no place on earth that can I make my home."*)

My longest time away from my family was when I went to Florence,
Italy, for my much-anticipated junior year abroad. My whole family
came to Boston's Greyhound Station to send me off; I was boarding
a bus for Montreal, where the flights to Italy were much cheaper than
they were from Boston.

As I looked out the bus window at them, Marcia stood
waving and calling out, "Happy Birthday! Merry Christmas! Happy
New Year! Happy Easter!" She covered every holiday we would not
spend together for the next ten months.

My scholarship money and savings would get me most of the
way to Italy, but I still needed to take out a student loan in the
amount of $900. I thought it was a princely sum. It was the only

student debt I ever incurred, and I couldn't imagine how I would ever pay it back, only that I would somehow have to find a way.

I spent the first six weeks of my Italian year in Perugia, a medieval Umbrian town, studying at the Università per Stranieri, the university for foreigners. There I would get an intensive advanced course in Italian to improve what I had already learned in Italian classes. Then I would attend a full academic year at the Università di Firenze, in Florence, taking all classes in Italian alongside native Italian students.

If I thought I would find some commonality with Italians, I would be quickly dissuaded. With our long hair and hippie-era clothes, the American students stood out like wild untamed bandits against a population of slim, elegantly dressed young Italians. They wore jeans, as we did, but they were nothing like the ragged, faded, patch-covered Levi's that I wore. Theirs were dark blue and crisply pressed, tailored to fit closely against their fine slim limbs, and they wore elegant fitted blouses with cashmere sweaters that they folded expertly like a belt around their tiny waists when they weren't wearing them. Florence was a mecca of high fashion and wealth, the center of the universe in Florentine eyes. And when their university offered a course on the history of art, it began and ended with the Florentine Renaissance, as if no other art existed.

The Italians I boarded with, both in Perugia and Florence, were people who made extra money by taking in foreign students, turning their homes into *pensiones*, but that experience did not immediately translate into an appreciation of other cultures. I found my Italian host family in Perugia completely insular, homebodies whose social lives began and ended with their immediate families. I wanted to go out dancing and listen to rock and roll music, as the other American students did, but the Italians I knew simply did not go out in the evenings.

I found greater camaraderie with the scores of Iranian students who lived in Italy, or "Persians" as they called themselves, all of them from affluent families who prospered under the rein of Shah Reza Pahlavi, and they all adored American rock and roll.

I caused quite a stir one evening in Perugia when a young Iranian man came to the door of my *pensione* to invite me out. Es-Hagh, or Essi as he was known, was a fellow student I knew from the Università per Stranieri. The lady of the house saw Essi's dark hair and beard and flew into a rage, sending him scuttling away.

"Dirty filthy drunken Arabs," she screamed at me in Italian. At least those were the words I understood in her long stream of expletives. "Drunks and troublemakers! They're not welcome here!"

"He's not Arab," I countered reflexively, not thinking about the fact that it didn't matter.

"Never again! I won't have it!"

Unfortunately the other American students boarding in the same house all suffered from my transgression. For the remaining week we had at their *pensione*, the host family shunned us and would not take meals with us at a communal dining table, as they did previously. The family ate in the small kitchen, while the student boarders dined on cold boiled potatoes and other paltry leftovers in the formal dining room.

When we got to Florence, at least the lady of the house at our new *pensione* was upfront about the rules.

"*Una preghiera*," the Signora said to us. "I beg you. If you come home in the evening with a young gentleman, say goodnight to him around the corner of the street, and not in front of our building where all the neighbors can see."

That seemed fair enough. We were warned. It would be a courtesy to her to spare her from the wagging tongues of her neighbors. But I continued to meet young Iranian men in the center of town, and ride off with them on the back of their Vespas.

The Signora of the house in Florence was a Fellini-esque figure who wore exotic turbans and thick black eyeliner, and she smoked serenely with a cigarette holder from her regal perch at the head of the table. She was a long-divorced piano teacher who occupied the elegant penthouse of a six-story apartment building. She had no children and seemed to enjoy the youthful company of her boarders, filling her spare bedrooms with American, British, and

Swiss students—she tolerated no other nationalities. She liked to move her entire dining table—linens, china, crystal and all—outdoors to her rooftop patio, and linens would blow and flap in the wind as we sipped Vin Santo and delicately ate blood oranges for dessert with silver forks and knives.

For one year, I was thoroughly imbued with Renaissance art, Italian cinema, and literature from Dante to Lampedusa, all filling my head with their gorgeous metaphors and translucent color, but on the street, I was a stranger, an obvious American. I was big, like all the other beef-fed Americans were, not tiny and delicate like Italians. When I tried on tall leather boots at a fashionable shop on Via Tornabuoni, the boots wouldn't zip up all the way. I weighed just 135 pounds, not bad for my five-foot-seven frame, but I was a giant by Italian standards. And my loose ragged hair trailing down to my waist instantly gave me away as an American.

The assumption was that any American girl was "easy," so the catcalls were incessant. I could not walk anywhere without being assaulted with male voices calling out at me. "Ti sposo," they would call out while whizzing by on their Vespas—"I'll marry you!" Or, "Sembra La Maddalena!" was another frequently heard cry—"She looks like Mary Magdalene!" That's because Mary Magdalene was always portrayed in Renaissance paintings as a woman with long reddish-blond hair. In Donatello's bronze statue, Mary Magdalene's hair trails down to her knees. It seemed Italian men always compared a woman to a famous painting or statue, never to a movie star or TV celebrity as they did in America.

The disrespect accorded by Italian men to American women was perhaps another reason why I found commonality with the Persian men in Italy, who were much closer in sensibility to Americans than the Italians. When I confided to La Signora at my *pensione* that I was dating an Iranian, she was horrified. "But Iranian men hold women down, like this!" she said, pushing her thumb down hard against the dinner table.

"And Italian men?" I replied. "Gli uomini Italiani, che cosa fanno?" What do *they* do?"

Despite her admonitions, I could never shake my attraction to Persian men. When winter break arrived and I had no money to fly home to the States as all the other American students did, I seized the opportunity to go back to Perugia and pay a visit to Essi, the one who caused such a stir when he visited my *pensione* there. He and his brother Mehrtash were still sharing an apartment near the ancient center of Perugia, close to the university, and they had invited me to join them.

Before I left town, I boxed up the little Christmas presents I bought for my family, trinkets from the San Lorenzo street market: leather wallets, scarves, handkerchiefs, and such. The kind of things one haggles for and still fears paying too much. They all went into one big box that I dropped off at the Post Office, addressed to "13 Prairie St., Milford, Mass. 01757"—and below, in giant letters, "USA."

The trains from Florence to Perugia were frequent and affordable. I loved train travel, and the small intimate compartments made it easy to socialize with fellow travelers. The evening train I chose to Perugia was fairly crowded, and as I walked the narrow aisle, peering into one compartment window after another, looking for an empty seat, I saw a young man sitting by himself who smiled and waved and beckoned me to join him. I took the seat facing his.

He quickly introduced himself as Lorenzo. A fair-haired and boyishly handsome young man with tight curls, pale-green eyes, and pink cheeks, he explained he was from Rome, but studied in Florence; he was going to visit friends in Perugia.

"I, too, am going to Perugia," I said in my clearest Italian.

Confident I would not miss my stop with a native Italian traveling companion, I settled in and got comfortable for the two-hour journey. Lorenzo and I were soon engaging in small talk about the difficulty of learning a foreign language, and his struggles with the double meanings of English words.

"The word *'jam'*—you say 'traffic jam' when you have a lot of cars in one place, and you also put 'jam' on your bread!" he said in English, with an amazed expression. "But now I remember the word for traffic jam, I don't forget, because I think of all those cars like fruit stirred up in a pot!"

Our laughing banter soon escalated into outright flirtation. Before long he was touching my hand, remarking how soft and white it was, turning it upward as if to read my palm. I was completely drawn in, thinking he was more pretty than handsome with his delicate complexion, translucent as bone china.

Then we heard the train announcer calling out the next stop: "Prossima fermata—Assisi."

Lorenzo and I were so caught up in making eyes at each other, we hadn't been paying attention to the train stops.

Assisi—the famous home village of St. Francis—was the stop *after* Perugia. Had we missed our stop? Lorenzo and I gave each other a momentary look of panic and quickly grabbed our belongings before rushing off the train.

After stepping down on the platform, we saw Assisi did not have a full train station—just a small, open, unmanned depot, a structure used mainly for shelter from the rain. The town of Assisi itself was high up on a cliff in the distance, and since it was after 11:00 p.m., there was no point in making the long hike to go there. Nothing would be open.

Lorenzo and I looked at each other, frustrated and sheepish. Here I was, en route to see a gentleman friend, and by flirting with a train passenger on the way, I missed my stop. Poetic justice, yes, but there was no time to think about that. We quickly located the timetable posted on the wall at the terminal, and the next train back to Perugia wasn't scheduled for another two hours. It was about a half-hour away by car—too far to walk, especially on a cold December night—but there were no taxicabs in the area. It was utterly silent, utterly dark, except for a single light bulb swinging on a long wire from the depot's ceiling.

Maybe we could hitchhike?

Lorenzo headed out toward the main road as I followed behind, my small suitcase in hand, but there wasn't a car in sight.

When a lone car finally appeared, it sped right past Lorenzo, despite his waving wildly to flag the driver down.

With our coats flapping in the winter wind, we finally admitted defeat and returned to the shelter of the train depot. There was nothing to do but wait, which we did, in complete silence. When the return train finally came through around 1:00 a.m., we had to pay a surcharge for buying our ticket on the train, but at least we were going in the right direction.

It was sweet relief when our feet finally touched down on the platform at Perugia's train station, and Lorenzo gallantly walked me to my destination before going to his own. Standing outside Essi's apartment house, a narrow stucco building in a long line of attached buildings on a dark side street, Lorenzo seemed uncomfortable leaving me there.

"Are you sure you'll be okay?"

"Yes, I'll be fine. Thank you for walking me here."

We looked at each other with a mix of sadness and weariness, and I watched him turn and disappear into the night.

I ascended the stairs as quietly as I could and knocked softly on Essi's door.

"Essi! Sono io, Caterina!" I whispered. *"It's me!"*

I didn't hear any response or any movement inside. So I knocked a little harder. "Essi! Essi!"

Suddenly a door on the lower landing flew open, light flooded the hallway, and a heavy woman in a flowered bathrobe emerged, glaring up at me from the base of the stairs with something resembling a baseball bat in her hands.

"Puttana! Va via! Va! Ti ammazzo!"

Her eyes were glowing with rage. There was no point explaining to a woman who was threatening to kill me that I was not a prostitute. My heart racing, I flew down the stairs and scurried past her, flying away as fast as I could, with the menacing woman inches behind me.

Now what? I was exhausted, cold, hungry, and alone on a dark Perugian street, not a streetlight in sight. I started walking. I was hoping to find a hotel of some kind, but the town was shuttered up tightly, as if it were expecting an alien invasion. Heavy metal grates were pulled over every storefront. I didn't know what else to do but to keep walking.

The streets of Perugia are a tangle of narrow cobbled pathways, stairways to nowhere, and winding streets barely wide enough for a FIAT. I was in the ancient part of the city, with massive stone walls of pale travertine blocks dating back to the Etruscans. I had no idea where I was heading. Not a window was illuminated. Not a soul was in sight. Only the moon and stars lit my path.

Just as I began contemplating the prospect of a doorway in which to curl up and sleep, I saw a figure emerge from around a corner, walking toward me in the dim starlight. He was a street sweeper, dressed all in black, carrying a long crude broom that looked as if the bristles were fashioned from tree branches and twigs. At last, a human being! What luck! This was surely a man who would know his way around this town. I approached the man, hopeful he could give me directions to a hotel, and said, "Signore, mi scusi…"

The man ignored me! He didn't pause or flinch, keeping his eyes trained straight ahead, and walking right past me as if I were invisible.

Now I was truly frightened. Nearly hallucinating from exhaustion, I began to wonder if I actually might be invisible. Strange thoughts and random associations were forming in my head. I remembered the story of the ghost of Hamlet's father, and how the ghost disappeared when the cock crowed at the break of dawn. I started thinking that I might be a ghost. Maybe I had died I in a train wreck between Florence and Perugia, and now I was sentenced to an eternal hell of wandering through what looked like an M. C. Escher lithograph.

I persuaded myself that if I were still alive when the first light of dawn appeared, I would have proof positive that I was not a ghost. I looked around me for the highest spot in town and headed there, hoping to get the first glimpse of morning light.

I was drawn toward the ancient Pallazzo dei Priori, a familiar sight, with its crenellated roofline and its dramatic stone steps at the grand portal facing the town square. I climbed the stone steps as high as I could go and finally collapsed in exhaustion, dropping my small bag and purse at my side. I stayed there, shivering under the bronze griffin and Guelf lion mounted above my head, waiting for the dawn's light to determine my fate.

The morning arrived uneventfully. I don't remember if I had nodded off, but I do recall the joy of opening my eyes and seeing my own jagged shadow against the Pallazzo steps. Sunlight! The weary traveler was not a ghost after all. I stretched and yawned, just as the sound of shopkeepers lifting their metal grates broke the silence of the long night. A café was in sight. Hot espresso beckoned. And before the morning was out, I would be back at Essi's door with a fantastic story to tell.

৪১৩৪

My last week in Florence compelled me to make one last visit to the Uffizi Gallery, one of my many visits to the former palace of the Medici family. The word "Uffizi" means "offices," a place once used to conduct business. The same ruthless bankers who invented the general ledger and double-entry accounting were also patrons of the arts, amassing the world's greatest works by Botticelli, Caravaggio, da Vinci, Mantegna, and Michelangelo. Wandering the galleries, I was struck by a group of schoolchildren, no more than eight years old, carrying tiny folding chairs. I followed them as they set up their seats in front of Giotto's famous Ognissanti painting of the Madonna and Child. And so began a makeshift art class with a young schoolteacher presiding.

"What do you notice about this picture?" their teacher asked. All the little hands flew up. One answered, "The Madonna's face and hands—you can almost touch them." One of them used the word *plasticità*—meaning malleability, a tactile quality, unlike the flat two-dimensional paintings before the time of Giotto. Whether by observation or by prior training, these children fully grasped the meaning of perspective, the defining quality of Renaissance art. I was impressed.

Meanwhile, two American tourists wearing clumsy white sneakers and baseball caps walked over to see the Madonna that everyone was looking at. One of them scoffed, "What are they all looking at? How many pictures do we need of the Virgin Mary, anyway? She's not even *pretty*!"

I felt my heart torn in two. Where did I fit in this crowd? There was no question I was American, not Italian, but moments like this made me want to disguise myself as anything but an American, a citizen of a country uniquely my own. Other times, hearing the obscene catcalls of Italian men on the street, or feeling groping hands on my thighs in a crowded bus, I yearned to be on American soil again, where I could walk down a street blissfully unnoticed, without anyone thinking I was one of those easy foreign women. Or worse, without their thinking I was a tourist.

I thought I would find something about my Italian roots in this country, something that might illuminate my family's story, but I didn't. I learned a great deal—the history of Italian cinema, the aspirate "h" sound that defines the Florentine accent, and how to think in another language. I could identify the exquisite symmetry that defined Michelangelo's Palazzo Farnese. I had my breath taken away at the sight of the Duomo, the great cathedral of Santa Maria del Fiore, covered entirely in stripes of rose, green, and white marble. I saw the Battistero di San Giovanni, where Dante was baptized, and Ghiberti's Gates of Paradise. I wouldn't have traded the experience for anything. But I didn't come any closer to knowing who I am or where I come from. I still hadn't found any clues to my place in the world.

My last night in Florence, I remember lying half-awake in bed, and my roommate Helen was nodding off in the twin bed across the room. Helen was intense and intellectual, small and olive-skinned, the American child of Italian parents who somehow were transplanted from Genoa to a dusty Texas town. While I was spending my spare hours with handsome Persian men and riding around Florence on the back of Vespas, Helen was attending political rallies for the Italian communist party.

Just as I was about to drift to sleep, I heard Helen say in the dark, "Catherine—do you hear elephants?"

Without thinking about the absurdity of the question, I said, "Helen, you know there are no elephants in Florence."

Immediately, we both sat up in bed when the same realization dawned on us both: the circus was in town. We had seen the posters while walking home from class that day. We threw on our robes and ran out to the balcony. Looking down to Viale Belfiore, we saw five or six elephants that had apparently broken loose. They were taking over the street, four lanes of traffic, causing little Italian FIATs to swerve onto the sidewalks, while hysterical circus men in purple-and-white-striped satin pants came running after them, trying futilely to corral them together with their tiny whips. One of the elephants was grabbing the tiny trees that lined the street and uprooting them one by one with its trunk, as if they were lollipops.

Elephants, ghosts of Hamlet, naked statues of David, and marble facades of cathedrals in red, green, and white candy stripes. It was a lot to take in. I didn't understand at the time how young I was, and how many years it would take to process everything I saw. But I knew with great certainty I would never see myself as anything but an American, born and shaped in a one-room house in Milford, Massachusetts.

When I arrived home in Milford at the end of my junior year, my mother greeted me with a crushing embrace, an uninhibited ferocity of love. I found they had never opened the box of Christmas gifts I had mailed them. My family was waiting for me to get home to open the box in my presence. And likewise, they had saved for me a pile of Christmas and birthday gifts, waiting patiently to be opened in June.

17

MARCIA

"There's someone here to see you, Catherine," a voice called up the stairs. "I think she's your mother."

I knew that could only be one person: my sister Marcia.

No one ever guessed my real mother was related to me, with her dark hair and much shorter stature. Marcia had the same fair coloring as I did, although her features were quite different, and she always appeared to be a good twenty years older than me.

It was my senior year at Tufts. Marcia had stopped by my college dorm for a surprise visit, and she was sitting primly in the reception area when I came to greet her. She was dressed in her usual outfit, a plain dark-brown A-line skirt with a matching cardigan, a white cotton blouse buttoned all the way to the collar, opaque stockings, and sturdy oxford-style shoes. Although it was a warm clear day, she had her black raincoat folded neatly over her arm, "just in case it rained." Her shy smile quickly put me at ease that, for once, she had not come to bring me bad news.

While Marcia's short hair was curled tightly and stiffly sprayed, my long hair was loose and jagged and trailed well below my waist. I was wearing a blue denim man's work shirt with the sleeves rolled up, men's white carpenter pants that I bought from an army surplus store, and bare feet.

With just eight years between us, the gulf seemed like many generations. I had come of age at the height of the sexual revolution—a longhaired, bra-less, unshaven, unfettered hippie. Meanwhile my sister yearned for everything I rejected—a traditional role as wife and mother, home and hearth, everything safe and warm and predictable.

She loved to hear Robert Goulet sing,

What are you doing the rest of your life?
North and south and east and west of your life.
I have only one request of your life –
That you spend it all with me.

Marcia would have liked nothing better than to hear a man propose marriage to her in those exact words. And with her striking natural coloring, she could have been quite attractive if she chose to be. Instead she followed the plain and matronly style of the factory women she always worked with, all daughters of immigrants, never leaving the town where they were born.

As deeply as Marcia wanted to be rooted in one place, I was equally determined to break loose and fly away to see the world. I rarely thought about my sister, but when I did, I imagined her finding a like-minded man who would give her a home and family and all the domestic pleasures she dreamed of. The one who would ask her, "What are you doing the rest of your life?"

She in her world, I in mine.

All that changed when she appeared at my college dorm that day in my senior year. I couldn't have been more surprised by her news.

"I've just moved to Boston," she said, climbing the stairs behind me. "I rented a room, over in the Back Bay. And, oh—I need to borrow your typewriter."

It had been years since Marcia took typing classes in high school, and she wanted to brush up on her typing skills and apply for an office job.

"Well, I can't spare the typewriter now, not with term papers coming up. But you can practice here in my room any time you like!"

She took me up on my offer immediately. Settling in at my cramped student desk, while I perched on the bed with a stack of textbooks, she tapped away diligently at my Olivetti electric typewriter for more than an hour until she was satisfied her typing speed was back to a respectable seventy words a minute.

"That's it. I'm done. I can pass any typing test now."

Before long she had secured a job with Prudential Insurance, one of the largest insurance companies in the country. The Pru was a soaring office tower, then the tallest building in Boston, and its massive presence was symbolic of my sister's towering achievement. It was just a data entry job at first, but the milestone was dramatic nonetheless. She had broken free of her town and her destiny, choosing a path of her own.

Her prospects seemed bright. She was disciplined and hard-working, and in just a few months, she progressed from data entry operator to an entry-level insurance claims examiner. We met often for dinner at local Boston restaurants, seeking out simple Italian fare in the North End, and she delighted in fighting me for the check. We had never been closer to each other than we were in those months in Boston.

I could never escape the feeling, though, that her dinnertime conversation was strange and stilted, as if she had been rehearsing the lines all week. At first I chose to ignore the feeling. Even if she had, it made me think more warmly of her, as if these dinners were so important to her, she just wanted to make a good impression on me.

On the day of my college graduation, Marcia took the subway and connecting bus from Boston to the Tufts campus in Medford, joining my mother, Celia and Jerry, who drove in from Milford. The four of them sat together on the slatted wooden lawn chairs, alongside families that owned summer homes and vast diversified portfolios of mutual funds. For a few hours, at least, they were all on a level playing field.

'After the ceremony, my boyfriend Stan came by to give a congratulatory kiss. I briefly introduced him to my family, and my mother predictably snapped a Polaroid of Stan and me together. He was a graduate student at the Fletcher School of Law and Diplomacy, a part of Tufts, and briefly one of the renters in my off-campus apartment house, where we had met. He was handsome and blue-eyed and more than polite to my family, but social interactions with strangers were always difficult for them.

Our gathering quickly dispersed after the ceremony. There was no celebratory dinner in a posh Boston restaurant afterward, no cocktails or theatre tickets, as there were for most of my classmates. I went back to my apartment, and resumed work on my graduate thesis. I had finished all my coursework for my combined degree program, but now I had to finish writing my thesis to get my master's degree.

Back to the typewriter. Just another day.

After graduation, I continued seeing Marcia frequently, hoping I could snap her out of her shell. She was so painfully shy. I encouraged her to trade up from her boarding-house room and get a nicer apartment, and use some of her hard-earned bonus money to buy herself some new clothes. I offered to go shopping with her. I thought it would make her feel better about herself to try a new look, something that might make her look younger. She refused. Instead, her lifestyle grew ever more stoic. Her outfit was always the same, no jewelry, no makeup. She could have afforded an entire new wardrobe, but her self-imposed uniform never varied.

After a time, she started bragging that men at the office were flirting with her incessantly.

"You wouldn't believe the offers I get! It's all I can do to fend them off!" she said. I found it odd that one who dressed so plainly could attract such attention. As the bragging grew more and more outlandish, I started to become concerned.

She started claiming she had a steady boyfriend, but there were never any details she could share. From what I could tell, there seemed to be no trace of evidence in her humble boarding-house room that any man had ever visited there. There was never more than a single coffee cup in the room, sitting next to the same jar of freeze-dried instant coffee, and the same single plastic spoon, next to the same lonely hot plate and kettle.

I couldn't imagine her allowing any man to be close to her. If I touched her lightly on the arm, in the course of conversation, she would stiffen and recoil. It made me wonder what had happened to her, to make her cringe at human touch. I started to think there was something terribly wrong.

ဆဣ

Months went by, and I saw less and less of Marcia. I was consumed by my master's thesis, a linguistic comparison of the poetry of William Wordsworth and William Carlos Williams. It wasn't a theme anyone encouraged. Most of my professors were caught up in the literary fashion of the time, which involved dissecting literature according to psychoanalytic principles. I felt like the only one who cared about linguistics, the language of poetry, and not Freudian code words like *phallic* or *anal*, which I thought only diminished poetry into formulas rather than expanding its richness. I loved the English language and wanted to dig my fingers into the dirt of that language, not stand aloft and talk about horticultural theory.

My thesis written and successfully defended, it was time for a very different writing project: my résumé. I cataloged all my academic distinctions: MA, BA Summa Cum Laude, Phi Beta Kappa, twice first-place winner of the Academy of American Poetry Prize, high school valedictorian. Education entirely self-funded. I fancied I would be quite the catch for one of the big publishing houses in town.

I was in for a surprise. At the height of an economic recession, I quickly learned how little my report card mattered in the real world. I knocked on the doors of Little Brown, Houghton Mifflin, The Boston Globe, and every publishing house in town, hoping for a receptionist job, anything, just to get a toe in the door, but there were simply no openings of any kind.

I took the only work I could find, waitressing in Harvard Square, until a more solid job materialized. It was enough to pay the rent for a modest apartment on the wrong side of Boston's Beacon Hill. In the late 1970s, Beacon Hill was split down the middle by Pinckney Street, with lavish mansions of the Boston Brahmins on Chestnut Street and Louisburg Square on one side, and on the other side—student slums, formerly servant housing. I had a run-down one-bedroom flat on Myrtle Street, which I shared with an army of cockroaches.

I was waiting on customers at a Cambridge counter-top restaurant, part of a chain called Zum-Zum, which featured German sausages. Dozens of fake plastic bolognas and bratwursts were hanging from the ceiling. My uniform consisted of a white dress and apron, and a rather embarrassing German bonnet. All my years of education, my fancy college degree and my gold Phi Beta Kappa key, had all come to this.

One day while taking down an order, I looked up from my order pad to see my mother standing with my brother Jerry in the restaurant doorway. They thought it would be fun to come in and order something from me, and had driven forty-five miles to do so. My mother was standing there smiling at me, her face beaming with pride. I didn't understand why. After they settled into a booth, I went to take their order—and to ask why she was smiling.

"It's so good to see you working, out on your own in the world. I'm so proud of you."

"But it's such an awful job," I whispered, not wanting my boss to hear me.

"I'm waiting on the same people I went to college with. It's embarrassing! I can't seem to find a decent job anywhere."

"But you will, honey. You will. You'll do better and better every year. And you're already standing on your own two feet—not everyone can say that."

I sighed. In my mother's eyes, it wouldn't matter what I did. I could be digging ditches, cleaning out bird cages, scrubbing floors, doing anything at all, and my mother would always be proud of me.

My first publishing job finally arrived. It was with a little hole-in-the-wall magazine publisher called Berkeley Enterprises of Newtonville, Massachusetts, founded by Edmund Berkeley, a pioneering but eccentric computer scientist. Its publications included *Computers and People*, said to be first or second oldest computer magazine depending on whom you asked, as well as a political rag called *People and the Pursuit of Truth*, an organ for the editor's convoluted conspiracy theories about the JFK assassination.

The job paid minimum wage. Besides typesetting on an old IBM Selectric typewriter, taking calls, and answering subscriber complaints—which were numerous—my duties included tending the tomato plants that Ed Berkeley grew in the tall south-facing office windows. I was instructed to vacuum the plants daily to remove the white fly infestations. My job also included refreshing dried-out bottles of rubber cement, as well as cutting old press releases into small squares to be recycled as notepaper.

Just down the hall from Berkeley's dusty and cluttered little office was the headquarters for *Computerworld*, a thriving trade magazine. After a year in the salt mines at Berkeley, I soon shifted my focus to *Computerworld*, initially taking a job as a copy editor. I would later move up to copy chief, then senior features editor. I didn't know anything about computers; I was just interested in writing and editing, and I thought *Computerworld* would be a stepping-stone to a "real" publishing job at a more glamorous place like *The Atlantic Monthly* or *Harper's*. As it turned out, *Computerworld* would be much more seminal to my career than I could ever have anticipated, a place where I formed lifelong relationships. I was surrounded by young, smart, funny, quirky, and memorable people, one of whom I would later marry.

It was the late 1970s, the end of the hippie era. I was no longer bra-less and barelegged, but was now carefully cultivating a professional persona. I traded my Indian peasant skirts and androgynous painter pants for tailored suits, and my Dr. Scholl's sandals for high-heeled pumps. Although I was still sewing my own clothes, I was gradually getting accustomed to shopping at Saks Fifth Avenue and Bloomingdale's. I was meticulous about my appearance, taking two-mile runs every day, interspersed with Jane Fonda workouts on videotape. I got my teeth straightened, too—something most people did when they were kids. It was all about looking the part in this strange new world of the upwardly mobile.

My unintended entry into a technical field could not have come at a more auspicious time. At the dawn of the 1980s, the computer industry was booming on both the East and West Coasts. The availability of venture capital exploded after the initial public offering of Apple Computer in 1980. Advertising money was pouring into publications like *Computerworld*, and I was becoming, as one friend called me, an "expense account *bon vivant.*" It was not unusual for *Computerworld* to send the entire editorial department on junkets to Caribbean resorts. I remember a particular group dinner at the Paradise Island Hotel in the Bahamas; our editor barked at the waiter, "More Dom Perignon for the table! And keep it flowing!" That one dinner cost more than my annual salary.

The 1980s were sprawling out in front of us like a bejeweled odalisque. I was learning about 401(k) plans and mutual funds, vintage Moët & Chandon champagne, and posh bed-and-breakfast weekends. Around this time, I got my first car, a brand-new Toyota Tercel, sapphire blue, like the color of my first new bicycle—which I also purchased with my own money. I was making up for years of deprivation, savoring every new pleasure, but careful never to spend beyond my means. I was also saving money religiously, hoping to be able to buy a new house for my family one day. And I was still trying to cultivate an inner life, too, reading and writing poetry, and going to the theater, museums, and poetry readings.

Although I was still living in Boston, I saw little of Marcia in those days, preferring to spend my weekends with Tom, the tall green-eyed typesetting manager I had met at *Computerworld*. And it was always so sad for me to see Marcia, wasting away in her boarding house, spinning tall tales about imaginary suitors.

In late 1982, I called Marcia with some news. I had been offered a plum job with an international consulting firm, The Diebold Group in New York City, and I wanted to tell her all about it. The firm's founder, John Diebold, was an industry luminary, a pioneer in the field of automation, and I had done an in-depth interview with him for a feature in *Computerworld*. He was so impressed with the extensive homework I had done before the interview, he offered me a job on the spot.

I would be his personal speechwriter, ghostwrite his articles and books, and handle his publicity. It would double my salary, and I didn't even have to move to New York. I could work from my home in Boston—a novel arrangement at the time—and transmit my work electronically to the Diebold offices in New York. It was very exciting news, I thought, to land a job with a famous and well-respected captain of industry, and I wanted to share the news with everyone.

I called Marcia.

"You won't believe it, Marcia. I have a new job! With an international management consultant. I'll be meeting the most amazing people, and doing a lot of writing, and—"

"Oh, I wouldn't do that if I were you, Cath. I know about consultants. There's something shady about them."

"What are you talking about?"

"You don't know what you're getting into. I think you should hire a private investigator. Have him tailed."

"What?"

"I think you're being very, very foolish, Cath. Very foolish. Is there any way you can back out?"

I erupted. "What is wrong with you? Why can't you just say 'Congratulations' and be happy for me? Don't you think I'd know better than to take a job without doing some research? Without knowing what I'm doing? Do you even know what a consultant is?"

I could feel the blood rushing to my face and realized I was screaming into the phone. I was sounding crazy, while my sister was sounding calm and serene, tendering measured words of caution and advice. The voice of reason on her end of the line, the voice of hysteria on mine.

I don't know why I even cared what she thought. A woman who had so little in common with me, who lived like a cloistered nun, who tormented and teased me as a child, who threatened to cut off my long braids at night while I slept—why did it matter to me what she said?

"Just send him a letter in the morning," she continued. "Type it in triplicate. Get it notarized. And send it certified mail, with a return receipt requested. Let him know you don't work for consultants. In no uncertain terms!"

She was still talking as I gently hung up the phone.

18

INVESTMENT

In 1983, while still in my twenties, I bought my first home. It was a condominium in a stately yellow brick building on 11 Park Drive, Boston. It had expansive views of the Fenway, a marshy waterway or "fens" overgrown with tall rushes, with a backdrop of the Boston skyline beyond.

The Fenway, apart from giving the nearby baseball park its name, was part of a long string of green parks known as the "Emerald Necklace," designed by Frederick Law Olmsted, the same man who designed Central Park in New York. The section of the park across the street from my building had been tilled during World War II, giving birth to the Victory Gardens, where local residents grew vegetables for sustenance at a time when foods were rationed. Decades later, the land was still gardened in neat, well-tended urban garden plots, and I rented one myself to grow tomatoes, basil, and lettuce.

I could walk shady, tree-lined streets to the Museum of Fine Arts, the Isabella Stewart Gardner Museum, or Symphony Hall. I could peruse the disco dance floors at the 1270, one of the nearby gay men's bars on Boylston Street, where my girlfriends and I could just dance to the music and feel free and safe, and never be pestered by men. And on open-windowed summer nights, I could hear the crowds cheering a home run in Fenway Park.

It was also a short walk to my sister's boarding house.

As much as Marcia annoyed and frustrated me, I was also deeply worried about her. I tried to check in on her from time to time, inviting her to my new living quarters and accepting invitations to hers. She had been living in the same drab room for more than seven years. But every time I spoke with her, she seemed to be getting worse, moving further and further away from herself, into an unrecognizable territory.

It was around this time that I met a young woman named Carmen. I had posted an ad for a research assistant at Harvard University. I needed someone who had access to Harvard's Widener Library, and only Harvard students or alumni had that privilege. I needed someone to locate and photocopy some hard-to-find reference materials for a book I was writing for John Diebold.

Carmen answered the ad. She had access to everything I needed at Harvard, and she was smart and reliable. I liked her immediately. I met her at a coffee shop in Harvard Square one evening to pick up her latest assignment and to hand her a check, and we got to talking. Apparently she was a psychology major at Harvard and was hoping to get her doctorate at Hofstra. She was born in the Dominican Republic and raised in New York City, a native Spanish speaker, but she had not a trace of an accent.

After hearing about Carmen's academic specialty, I was emboldened to tell her about my sister. Marcia's delusions about her social life, her fictitious boyfriends, her suspicions over my working with a consulting firm, and her urging me to hire a private investigator. I laid out her whole history.

Carmen was quick to put a name to Marcia's affliction: paranoid schizophrenia.

"Now, I have to say—no one can diagnose a mental illness without examining the person. But from what you're describing, it sounds like a textbook case," Carmen said.

I had never taken psychology in college and knew next to nothing about mental illness, so the word *schizophrenia* threw me.

"Doesn't schizophrenia mean split personality?"

"No," Carmen explained patiently. "That's a misconception. Schizophrenia is when a person experiences delusions, or hears voices. Paranoid schizophrenia is a variant of the disease in which the person feels persecuted and thinks people are plotting against them."

That made sense to me. I never had any exposure to mental illness, not that I knew of. But the knowledge that Marcia's illness had a name was somehow comforting. It made me feel I could do something about it.

Armed with this small scrap of knowledge and fresh perspective, I walked to Marcia's boarding house one Sunday afternoon to bring her a bag of tomatoes and lettuce from my garden. Maybe I could find a way to talk to her about seeing a doctor. I expected she would be offended if I even hinted at the idea of a mental illness, but maybe I could get her to see a general practitioner for a regular annual checkup. That way, the doctor might see the problem and refer her to a therapist. It was worth a try.

"I'm glad you're here," she said upon my arrival, taking the bag from my hands and motioning for me to sit down. It was as if she had been waiting for me and carefully rehearsing what she would say. I settled gingerly into one of her rickety wooden chairs.

"I have an announcement to make," she said.

"Oh?"

"I'm engaged!"

"Marcia, I'm—well—okay. I guess I'm—I'm stunned. Who's the lucky man?"

"Oh, I can't tell you now," she said, blushing. "You'll find out soon enough."

I looked at her hands. There was no engagement ring. And glancing around her room, I saw nothing had changed. There was no photo of the man, no flowers, nothing at all to signal her upcoming nuptials. This was worse than I expected. No longer just tall tales of men flirting with her. Now she had put a very deep stake in the ground. An engagement. This was serious.

"Marcia—have you ever—I mean, do you have a regular doctor that you go to?"

"Oh, you mean for a blood test? Don't worry. There's plenty of time for that."

"I mean, have you been to a doctor lately, just—you know, just for a checkup?"

"Oh, no, not me. Don't need to. I never go to doctors. I'm healthy as a horse!"

My heart sank. "I can't stay," I said suddenly. "Let me know if you need any help with….your wedding plans. I've got to go."

Over the next few weeks, I asked Marcia repeatedly if I could meet her fiancé, to know his name, but she brushed me off and made excuses every time. Then, without blinking an eye, she called me one day to announce that she was already married! And still, there was no change in her living arrangement, no variation in her nun-like attire, no introductions to the man, and no wedding ring.

It was time for a talk with my mother and brother. They had driven in one day to see my new home in the Fenway. It would be the perfect opportunity to present my case. After I served lunch and the plates were cleared, I handed my mother a cup of coffee and laid out my concerns.

"Ma, I don't know if you've talked to Marcia lately, but I'm very worried about her. There's something wrong with her."

My mother fidgeted and looked uncomfortable.

"Ma, you should hear her. She's been making up stories about having boyfriends, multiple boyfriends. She's practically beating them off with a stick. Next thing you know, she says she's engaged. Now she actually thinks she's married. Married! Can you believe it? I mean, she is seriously delusional!"

"Oh, you shouldn't say that. You don't know that," she said with a wary look and furled brow, shaking her head.

I knew mental illness was not something my mother's generation accepted easily or even talked about. It was a stigma,

144

something to be hidden away or denied. People who weren't right in the head were "put away," harnessed in a straitjacket and locked up in an institution, never to be spoken of, never to be heard from again. That's how people dealt with the issue in my mother's day.

"I think she has a disease," I said gently. "It's called paranoid schizophrenia. I'm not a doctor, but I have a friend—she knows about these things. It's a textbook case, she says."

"But she *might* be married," my mother offered weakly.

"Ma's right. I don't think you can jump to conclusions like that, Cath," my brother piped in, supporting my mother's position.

Their denial stunned me. "But how could she be married? Think about it. She has wanted to be married all her life, and she doesn't even invite us to her wedding? Wouldn't you think she'd be dying to show the man off? And... and... and where's the ring? And why on earth is she still living in a women's boarding house?"

I was exasperated. Why couldn't my family see what was so plain and obvious? But when my mother stepped away to the bathroom to wash her hands, my brother took me aside.

"Hey, Cath, you might want to lay off all this mental illness stuff."

"What do you mean? I'm not saying it to upset anyone. I'm really worried about Marcia!"

"I know, but it's kind of a touchy subject. You know, Dad used to go to a shrink."

"Huh? What are you talking about?"

"It was a long time ago, before you were born."

"So how do you know?"

"Ma told me, not too long ago. She never said nuthin' about it for the longest time. Dad had some kind of a nervous breakdown. Went to a psychiatric clinic in Boston."

"What do you mean, a nervous breakdown?

"I dunno. It was around 1953, '54, something like that. Right before you were born. That's why he ended up as a cemetery caretaker. It was a nice quiet job. He couldn't handle any stress."

"But where would he get the money to go to a shrink?"

"Some charity clinic in Boston that takes poor people."

"Oh, so now maybe we're looking at a family history of mental illness? Great. What else don't I know about?"

"Yeah, you know, Grampa Stefano had something going on with him, too. In those days, people didn't go to a shrink. I heard he went to an exorcist."

"An exorcist? You can't be serious?"

"Just don't talk about it, okay? Sh-h-h-h, quiet, here she comes now."

I was reeling. My sister was seriously ill, and my family didn't want to talk about it. Too touchy a subject.

I decided I would have to take matters into my own hands. The following morning, I pulled out the phone book and tried to find a psychotherapist, dialing the numbers one by one until could I find one who would speak to me by phone. I finally found one. He suggested that I have my sister come in for a consultation.

"And what if she refuses?" Remembering my conversation with Carmen, I asked him, "Isn't it a mark of the disease that you don't acknowledge you have anything wrong with you?"

"There is nothing you or I can do to make her to seek treatment. The laws now protect people from being institutionalized. No one can be forced into treatment against their will. There's one exception: if they pose a danger to themselves or to others. Then you can do something."

But Marcia posed no danger. Just as she did when she worked in a factory, she quietly blended in, doing the most mind-numbing work every day, with never a complaint or a fuss.

Whenever I talked with my sister, I began to challenge her wedding claims, gently at first, but ever more insistently. "If you don't introduce me to this man, I'm going to think you're making this all up," I prodded with a very weak smile. All the while, her stories only escalated.

On my next visit to her boarding house room, I noticed scraps of yellow flannel, pinking shears, thread spools, tissue patterns, and pin cushions strewn over her bed. I had interrupted a sewing project. I was afraid to ask, but she seemed to be making baby clothes.

"You want to touch my belly? You can feel the baby kicking!" she said proudly.

"No, thanks," I said. It was just too much for me to bear. The sight of my sister stitching tiny baby clothes broke my heart.

I grabbed her shoulders and gave her a good shaking.

"Marcia, look at me. Look at me. I want you to tell me, right now. Why haven't I ever seen your husband?"

As if she were anticipating the challenge, she calmly said, "I'll show you."

She produced from a bureau drawer a newspaper clipping, showing a Boston police officer sitting on a motorcycle. He was part of a police escort for a visiting celebrity, Erik Estrada, an actor who played a motorcycle cop on TV.

"There, there's your proof, there he is," she said calmly. "That's him, the one in the front. You can see his name in the caption. Officer Paul Halloran."

"But this only proves that this man exists, not that you're married to him!" I shouted, slapping the clipping down against her table.

This final challenge had visibly offended her. She clammed up, folded her arms, and turned her back on me, saying, "I think you'd better go now."

My doubts had started a rift that was difficult to mend. Marcia began to avoid me from then on. She was never home when I rang her buzzer, and she became a no-show at family events, like the annual Thanksgiving dinners I cooked for my family. She didn't drop out of sight completely, though. She left odd messages on my answering machine, warning me to be careful—people were trying to brainwash *me* and control my mind, she warned. She mailed me envelopes full of strange newspaper fragments, folded and wrapped tightly in aluminum foil, with instructions that I should carefully unwrap the clippings and read them repeatedly, several times a day, to deflect mind control.

I called mental health professionals repeatedly, but was told again and again there was nothing I could do. Marcia seemed to be holding down a job and acting as a productive member of society. There was no imperative to intervene.

But my disbelief had struck a nerve in my sister, and it bothered her that I, and I alone, didn't accept her stories at face value.

She made one last-ditch effort to convince me. She appeared at my door one day with a mission. She wanted to tell me everything. All would be revealed. She had brought the plastic shopping bag she carried everywhere, with a jar of freeze-dried coffee and a plastic cup and spoon inside, and who knows what else. She fixed us both a cup, which I sipped with a wince and allowed the rest to go cold. Settling in at my kitchen table, sitting across from me, she took a deep breath and then began unfolding a carefully rehearsed tale that was so meticulously embroidered, so complete, so perfect, it was far more perfect than reality itself.

It all fit together, all making a kind of undeniable sense. As Marcia explained it, people I believed to be dead were actually living. People I believed to be living were really dead. Nothing was what it seemed to be. Her husband, the police officer, was working undercover—they had to keep their wedding a secret for her protection. Spiteful relatives who were jealous of her had kidnapped her children, who were then placed in an orphanage— the fabled New England Home for Little Wanderers. That's why I never saw them.

She also revealed that I had been kidnapped myself fairly recently, that she had actually seen me being attacked and forced into a car, flailing and screaming, while strange men injected me with mind-control drugs. That's why I was the only one who doubted her. "They," whoever "they" were, had manipulated *my* mind.

Somehow her engagement, marriage, the birth of multiple children, and their subsequent kidnapping all occurred in the space of mere months. As she continued to weave this fantastic story, my heart slowly sank.

And she saw it in my eyes. She said finally and grimly, "You don't believe a word I say, do you?"

She got up to leave, holding her nose high in the air and her lips pursed, looking deeply wounded.

"Marcia, I beg you, please see a therapist. Or a doctor. Somebody. Please, just talk to somebody."

Marcia hurriedly retreated, and it would be a long time before she spoke to me again.

19

CELIA

On a warm summer night in June 1983, I was enjoying a small gathering with my now official boyfriend Tom. A hot-blooded attraction had turned into a long-time affair. Now I was joining his family for an intimate dinner at his home in Boston's South End. His parents, Lynn and Roger, had driven down from New Hampshire, and his older brother Bruce had arrived from Connecticut with his long-time partner, Hugh.

When Tom had introduced me to his parents some two years earlier, they both charmed me instantly. Sitting next to me at St. Botolph's, a fancy restaurant in Boston, Lynn made me her co-conspirator, buzzing about restaurant diners around us. She whispered in my ear, "That woman over there in the white fur—" I looked over and saw a stunning bejeweled woman in a fox jacket, dining with a man who looked very much like a wart-covered toad.

"Don't you think she's a prostitute?" she said. She started me giggling.

"Well, isn't she?" Lynn insisted. "How else do you explain her being with that awful man!"

From that first conversation, Lynn and I were instant friends. She was the same age as my mother, born in 1920, and she was quickly becoming a second mother to me. Although she enjoyed a comfortable life, supported by Roger's successful career as a salesman, she was warm and down-to-earth. I liked her. I liked the whole family.

Their son Bruce was an antiques dealer, a towering man with movie-star looks, a cross between Clark Gable and Tom Selleck, and an easy laugh. His partner Hugh was an elegant, silver-haired former advertising man from a Madison Avenue agency. Fourteen years older than his brother Tom, Bruce had come out as a gay man in the 1950s. Such things were never discussed in that era, but Roger and Lynn seemed completely accepting of their son. I admired them for that. They all had an exuberance, a love for life, and it was always as fun to be with them as it was on that sultry June night.

We were enjoying dessert when, with a glass of champagne in one hand, I picked up a call from my brother. I had forwarded my calls to Tom's phone for the weekend.

Jerry's tone was dark.

"It's Celia. She had some kind of an attack at home. She started convulsing on the floor. Ma didn't know what to do."

"Oh no! Where is she now?"

"At the Newton-Wellesley. They moved her there from the Milford Hospital."

"Should I come right now?"

"No, it's late, and she's not conscious. I thought I'd have some good news for you by now, but they just told us she's lapsed into a coma. I'm driving Ma home now, and we're coming back in the morning."

"I'll be there in the morning, too."

When I put down the phone, I noticed Bruce was standing next to me with his hand on my shoulder. I was so absorbed in the call, I didn't immediately notice his gesture of comfort and kindness. He seemed to understand everything. He took my hand and squeezed it tightly, without saying a word.

Celia was no stranger to hospitals. From early childhood she had suffered hearing problems that required repeated surgeries, and in her twenties and thirties, she was prone to benign brain tumors that led to further operations. She had been to a litany of hospitals—Mass. General Hospital. Mass. Eye and Ear Infirmary. Leonard Morse in Natick. Milford Hospital. And now Newton-Wellesley. Every time she was hospitalized, she always recovered and moved on. So my first response was concern, but not surprise.

This seemed different, though. Before it was always a doctor's visit, followed by a scheduled surgery. This time she was rushed to the hospital in an ambulance.

I drove out the next day to see Celia at Newton-Wellesley. When I arrived, the doctor was already talking to my mother and brother at Celia's bedside. Celia, he explained, had been diagnosed with encephalitis, a brain infection.

"Your daughter has entered into a hopeless state," he told my mother. "There is no brain activity at this time. There's nothing more we can do."

We all looked at Celia. She had a respirator's tube taped to her mouth to help her breathe artificially. Her chest heaved and fell rhythmically like a soft balloon.

"We can keep her like this indefinitely, or we can let her go at any time. It's your decision."

My mother didn't have to think long. "I've talked to Celia about this before. I know what she'd want. She wouldn't want to be kept alive like this, hooked up to—to a machine." She was choking back tears.

"Then give us a few moments," the doctor said, gently leading us out of the room. A small group of nurses came in, wearing their light blue scrubs—through watered eyes, they seemed like a fluttering of pale doves. They pulled the tape and tube from Celia's mouth, unpinned the intravenous, clicked off the machines, and wheeled all the equipment away.

When they called us back into the room, Celia was lying perfectly still in her clean hospital johnny, as if she were peacefully sleeping, covered with an immaculate white bed sheet pulled neatly up to her waist.

My mother gently drew the sheet back to touch Celia's hand, then her feet, the way a young mother might check her newborn's fingers and toes. Celia was thirty-six years old.

I volunteered to make the dreaded call to DePasquale's Funeral Home, a place that knew my family well. I located the hospital pay phone, and got all the arrangements in motion. After I finished that call, I telephoned Marcia at work, to let her know her sister had died.

"Ma and Jerry just want a very simple ceremony. I think that's best, too. Just a few words at the funeral home, nothing in a church, and very brief calling hours."

"I understand. Thank you for calling," Marcia said stiffly, as if not wanting her co-workers to hear.

When the day came to pick up Marcia in Boston and drive her to the funeral home in Milford, she was talkative at first, looking pensively out the passenger window as I drove onto Commonwealth Avenue in the Back Bay, heading for Massachusetts Avenue.

"You know, Celia and I were so close in age, not even a year apart," she said. "We were practically twins."

I said nothing. My sisters were close in some ways, yes, but I never thought of them as anything like twins. I remembered their sharing close quarters, sleeping in the same big bed until they were both in their late teens. I remembered their effortless intimacy, sitting on their bed in the late evening, baring their backs and taking turns at squeezing each other's back pimples. But that intimacy could quickly flare into a violent argument over something trivial, like who had used up the last of the Noxzema cold cream. They were polar opposites in my mind: one shy and the other spitfire; one light and the other dark; one matronly and the other childlike; and both constantly at each other's throats.

"We used to play in the gladiolus fields, when we were little. The flowers were so tall, they grew way over our heads. We played hide and seek. It was so easy to hide between the rows."

"What are you talking about?"

"Oh, this was a long, long time ago, before you were born."

"I've never heard you mention gladiolus fields before." My sister's mind was wandering to a place I had never seen, a place that may never have existed, for all I knew.

I was driving through congested streets toward the turnpike exit, when my sister suddenly rolled down the car window and, for no apparent reason, shouted at a passerby, "Fuck you!"

I was horrified. It was all I could do to keep my eyes on the road.

"Marcia! What the hell do you think you're doing?"

She extended her arm out the window at another passerby, lifted her forearm at a right angle, and violently whacked the crook of her elbow in an obscene Italian gesture.

"Vaffanculo!" she yelled.

"Marcia, what the— Shut that window, right now! Shut it now!"

She reluctantly closed the window, folding her arms petulantly as she sat in the passenger seat, like a spoiled child. But I could see her, from the corner of my eye, turning her face slyly toward the window and silently mouthing vulgar words at strangers.

Thankfully we were soon on the Mass. Turnpike, and I doggedly stuck to the far right lane so there would be no cars to harass in the lane next to her. The monotony of the highway seemed to calm her. After about a half hour on the road, as we approached the exit for Milford, she turned to me and asked, "Do you believe in curses?"

"No," I said flatly.

"You don't believe a family can be cursed?"

"I don't."

"Oh, you should, Cath, you should," she said in a spooky low voice. "Our family is cursed. Someone gave *you* the *malocchio* when you were born. That means 'evil eye.'"

"I know what it means, Marcia. I speak Italian. I lived in Italy a year—remember?" I was quietly fuming.

"You don't know about these things, Cath, you just don't know. But I know. I know. Oh, and the house is cursed, too."

I took a deep breath. "Marcia, we are going to our sister's funeral today. Could you try to remember that? Could you just try to behave normally today?"

"I'm not going to open my eyes when we go into the house. That's what I'll do. I'll keep my eyes shut. *That's* how I'll protect myself from the curse."

I sighed heavily as we arrived at our old house and pulled into the long dirt driveway. True to her word, Marcia closed her eyes as she stepped into the house and started feeling her way around like a blind woman, knocking things over, until she found a chair. My mother and brother looked on with baffled faces.

"She thinks the house is cursed," I said loudly, my hands flailing in the air with exasperation. "She's keeping her eyes shut to protect herself from the terrible family curse!"

I turned to my mother and said, "Now do you believe me? Now do you see? There is *something wrong with her!*" My eyes were wet with angry tears.

"It's all right, honey," my mother said. "You're just hurting right now. We all are."

But it wasn't all right. My mother was still refusing to see Marcia's illness, sweeping it under the proverbial rug.

Somehow we all managed to attend Celia's wake and funeral services, along with a small gathering of relatives, without incident. There was no outburst from Marcia. It made me wonder if this was how Marcia functioned at work every day, quietly restraining herself while she was in public, and only unleashing her bizarre behavior when she was alone or among family members. How else to explain her long tenure working at the Prudential Insurance Company?

∞⌘

The following year my mother received $40,000 from Celia's life insurance policy.

It was completely unexpected. It was enough to buy a modest prefabricated house. But she would need more money to bring town water and sewer lines to the property; that would be over $20,000 alone. Then there were permits, perc tests, surveyors. We had to grade the land, which flooded every spring, and build a foundation. Not to mention the furniture they would need. They needed everything; there was almost nothing worth salvaging from the old house, except maybe my mother's heavy old cedar chest, but even that was showing signs of decay after forty years in a damp, leaky house.

We were soon looking at floor plans for their new house—a design we picked from a catalog. I was hoping they wouldn't have to spend all the insurance money and could set a few dollars aside in a savings account of some kind, a little nest egg, and use only half as a down payment on the new house. I helped them fill out the application to prequalify for a small mortgage, but the banks turned them down flat.

It was not that my mother and brother had a bad credit history. They had *no* credit history. They were practically living off the grid. Even though my mother now had $40,000 sitting in the Milford Savings Bank, she could not qualify for a $25,000 mortgage from the same bank.

By then I was established in a good job and had money set aside. I was able to help. In 1986, my family would finally have their new house.

20

NESTING

Just as my mother's long-awaited house was taking shape, Tom and I were making plans of our own. We had been a couple for five years, and now we were looking to buy a home and live together. We were each doing well, each of us moving up in the world. I was gainfully employed by The Diebold Group—despite my sister's dire warning about the evils of the consulting trade. Each of us owned a place in Boston. Now we planned to buy a home to share.

I was working full-time from home, an unusual arrangement at the time. Since I did not want to move from Boston to New York to take the job, Diebold allowed me to do what the futurists had predicted: it was called "telecommuting," the electronic cottage of the future that Alvin Toffler had foreseen in his book by that name. I was happily tapping out speeches, articles, press releases, and even books on a DEC Rainbow desktop computer, then transmitting them via dial-up modem to New York. There they were downloaded, printed out on a Wang word processor, and placed in John Diebold's hands.

This type of work arrangement was so rare in the early 1980s, an Associated Press reporter interviewed me for a story about working from home. He sent a photographer to take a photo of me in my home office, with Tom's Siberian husky nestled at my feet. The article and photo were syndicated nationally, with the bold headline, "PAID TO STAY HOME." For days afterward, people were calling me from across the country to ask how they could get a job like that.

Now Tom and I were hunting for houses, and we needed a place that could accommodate my home office. I had no thought of getting married at the time. I had lived through women's lib, the bra burners, the Equal Rights Amendment, open marriage, and the Pill. I had grown up questioning every institution presented to me—most especially marriage. Children's fairy tales, from *Snow White* to *Cinderella*, had taught me that young women's adventures ended when they got married—at least that's how I interpreted the "happily ever after." Marriage meant "end of story." If I looked to my parents' example, their union was no inspiration to me, resulting in poverty and subservience for my mother. And I saw nothing to prevent me from living with a man without being married. As Joni Mitchell put it, "we don't need a piece of paper from the City Hall, keeping us tied and true."

Even though I was making slightly less money than Tom at the time, I insisted on dividing all the expenses equally. We signed an agreement, similar to a prenuptial, in which we agreed to split everything fifty-fifty. We would be equal partners. That was how I envisioned a relationship should be in the enlightened 1980s, not the way it was in my mother's time. I was determined not to repeat the mistakes of my parents, buoyed by the youthful confidence that my generation had all the right answers.

We found a Queen Anne Victorian, a former governor's mansion that had been used as a nursing home for many years and was recently renovated and divided into condominiums. It had tall ceilings, massive fireplaces, exquisite architectural details, and fine parquet floors that had previously been covered with linoleum. It was on Sumner Hill in the Jamaica Plain section of Boston, a tree-filled suburban neighborhood where all the houses were Victorian masterpieces. Built by wealthy merchants in the late nineteenth century, the once-stately homes had fallen into disrepair by the 1960s and were occupied mostly by artists, musicians, students, and working-class families. The condo conversions of the mid-1980s were not very popular in the neighborhood, pushing up rents and property taxes, nor was the arrival of young upwardly mobile professionals like Tom and me. However, quite a few architectural treasures were salvaged and restored in the process.

The day of the closing on our new home, Tom and I met at the office of the seller's attorney. At first, the attorney couldn't find our documents, because I had given him my last name. For some reason, my name wasn't anywhere in their records. Even though I had handled all the negotiations and written the down-payment check, they had filed everything under Tom's name. And when presented with the standard, pre-printed closing documents, I saw two signature lines—one labeled "buyer," and the other line, an inch below it, was labeled "wife." This was the standard template.

"But we are not husband and wife," I pointed out. "We are co-investors in this property."

The lawyer simply smirked. "I guess you'll have to take a vote on who gets to be on top!"

I was not smiling. Later that week I received, as requested, a letter of apology.

Despite this inelegant beginning, I was very happy with Tom in our new home. We were not far from Jamaica Pond, which had a wonderful running path around it that I circumnavigated on a daily basis, and we could easily walk to the subway, the Orange Line, which could whisk us into the center of Boston in minutes. The place had two bedrooms, one of which I designated for my home office.

Tom and I were now officially a couple, living together, looking to our neighbors like the perfect husband and wife. We were living the good life, *la dolce vita*. We entertained. I became a proficient cook. I was always a great admirer of Julia Child, the French Chef of public television, which I first started watching when I was in high school. Her exuberance made me want to do more than cook. She made me want to learn French, to travel, to see and taste the entire world. She was my first hero, and my cookbook collection included a precious few that were autographed by Julia herself. I had cookbooks from Italy and France, and the popular boxed set of *Silver Palate* cookbooks. If you needed a catch phrase to describe the 1980s, "silver palate" nicely summed it up.

During those years in Jamaica Plain, I made monthly trips to New York on the Eastern Airlines shuttle, getting there early enough to meet my boss John Diebold at the Union League Club for breakfast. He had a membership at the Club, a classic male bastion from another era, where women were only allowed in certain dining areas marked by feminine chintz drapes. Breakfast would be followed by a brisk walk down Park Avenue South to his office. He was tall and long-legged and remarkably fit for a man nearly twice my age; I could barely keep up with him, my high heels clicking at a mad pace as I hurried along beside him.

If I was there on a Monday, I might be treated to one of Diebold's famous Monday Luncheons, as he called them, where he invited the cream of business and literary society to dine in his elegant board room, with its French white marble fireplace and ornately paneled walls. Guests were handed glasses of chilled sherry as they walked in, and lunch was served by white-coated butlers and capped off with port and cigars. You never knew who would be there—Barbara Walters, Jack Welch, Gloria Steinem, Lewis Lapham…I could be assured of eating and drinking well, meeting interesting people, and dining at places like Lutèce or La Cirque whenever I went to New York.

On one of my flights home to Boston, I was waiting for my bag at the luggage carousel at Logan Airport. Whom should I see but the poet Denise Levertov, one of my professors at Tufts, picking up a bag from the same carousel. I hadn't seen her in ten years. I remembered how hard I had worked to get into her poetry writing class, and how much she terrified me once I was in it. From a poet I so admired, a single word of criticism—over an ill-chosen word, an ill-timed pause, or even a comma—could be devastating.

She looked at me in my business suit and Coach briefcase, and her expression was entirely disapproving. I remembered that same look after I had read aloud one of my lesser efforts in her poetry class.

"Catherine," she said, "you know what you should be doing with your life. You shouldn't be wasting it on some *job.*" And then, after dropping that bombshell, she fluttered away.

Her words cut me to the quick, a *deus ex machina,* a proclamation from the gods. I had often thought I was ignoring my inner life too much, spending too much time entertaining and living well, devoting my time to gaining a solid financial footing, and not enough on writing the kind of poetry I wrote in my student days, the poetry that was in my heart of hearts. I thought about it often.

How is it that some artists and writers can commit themselves totally to their craft, sometimes starving, sacrificing everything for the sake of their work? There was no way to make a living writing poetry, and in my experience, there was nothing poetic about poverty. Was it wrong to delay these creative pursuits, to focus on a career first, and on writing later, once I was financially secure and on solid ground? I didn't have a patron of the arts. I was going to have to be my own patron.

I was of two minds. My practical side was telling me to be hard-working and industrious, to stockpile my savings for the future, and my artistic side was telling me to throw caution to the wind, fly away to a Greek island, and devote myself to writing. But how would I live if I did that? I thought the choice was clear. I didn't want to be a dependent or burden to anyone. I would feather my nest first, and settle down to do writing and all the things that mattered to me later. It was the only thing that made sense to me then, when the years ahead of me seemed an endless open canvas.

I was no longer Catholic, but I had not forgotten the brutal penance of guilt.

21

HOMECOMING

"Hello, this is Officer Paul Halloran calling. Is there a Marcia Marenghi there?"

"No, Officer, this is Catherine Marenghi. I have a sister named Marcia, but she doesn't live with me. Can I help you with something?"

"Uh, maybe. Maybe you can. I've been calling every Marenghi in the phone book. There's a Marcia Marenghi who sent a letter to my boss. Do you know anything about that?"

I thought for a moment. Paul Halloran. It sounded familiar. Now I remembered—the newspaper clipping that Marcia showed me, with a Boston police officer posing on his motorcycle. The one she claimed was her husband. His name, as I now recalled, was Paul Halloran.

"Officer, I think I may be of help here. You say my sister wrote a letter?"

"Oh, she had quite a few things to say about me."

My heart sank.

"Officer, something you should know—my sister is—well, she's very disturbed, and I'd like to help you set things straight. Can you tell me what she said about you?"

"You're her sister?"

"I am."

The voice hesitated at first, but my calm tone had finally set him at ease and won his trust

"Well, she said some pretty nasty things. For one thing, she said I fathered her children and then walked out on her. She accused me of abandonment. Ma'am, I'm already married, and a thing like this could ruin my career."

"Officer, I'm so, so sorry. My sister is not well. She is suffering from a mental illness. Paranoid schizophrenia. I was told we couldn't force her to get treatment, legally, unless she posed a danger to someone."

"Well, she's posing a danger to my job!"

"Please," I said, "let me come in and speak to your boss. I'm sure I could straighten out everything."

"I'd really appreciate that, ma'am."

"And if you could share with me that letter, maybe that would be something I could use as evidence, to get my sister into treatment. To show she is causing some harm. Could you do that?"

Officer Halloran gave me directions to his station, near Franklin Park, and promised to share a copy of the letter with me. But when I arrived there at the appointed time, there was no record I had an appointment, and the officer was out. I tried to reach him after that, but he never answered my calls, and I never saw the letter. I didn't know if he had resolved the matter and didn't need my help any more, if he forgot the appointment, or if he just wasn't comfortable meeting with the sister of a mentally disturbed person. I never heard from him again.

For a while I heard nothing about my sister, either from her or from others. I didn't know how long she could continue living and working in the city without someone noticing her condition. Finally I received word that the inevitable happened: Marcia was leaving her job and leaving Boston. She had been there a dozen years.

The circumstances of her departure were not entirely clear. I only know what my brother later told me. Marcia had called Jerry one day and asked him to come to Boston right away. She had been kicked out of her boarding house room, and she was calling from a pay phone in front of her former residence. Jerry dropped everything and drove to Boston immediately. He found Marcia accompanied by a marshal on the sidewalk in front of her building, with her meager belongings in a few plastic bags on the sidewalk.

Marcia had been evicted for being loud and disruptive, disturbing her neighbors with her nightly tirades, shouting profanities at the voices she heard in her head. Apparently these nocturnal outbursts also caused her to fall asleep at her desk during the day, forcing her employer to terminate her job. From what Jerry could tell, The Prudential was kind to her in honor of her many years of service, gradually phasing out her job and giving her some severance money.

Everything my sister owned fit easily in Jerry's trunk, and he brought her home to occupy the third bedroom in their Milford house.

That's when the nightmare began for my mother and brother. If my mother still harbored any doubts about Marcia's mental state, they were quickly put to rest. The once-peaceful house, the long-awaited dream house, was now inhabited by a host of invisible demons, and Marcia could be heard railing against them day and night. Enjoying a peaceful night's sleep would be a thing of the past. Even worse were the times Marcia vanished for hours at a time, with no hint of where she was going. She terrified my brother by repeatedly stealing his car keys and taking off with his car...

One day I got a rare phone call from my Aunt Lizzie. She asked, "What is wrong with Mahsha? She comes to my house and stahts accusing me, saying I was hidin' her husband. I was scared to let her inside. She was cursing at me. Something about a Paul Halpin, Haslin—something like that. I don't know any Paul. What is wrong with her?"

"Marcia isn't well. She isn't right in the head. She's sick."

"What kinda sick is that? She should go to a doctuh!"

There were more than a few incidents like this, with Marcia standing on the front lawns of neighbors and relatives, hurling bizarre accusations, shaking her clenched fist menacingly at the houses. As time went by, though, the incidents seemed to dwindle. Marcia's hostility melted into reclusiveness. She never went out any more, rarely even left her bedroom, locking her door and never emerging except to use the bathroom or get something to eat.

My brother, though, was fully aware of her presence every night as he lay sleepless in the bedroom next to hers. He could hear her night after night, quarreling with ghosts, often turning up her radio to drown out the voices, the voices that screamed at her as she screamed back, the voices that never left her alone.

22

UNION

Tom and I had been together seven years when I started thinking about having a child. It was an idea that first took root in my heart when I lost my younger brother. My belief in the possibility of new life was the only thing that carried me forward.

I was in my early thirties. My window for childbearing was closing, and I could not imagine having a child with anyone but Tom. The strong physical pull that first drew me to him had grown into a comingling of our lives and fortunes that I could not foresee untangling. His business footing was still a little shaky, having recently launched an online publishing company—years before anyone had heard of the Internet. The idea consumed him. He spent every waking moment thinking and talking about his new venture. It hadn't made a penny yet, but my paycheck was enough to keep us both afloat. And I loved him and believed in him, and was certain we could conquer any challenges together.

Having children was the only reason I could think of to get married. I would not want any child of mine to be made to feel "illegitimate" in any way. It may have been an old-fashioned idea, especially for one who was once an anti-establishment hippie, but I thought a child should have the stability and permanence provided by two married parents.

I started dropping hints about getting married. I inserted oblique comments into conversations, like, "Tom, are we going to go on living this way forever?" Or, "Tom, I don't want to wake up one day and find that life has passed me by." As I think about it now, Tom and I were never very good at talking "about" things. We talked "around" things, circling around and around a topic, nibbling away at its edges, until we arrived at a point where we both agreed on something—more or less.

There was no marriage proposal, no bending down on one knee, no limousine sent to my door, not even a romantic dinner. We simply had a conversation. I remember hearing him say, "What do you think about getting married?" one Sunday morning while reading the papers in bed, spoken in the same tone as, "How would you like another cup of coffee?" Since I had never expected to be married, I had never put much thought into how a proposal should look or sound. In hindsight, I wish I had said, "You'll have to do better than that, fella!" But I simply said, "Okay."

Even the ring was an afterthought. We later went shopping for rings together. At my insistence, it was a modest ring, so we could preserve our savings for more important things, like furniture or retirement savings. We first talked about getting married in February 1988 and set a date for June the same year.

As we began to think about the invitation list, the first name I thought of was Marcia. What were we going to do about Marcia? Could I discourage her from coming? Did I have to invite her at all? I imagined a lovely ceremony with flowers and lace and all my assembled friends in the world, and just as the vows were being exchanged, Marcia suddenly standing up and shouting, "Vaffanculo!" When I called my mother and brother to tell them the news of my engagement, I asked them specifically not to tell Marcia. They completely understood and somehow managed to keep the wedding a secret from her.

In the weeks that preceded the wedding, there are exactly two moments I can recall when I came within inches of calling the whole thing off. One was the evening when I was addressing the envelopes for the wedding invitations. It was the end of a long and stressful workday for me. I had carved out a couple of precious hours after cooking and cleaning up after dinner, time I had reserved for the task of getting the invitations finished and sealed and ready to send.

I had arranged on the dining table bundles of cream-colored envelopes, a stack of invitations and return envelopes, a roll of stamps, an address book, a handwritten list of names, and pair of my finest felt-tip pens. The assembly line was ready. I wanted Tom's help finalizing the list and stuffing the envelopes.

As I began hand-addressing the envelopes, I called out, "Tom, where are you? I thought you were going to help me with this?"

Tom emerged from my office with a yellow pad of paper in hand and pulled up a chair. He had a completely different project in mind. "Let me ask you something," he said, looking quite pensive and holding his pen aloft. "How should I organize my business?"

I exploded. "Are you out of your mind? Once, just once, could we *not* talk about your business? Morning, noon and night, that's all you ever talk about! Could we please focus on something else here?"

"Sheez, okay, okay, I'll leave you alone."

"I don't want you to leave me alone! You promised to help me with this!"

"If you don't want to talk to me, you can do it yourself!"

I sighed and put my face in my hands. Was this the way our married life would be? I was uncomfortably eyeing my future, the way you might glimpse into a room through a barely open door, trying to piece together the activity in the room from that single sliver of a view. Would his priorities never align with mine?

The other moment of doubt came when I was riding home in the car with him one day, and the subject of last names came up. Earlier that day I had learned that, in Massachusetts, a bride can legally change her last name to anything at all when she marries. It could be a completely new name.

"I have to admit, it's an interesting possibility," I said. "It might be nice for a change to have a last name that other people can actually spell!"

No response from Tom. He kept on driving.

"I've had my name for over thirty-three years," I went on. "It's hard for me to imagine changing it to anything else. So many people know me by this name. And besides, the ethnicity of a name—I identify with being an Italian. Could you imagine changing *your* name? It would be like changing your identity."

Before I could finish, Tom was verbally barraging me with so much venom and contempt, I didn't hear any of the words—only the tone. He was plunging his verbal knife so deeply, I couldn't remember what he said, only how I felt when he was done. Anyone passing by would have seen a man behind the wheel, his face distorted with rage, his eyes on fire, and a woman shrinking in terror in the passenger seat.

Tom didn't say anything about what I had said; he had a habit of getting angry over one thing, but expressing his anger over something that seemed unrelated. I always had to guess what he was really angry about. Although he didn't come right out and say it then, I later understood he had wanted me to take his last name, a prospect as unthinkable to me as it was presumed inevitable by him.

I brushed off these ugly moments as just that—moments. Just typical pre-wedding jitters. Inconsequential in the larger scheme of things, like tiny chips and cracks in the bone china that one hopes no one will notice. By now the wedding was gaining momentum, barreling forward with a will of its own. There was no stopping it.

As the big day approached, I wanted my mother to look like a queen. Although she had met Tom a few times, after she had moved into her new house, this was the first time she would be meeting all my friends and coworkers, and I wanted her to feel proud and confident among them. She was finally fitted for dentures, after living with missing front teeth for decades. I took her with me to the Elizabeth Grady salon, where we both had facials.

It was the first time we had ever done such a thing as mother and daughter. They waxed the thick hairs from my mother's chin and upper lip, and shaped her eyebrows. I bought her a suit, a pink and beige Chanel-style bouclé, and bone-colored shoes. I made sure she had hairdresser and manicure appointments lined up. And when the professional cosmetician I hired came to do my makeup on my wedding day, I had her do my mother's face as well.

It was the first and only time I had ever seen my mother wearing makeup. She looked as if she had just arrived for afternoon tea at the Copley Hotel. It was such a transformation, anyone who knew her would have been astonished. One of my aunts later told me that my mother was showing herself off to her sisters at the reception, twirling around like a little girl, and saying, "Look at me! Look at me!" I was deeply relieved to hear she was happy with her new look, and not annoyed with me for practically forcing it upon her.

Both wedding and reception took place at the Boston Rowes Wharf Hotel, an elegant new waterfront building that managed to look like a meticulously restored antique. We chose its massive cupola for our ceremony. The cupola looked as if it belonged on a Florentine cathedral, with lovely sunlight streaming in from a circular window at the top. It had 360-degree views of the city, with Boston skyscrapers on one side, Boston Harbor on the other.

When the guests were assembled and the ceremony was about to begin, the music seemed to be droning on a bit too long. My Aunt Lizzie was late for the wedding ceremony, and we held it twenty minutes to accommodate her. She had never learned to drive a car and was driven in from Milford by her neighbors, who were probably unaccustomed to Boston traffic. When she finally appeared, all eyes turned to her. Lizzie had all the bearing of a countess. She wore a fine navy silk crepe dress, something she might have worn on special occasions for many years, and a pearl choker. I always thought of her as the matriarch, even though she had no children, presiding over the family's ancestral estate. Her lush white hair was pulled up in her trademark French twist, with a tortoise shell comb, and with her broad nose and warm dark eyes, she had the map of Italy written on her face.

When the first notes of Mendelssohn's "Wedding March" started, I walked down the aisle with Tom. I could have asked my brother Jerry to escort me, but I was never comfortable with the wedding tradition of giving the bride away, a practice that originally signaled a transfer of property from father to groom. So I walked down the aisle arm-in-arm with Tom.

Equal partners, all the way.

I didn't want a grand dress with a skirt the size of a house. I had a simple tea-length dress in sheer ribbon silk, a soft cream color, with a peach satin ribbon tied around my waist. Nor did I want a religious ceremony. We had a justice of the peace preside, who showed up for the occasion in a lemon-yellow suit jacket and a brightly flowered tie. Our friend Rich, because he was best friend to both Tom and me, stood with us, not as best man, but as best person, and he read a Robert Frost poem as part of the ceremony. I had no bridesmaids or matrons of honor. It was just Tom and I, and Rich—we were the entire wedding party.

My employer, John Diebold, was there, too, with his young second wife Vanessa. He looked like the worldly millionaire that he was in a glen plaid Saville Row double-breasted suit. He made a special point of asking to meet my mother, who graciously took his hand and smiled in return.

The day was flawless. After champagne and plump pink shrimp and beef tenderloin and chocolate-covered strawberries, a small flute ensemble played my favorite love song, "My One and Only Love," as we sliced in unison into the hazelnut wedding cake with buttercream white roses. After all the photographs and well wishes, we finally made our exit to a waiting car, a classic gold Pontiac convertible with the top down, covered with crepe-paper streamers. The car started pulling away when our friend Rich, hamming it up, made a great show of trying to climb in with us.

We slowly cruised the streets of Boston while people waved and cheered at the car with the "Just Married" banners trailing behind. And thankfully, oh so thankfully, Marcia wasn't there.

23

NEW LIFE

Dr. Samuel Bielak pressed the Doppler stethoscope to my belly. Suddenly I heard a loud thump-thump, thump-thump, thump-thump—the most cheerful noise I have ever heard.

I was stuttering with joy. "Is...is...is that my baby's heartbeat?"

The white-coated Dr. Bielak nodded, expressionless. This was all routine to him. His head down, he kept jotting notes on a notepad, and in a matter of moments, he calculated my due date with a simple pencil and paper: "April 26, 1991."

He would turn out to be absolutely accurate. At this point, I was already four months along although I didn't have a clue that I was pregnant until a few days earlier. My monthly cycles hadn't given me any warning. I only knew my waistline was getting a little thicker, so I decided to buy an over-the-counter pregnancy test. Even when I saw the clear plus sign emerge on the test strip, I still didn't believe it. I wouldn't be convinced until I heard it from a doctor. But now there was no doubt. Someone's little heart was thumping away inside me.

A new life.

My worries about having difficulty getting pregnant in my mid-thirties were baseless. By my calculations, I was pregnant within a week of stopping my birth-control pills. It happened so fast, I was dumbfounded.

We didn't let my mother know right away. After an ultrasound confirmed that everything looked okay and revealed the baby's sex, Tom and I took a drive out to Milford. I wanted to tell my mother and brother personally. And I had a very important question to ask them.

Tom and I were seated at the kitchen table with Ma and Jerry, while Marcia remained down the hall in her bedroom, absolutely silent, with the door closed.

"I have an announcement to make. We're…"

Before I could get all the words out, Jerry was jumping out of his chair exclaiming, "I knew it! I knew it! I knew it!"

My mother, never one for high emotion, smiled warmly at me. "That's good news, Catrina. Very good news. I guess I'm old enough to be a grandmother by now!" She was seventy years old, about to have her first and only grandchild.

"There's something else," I said. "We know it's a boy. And I wanted to ask you both how you would feel if—well—if we named him Steven. Would that be all right?"

I was worried the mention of my brother Stephen's name would evoke terrible memories, and cause them more pain than joy. I needed to know it was OK to use that name. And I needed to hear it from my mother's lips.

Without hesitation, they both looked at each other and nodded in agreement. "That's a very good idea," Ma said softly.

And so it was decided. Steven, but spelled with a *v* and not a *ph* as in my brother's name. And he would take his dad's surname.

Steven and Stephen. I wondered, as we tossed these names across the table, if Marcia could hear us from her room down the hall. Her bedroom was on the same level as the kitchen, just a few steps away. I knew she was in there. I looked down the hall and contemplated, for a brief moment, getting up and knocking on her door, letting her know she was going to have a nephew.

Then I remembered that day in her rooming house, watching her stitch together tiny clothes for an imaginary baby. Would my announcement make her happy or stir up painful memories? I thought better of it, and Tom and I quietly left to go home.

From that day on, our baby would no longer be a nameless fetus, bobbing around in amniotic fluid. He had a name. He was Steven, my son.

24

A NEW PAGE

At the time I learned of my pregnancy, I had been gainfully employed at a Boston public relations agency. I had taken the job a few months after Tom and I were married. Tom's business still hadn't taken off, and the promise of a senior position with a generous salary was hard to pass up. Mine would be the only paycheck supporting the household.

Now, just as our family was about to expand, I was suddenly laid off from my job. In some ways, it was something of a relief; the job was high-stress, thankless, and utterly joyless. But now we were two parents without paying jobs, and I was worried my rapidly expanding waistline would make it complicated to find a new employer.

Who would hire a woman who would go on maternity leave as soon as she was hired? And I was quite certain little Steven would fully expect to be fed, sheltered, and clothed.

I soon found myself picking up writing projects. Business came from friends at first, in the form of small freelance assignments. A press release here, an article there. Encouraged by these small successes, I sent out letters to everyone I knew, announcing my writing services—speech writing, ghost writing, articles, books...you name it, I'd write it. I even posted a listing under "Writers" in the

Yellow Pages. That made it official: I was now a professional writer. Denise Levertov would have been proud.

One of my offers came from a friend at Arthur D. Little, a consulting firm in Cambridge. The firm had a practice devoted to green business—corporate environmentalism—and needed someone to help them write a book. I had ghostwritten a book for John Diebold, and had edited two collections of his speeches into books. Even at the public relations firm, I further honed my ghost-writing for the agency's clients. I had good experience and good references.

The lead consultant at Arthur D. Little could see, though, that my pregnancy was showing, and he was understandably worried I would not be able to finish the project. He had just gone through two prior writers, who were disappointing, and he needed assurance I could get the job done. I promised to write a chapter a week, starting in December, and would be finished with all twelve chapters well before my due date in April.

When I handed them my first chapter, the consulting head started reading it, and I could see the smile forming on his face.

"It's excellent. Exactly what we were looking for. Finally, we will have a book!"

In all my years in the corporate world, praise was rarely dished out so freely. It was thrilling to get such positive feedback. And it would be a substantial sum of money. I was already mentally socking away funds for my son's college education.

I was gaining weight at a healthy rate, exercising, cutting down on my beloved six cups of coffee a day, and doing everything right. In February, I breezed into the obstetrician's office with my business suit on and my briefcase in hand, ready to go to Arthur D. Little after my appointment. I let them take all their tests, weight, blood pressure, heart rate, and all, and I was hurriedly getting dressed to go when the nurse came back in.

"Hold on. You're not going anywhere."

She asked me to lie down on my left side and not move in any way for a few minutes.

Now I was getting worried. After fifteen minutes of lying on my side that way, the nurse came back and measured my blood pressure again.

"There, that's better. Your blood pressure dropped, just from lying in that position. Dr. Bielak will explain."

When the doctor came in, he wasted no time telling me what to do.

"Young lady, I want you to go home and go to bed."

"But I have an appointment—my biggest client—"

"Cancel it. Cancel all your appointments, not just today, but for the next few months. You are to go home, go to bed, and lie constantly on your left side, just like you're doing now. Don't get up, ever, unless it's to eat or use the bathroom."

Apparently my blood pressure was dramatically higher than normal. At the same time, my weight had taken a sudden spike upward as well. Both were signs of preeclampsia.

Further tests confirmed it. Preeclampsia, I was told, was the number one cause of maternal death in childbirth. My doctor spared me no details. He thoughtlessly told me about a patient of his who had preeclampsia, and she had a convulsion, and died, on the delivery table. Another had a coronary and required open-heart surgery within minutes of childbirth. I don't know why he was telling me these horrible tales. He couldn't say the same would happen to me, but it was imperative I stop everything and put my work on hold, unless I wanted to risk my life—and possibly my baby's.

As ordered, I went straight home, and Tom was out for the day. When he arrived home, he found me in my nightclothes, lying on my left side on the sofa. My eyes were wet and red.

I sat up and told him what the doctor had said.

"Tom, I'm scared. The doctor said I could die in childbirth. I could leave my baby without a mother!"

I was even more afraid of losing Steven, but I couldn't bring myself to put that fear into words. It was too unspeakable. And I was terrified of being bedridden, of being dependent. I had never been dependent on anyone before. I had been working for twenty years, since I was fifteen years old, and now I couldn't even rely on myself.

"Tom, what are we going to do? Your business hasn't been bringing in any money—just expenses. We can't go on like this. I thought I could work right up until Steven is born, but now I *can't* work. You need to do something!"

Tom glared at me. He sensed the implicit doubt in my words, the lack of faith that he would provide for me. It was a personal affront. His eyes were glowing with anger, and he pointed his finger at my face. "I am not going to give up my business. It's going to make us *rich*. Do you hear me? It's going to make us *rich*, *rich*, and you're just too stupid to see it!"

I curled into a fetal position and buried my wet face in my hands, while he stormed out of the room. I stayed on the sofa through the night.

The next morning I called the consulting head at Arthur D. Little.

"Joe, I'm so sorry I never made it in yesterday. But I hope you got my message."

"Catherine, we've all been worried sick about you. Don't even think about the book. You know we could never forgive ourselves if we made you do anything that put you at risk."

I closed my eyes and leaned my head back. If only I had heard such genuine concern coming from the mouth of my husband. Is there something about marriage, the most intimate of relationships, that keeps us from saying what our partners need most to hear? Why do every-day acts of kindness come so much more easily from those who barely know us?

"Joe, you're very kind. But I'll be bored silly if I lie around at home for weeks and do nothing. The book is almost done. I recorded all my interviews. They're all transcribed and just need to be edited. I can finish the rest at home. I have a laptop computer, and I can use it even in bed."

"Catherine, I don't want you to push yourself."

"I promise, I won't."

"If you need anything at all, we will bring it to your house."

And Joe did, as promised, make two trips to my house before the book was done, and one later on, after the printed galleys arrived, to give me a bound review copy. He was a senior consultant for an international consulting practice, and yet he found the time to drive to my house to show me a finished copy of my work.

"Catherine, I want you to put away a copy of this book, to give to your son some day when he's a teenager—just around the time when most kids start thinking their parents don't know anything! And then, you can open the book and read him this."

He peeled back the cover and read aloud the dedication:

"The authors wish to dedicate this work to Catherine Marenghi who, through her considerable skill and patient understanding, created a readable format and style from our rather stilted and often unnecessarily complex jargon. We would also like to thank her son Steven, who demonstrated equal patience and understanding by waiting until the draft was finished before arriving in this world."

80CR

Steven's birth was right on schedule. April 26 was an unseasonably warm day. I was lying on my living room sofa, reading a trashy biography of Frank Sinatra by Kitty Kelly, when my waters started to break. I laid a bath towel on the floor and sat on it while I called Tom. I was at the hospital around 2:00 p.m., and at 4:20, I heard my baby's first strange, throaty cry.

Because of my preeclampsia, I had intravenous needles in both arms, pumping me with magnesium sulfate, an anticonvulsant. Otherwise, there was no time to administer an epidural or any painkillers. Steven was in too much of a hurry to be born.

I remember holding his tiny body in my arms, touching his perfectly round little head with its soft light brown hair. He reminded me of the little plastic doll I played with when I was a girl, the one I had named Stephen. I was completely smitten. It was a rush of feeling, indistinguishable from falling in love. I have never seen anyone more beautiful than that baby.

My mother and brother had rushed to the hospital to meet the new grandson and nephew. The joy and love in their faces was wonderful to watch. Our friends Rich and Cindy were among the first visitors as well, everyone visibly elated and snapping dozens of pictures of the new arrival.

Tom, for his part, seemed happy to see his new son, eager to hold the little bundle in his arms. He seemed far less happy to see me. I noticed him shooting me ugly looks. He seemed surprised that all my extra weight, all the puffiness of preeclampsia, made worse by months of inactivity through my bed rest, didn't magically melt away the minute Steven was born. I don't think he understood how sick I was, that it would take time before I got my body back. I felt his eyes on me, constantly looking me up and down, with an expression of utter contempt.

The first few weeks after Steven came home, Tom's mother Lynn had come to stay with us and help with the baby. Lynn had always endeared herself to me, and here she was, helping Tom and me figure out the complexities of disposable diapers, all three of us standing over the changing table in a state of deep concentration, as if we were performing a delicate surgical operation. Lynn was a lifesaver, running to the store to get supplies, helping me quiet and soothe a very colicky baby—and deflecting the mounting tension between Tom and me.

It was a difficult time. I felt depressed and despondent, with my bloated breasts constantly leaking, leaving me drenched with a sour milk smell that was hard to get rid of. And with postpartum bleeding, I felt like a sieve, my body leaking from every direction. I was barely eating, unable to even finish a cup of tea before Steven started crying again and demanded my attention, and yet I was still bloated and puffy, feeling like a carnival-mirror distortion of myself in my over-sized T-shirts.

One evening, Lynn offered to stay home with the baby to give Tom and me a chance for an evening out alone. I drove in and met Tom in Copley Square, Boston, where he was renting a small office for his business, and I had spent hours getting ready. I squeezed into a new black-and-white print dress with the help of a high-rise girdle, the first time I had ever worn such a complex undergarment. When I got out of the car to greet him, he looked me up and down and gave a sarcastic "pheh," a forced exhaling sound. It was not the reaction I was hoping for.

All through dinner, as Tom stared down at his plate, looking embarrassed to be seen with me, all I could think about was Steven. I missed him. With all his crankiness and colic, I just wanted to be with Steven.

25

CRAZY

Our little two-bedroom condo in Jamaica Plain felt much smaller with a new baby in the mix. How such a tiny creature could require so much complex equipment amazed me—crib, changing table, bassinette, high chair, swing, strollers, plastic toys of all shapes and sizes...The second bedroom, once my home office, was now a nursery, with my writing desk pushed unceremoniously into a corner.

Tom was still struggling to make any money from his online publishing startup, and I was starting to resume my writing work again. I had imagined working from home while caring for a newborn, tapping away at my computer with one hand while nestling a sleeping baby on my lap; that turned out to be the most outlandish fantasy I've ever imagined. A newborn baby is a bundle of urgent needs, expressed in the form of a constant roar.

I needed office space. A quiet, distraction-free place to get things done. I loved my baby, but he was a world champion in the distraction department.

For a while I shared work space in Tom's small Copley Square office in the city, hiring a babysitter to care for Steven at home so I could get out and work. I was paying for the babysitter, the mortgage, and all the household bills, and even paying the rent for the office space I shared with my husband. I was paying everyone for the privilege to work myself to exhaustion.

We desperately needed a bigger home, preferably a house with a yard where a little boy could play, but did we dare buy a house when our finances—and increasingly, our marriage—were on such shaky ground? We had started seeing a marriage counselor, hoping it would sort things out.

Meanwhile, Tom had an idea. I could sell my share in the new Milford house to my family. They could pay me back what I invested in their home by getting a small mortgage, with the house as collateral. Then my brother or mother would own that property outright, and I would have the money to use as a down payment on a new house.

I was hesitant at first. Helping my family buy that new house was, in my mind, the singular good deed of my life. Nothing I had ever done had made me prouder. And now I was going to get paid back? I was going to retract my good deed? It made me uncomfortable.

I called my mother and told her, reluctantly, about Tom's proposal.

"I think it's a good idea," she said, without hesitation. "You'll get back everything you put into our house. You deserve that—it's your money. And your family deserves a real house."

I wasn't so sure it was good for my mother and brother. It meant Jerry, who still lived with and supported my mother, would now be straddled with a mortgage payment, but at least it was a small payment, considering they had a new house on an acre of land. And I would be giving up my stake in the Milford property; Jerry and my mother would own it outright. They both went along with the plan.

When my mother and I attended the loan closing, the bank's attorney looked on in silent amazement as my mother insisted on reading every line of arcane legal language in the lengthy mortgage documents. I remembered when I was in high school, and all the times I thrust paperwork in front of her, demanding that she sign them, without ever having the patience to let her read them. On this day, I was patient.

"She likes to read things before signing them," I told the attorney, with a knowing look.

With the investment from the Milford house now in my bank account, Tom and I started looking for a family house of our own. Housing prices were better the farther you went from the city, and we looked north, south, and west. We found a house that sat on four wooded acres along the winding South River in Duxbury, an ocean-side town thirty miles south of Boston. It was a spacious new construction, a beautiful yellow colonial with dark-green shutters. It had four bedrooms and a big yard—plenty of room to raise a family. Since I was the only one with an income at the time, the mortgage would be entirely in my name. It was a lot to take on.

I think we both knew it was a gamble to buy that big house, all the while Tom's business was flailing and eating into our bank account, and tension was growing thick between us. Yet we both harbored a blind hope that this lovely new home would turn things around. It would be a fresh start.

Steven was not even a year old when we moved in. I was still saddled with some extra weight from being bedridden and sick, but the pounds were steadily dropping off as I regained my health. Tom and I hadn't had a physical relationship in almost a year. The fact that he suddenly started showing an interest in me again, now that I was returning to my former appearance, only made me angry. Did I have to be a certain dress size to qualify for his affection? I had come from an Italian culture, where married women routinely grew plumper with every baby, and it never stopped them from having more sex and more babies. Surely it was possible for a married couple to stay intimate, long after losing their youthful bodies, if they truly loved each other? Was it naive of me to think so?

I had an aunt and uncle, Kay and Dave, whose marriage was always my idea of perfection. Although they were getting on in years, struggling to control their weight and dealing with chronic health issues, they still held hands and flirted, and looked at each other as if all they could see was the beautiful young bride and groom they once were. Why couldn't my husband see that I was the same woman he married?

Despite multiple sessions with a marriage counselor, I felt no better about my marriage. My pregnancy had been such a disheartening experience. Being bedridden had left me helpless and dependent for the first time in my life—the last thing I ever wanted to be. For once, I needed someone to take care of me, whether I liked it or not. But instead of help and support and kindness, I found contempt and rejection.

Somewhere along the line, I had come to the conclusion that my marriage wasn't the equal partnership I had envisioned when I walked down the aisle, side by side with my future husband. The marriage counselor seemed to suggest the fault was mine. He called me an "enabler." Perhaps I was, supporting myself, my child, my husband, and his failing business, paying for everything, without ever putting up a fuss. Was it all *my* fault, then?

The new house didn't work any magic on our relationship. Feeling empty and depleted, I contacted a divorce attorney—only a few months after buying the new house.

ℝ℞

The lawyer I retained, to his credit, didn't want me to give up on my marriage too easily. I knew nothing more than his name, a referral from another attorney, but I quickly found him asking me the most direct and personal of questions:

"So tell me—why do you want to get a divorce?"

I sighed heavily. How could I put this simply, in a way a total stranger could understand?

"Why? Because I feel let down in every way. When I needed him to be there for me, when I was very sick and unable to work, he wasn't there. I get no help or support of any kind, moral, financial, or otherwise. I feel completely alone, empty. I've felt this way for over a year. There's no affection, no intimacy. There's nothing I expected a marriage should have. Nothing."

I cleared my throat to steady my voice, and went on: "I wanted to build a home with his man. A life. A family. Instead I feel like—like an unwanted tenant in my own house. A renter. I'm there to pay the bills and nothing more. And one day I woke up and realized—I don't feel anything for this man. Nothing. I lost respect for him. When I lost respect, I lost love."

"There's no one else in your life?"

"No, nothing like that."

"What about him?"

"I'm sure he hasn't been unfaithful."

"This husband of yours—he doesn't sound like an ogre. He's not an ogre, is he?"

"No, I suppose not. He doesn't beat me, if that's what you mean."

"Well, I want you to try one more time with a marriage counselor. I'd like to recommend someone—she's very good."

So Tom and I tried a second counselor. Tom seemed to enjoy the first session, making a real connection with the therapist, talking freely about himself while she listened, wide-eyed, nodding and looking at him sympathetically.

"Would you want to have more children?" she asked us both.

"Yes!" he said, simultaneously with my emphatic "No!"

Tom looked at me and said, "I can't believe you don't want more kids. That is so sad."

Then, turning to the therapist, he explained, "My brother and sister were both a lot older than me, so I grew up alone. I was practically an only child. It was lonely! I wouldn't want that for Steven."

I was incredulous. "Tom, after everything you put me through, you actually think I would do that again? I was bedridden! I could have died! And you did nothing to help me. Nothing. All you cared about was when I was going to lose weight, so you could have a slim wife again!"

"Whoa, whoa, let's just slow down and take a deep breath," the therapist interjected. "You've both been through hell, haven't you?" Now the wide-eyed therapist turned her sympathetic gaze toward me.

"What about you, Catherine? Do you have sisters and brothers, too?"

My guts were churning. "You want me to talk about my family? I really don't want to talk about any of that right now."

"Catherine, I think it's important to understand where you're coming from."

"Look, the prospect of divorce is one of the hardest things I've ever had to go through. And if that isn't enough, you want to make it harder? You want to dredge up every painful thing that's ever happened to me? You want to pull the scabs off every single wound? I'm not interested. I'm not going to go there. I want to talk about what's going on in my marriage. The present, here and now."

"Okay, Catherine, let's change the topic. Let's talk about the present. Talk about the things you want to do with your life—right now. Is there a kind of work you like to do?"

"There's only one thing I've ever wanted to do. Writing."

Tom rolled his eyes. "Oh, here we go again, her *writing*," he said with a derisive sneer.

"You say that as if 'writing' was some sort of childish fantasy on my part! My writing is the only thing that's been putting food on the table for years!"

"Well, I guess not everyone can have a *calling* in life, like you," he said, holding his fingers in mock quotation marks.

I stopped and looked coolly at Tom, and for a very brief moment, I felt sorry for him. He had once told me that he never felt a particular calling to do anything. The fact that I always knew I was a writer at heart—whether I was actively honing my craft or not—had always seemed to make my husband uncomfortable. I don't think there was ever anything in his own life that he felt equally compelled to do.

I had once shown him a few poems I wrote, and he looked fidgety and anxious, not knowing what to say. I didn't fault him for that. A lot of people don't know what to say about poetry. But whether he liked my work or not, I had always longed to hear him simply encourage me, cheer me on, the way a good friend might do. Instead I found myself staring at a man who was being dismissive of the very thing I wanted to do with my life.

I tried to imagine, what if there came a time in the future when I could totally immerse myself in my writing, the kind of writing I always wanted to do? What if I actually published a book— not as a ghostwriter, but under my own name? What if my book was successful, even acclaimed? A bestseller? Would Tom ever be happy for me? Or would he minimize the achievement, pick it apart?

Here I was again, obsessing about the future, like the little girl and her imagined time machine. But Tom was already showing me my future life with him. If I excelled at something, he would not cheer me. If I lost my beauty, he would not touch me. If I was not useful to him, he would have no use for me. If a crystal ball were in my hands, the picture of my future could not have been clearer.

It wasn't long before I pulled the plug on marriage counselor number two. My suspicious nature was convinced the therapist was looking for many years' worth of lucrative therapy sessions, picking my whole life apart, all the while the meter was running. I wanted a simple, practical, direct answer to the question at hand: Did I marry the wrong man? That, to me, was the only question. And I was the only one who could answer it.

&)CR

In the fall of 1992, I was beginning life as a single parent, separated from my husband of four years, and the only man in my life for more than a decade. My family of three was now a family of two, and if that wasn't enough on my plate, I was starting up a new business.

One of my former clients referred me to a startup software company that needed public relations help. I really didn't want to do PR. I had done enough of that already, and I thought I'd never do it again. The PR agency that formerly employed me was a pressure cooker that left a persistent bitter taste in my mouth.

As a courtesy to the client who made the referral, I met with the software company's president and was bluntly honest. I felt I had nothing to lose. I told him what I could do, and what I couldn't do. I answered some questions with the almost unheard-of words, "I don't know." In the end, that was what he liked about me. I wasn't pretending to know everything. He felt he could trust me and offered me a monthly retainer on the spot.

A steady, predictable monthly check was hard to turn down. Divorce attorneys and marriage counselors had left me in debt, and so I had to consider it. I reluctantly accepted.

To my surprise, it turned out to be a positive experience. The smallest things I did for my new client seemed to make a real impact on his business, and I was appreciated for it. A single article I placed about the company in a trade magazine attracted positive attention, sales inquiries, and a lucrative new contract for my client, worth almost $1 million. I still had writing clients, too, but none would ever be as profitable as doing PR. And doing it on my own was a lot more pleasant than being a cog in an agency's gearwheel.

I was talking with an old friend who had also worked with me during my stint at a PR agency. June had left the agency as well, for health reasons. Severe stress had caused her asthma to flare up dangerously, requiring hospitalization. Her health was now fully recovered, and she was thinking about doing PR on her own. She suggested we go into business together.

The idea was intriguing. We could make our own rules. We could have a business that treated people with respect and humanity. Not one that squeezed every billable hour out of its employees, but a place that valued that elusive thing called work-life balance.

I couldn't stop thinking about it. I was a new mother; June was married and planning to be a mother; and we could flexibly arrange our work in the spaces around our lives, instead of the other way around. I started wrapping up my writing projects to focus on the new PR venture. While writing was my first love, there was no denying I'd earn more this way. I had a family to support, and everything I did, every choice I made, had to be with my baby's future in mind.

June and I started working together, informally at first, doing projects to test the waters. Soon we had pulled in our first big client: *Computerworld*, my former employer. Without ever writing a business plan, the plan seemed to be writing itself. June and I leased a small office in August 1992—the same month that Tom moved out of the house—and we hung out our shingle bearing both our last names.

Maybe I was crazy—starting a business while in the throes of divorce. No one in her right mind would attempt it. But I was propelled by all the ferocity of a mother protecting her young. I would do everything I could to provide for my baby, and I would do it by my own wits. I was launching a new venture, and I was launching myself.

26

PARTITION

When the letter arrived, it was late October. A difficult year was sputtering to a close. I was only beginning to come to terms with the strange new bargain I had made for myself.

The letter was waiting for me when I arrived at home, at the end of a long stop-and-go commute down Route 3 to Duxbury. Route 3 was also the main road to Cape Cod, and you could see the topography change from maples to scrub pine as you descended further and further south, past salt marshes and cranberry bogs. No matter how long the commute, no matter how weary I was from the working day, I knew I would come alive the minute I walked in that door and held my beautiful baby Steven in my arms.

The letter was waiting on the kitchen counter, atop a pile of junk mail and circulars. It bore all the marks of an attorney's correspondence, a plain white envelope with simple black lettering on the return address. I brushed it aside at first, not wanting to mar my precious moments with my son with what I assumed to be a divorce-related document. It would have to wait.

My first order of business was to fix a simple supper for Steven and the au pair, Dawn. She was a fresh-faced Iowan girl who disappeared every evening to spend hours on the phone with her boyfriend back home, while Steven and I began the joyful nightly ritual of bath time, stories, and songs.

When Steven was safely tucked into his crib for the night, and all the wheels on the bus had gone round and round, and he was "all bound for morning town, many miles away," I picked up the mail I had been avoiding and studied the white envelope. It was from an Attorney Adele Moroney of Worcester, Mass.—not a name I recognized, and not the divorce-related document I expected.

It contained a terse typewritten cover note with a copy of a "petition to partition the property at 7 Hayward Street, Milford, Massachusetts." My Aunt Chezz, one of the two Vermont aunts, had filed the petition, and the house in question was once my Italian grandparents' home.

Petition to partition. Such a strange alliteration. What did it mean? And why would the house on Hayward Street be of any concern me? As long as I could remember, it had been occupied by my Aunt Lizzie, along with her husband Emilio before he died. Before that, my grandmother Celesta lived there until she died in 1957. My grandfather Stefano had died in 1940. My grandparents bought the house shortly after they were married in 1903.

What did any of that have to do with me?

I brushed the letter aside, something to worry about later.

The following evening, I got a call from Aunt Chezz. She was born Cesarina, the feminine variant of Caesar, and later adopted the Anglicized spelling "Chesira." She was calling from Williamstown, Vermont, where she had co-owned a restaurant called The Gulf House with her sister Tillie. They were both newly married when they moved with their husbands to Vermont in the 1940s, and the restaurant did well for many years, situated on the main highway near the city of Barre, another granite quarry town like Milford. But when the new Interstate 89 was built in the early 1960s, tourists were diverted to eateries and rest stops along the interstate, and my aunts' restaurant began a slow decline.

In recent years, they had turned the restaurant into an antiques business. I always assumed they got much of their store's inventory from the ancestral Marenghi home, from elaborate Victorian birdcages to ornate armoires.

A call from Aunt Chezz was unusual. "Catherine, Tillie and I want to know what you're going to do?"

"I don't know what you mean?"

"What are you going to do? You got the petition, right?"

Before I could answer, she went on, "You know, when my father, your grandfather, was on his deathbed, he made me promise that I would always take care of the house. It was his dying wish. Please, he begged me, take care of the house. Your mother can't do it alone. You need to take care of the house. And I made him that promise, on his deathbed! On his deathbed, Catherine!"

Her voice rose in a steady crescendo of emotion. I could picture her wringing her hands as she spoke. I honestly had no idea what she was talking about. Her tone struck me as false and melodramatic. A deathbed proclamation to Chezz alone, when my grandfather had a wife and eight living children? She was alone ordained to carry out his final wishes? And what did she mean, "take care of the house"? She hadn't lived in that house for over forty years. From what I could tell, my Aunt Lizzie was living there, mowing the lawns, tending the gardens, and taking care of the place all by herself.

Chezz was a strange one. She was, in fact, my godmother, but ever since she assumed that role at my christening, I had never heard from her, not on birthdays or holidays or any time at all. I once got a package from her in the mail when I was fourteen or so, and it surprised me—I had never received so much as a card from her. I was thrilled to receive a gift from her. But when I opened it, I found it contained a filthy kitchen apron and an even nastier note.

Apparently Marcia had worn the apron on a recent visit to Vermont; my aunts had put my sister to work in the restaurant kitchen. Chezz wanted me to see how filthy Marcia's apron was. Rather than showing gratitude for my sister's unpaid labor, she wanted to turn me against her by sending me that foul object. From what I could tell, it didn't even look like normal kitchen stains—it appeared someone had deliberately smeared axel grease all over the apron in a suspiciously uniform manner. Chezz had gone to all this trouble, just to create drama between my sister and me. Why would she do that? I sent the package back to Chezz with a short note, admonishing her never to speak ill of my sister again. She was, after all, my sister.

I took another look at the petition to partition. It seemed to suggest that the house on Hayward Street was divided by some strange math into 720 portions, and that Chezz was apparently staking a claim to 60/720ths. Why not just say one-twelfth? I had no idea what that was all about. Why was my name even on this petition? Why would I care how many 720ths she has?

The petition made a reference to my grandmother's will, and I asked Attorney Moroney to send me a copy of it. When I received the document, I saw it had been filed in 1957, when I was three years old, and the whole thing seemed a bit sloppy to me. In addition to numerous misspellings, it listed my father's name as Jeremiah, which was never his legal name. He was born Gerolamo and went by the nickname Jerry. Even after reading the will, I did not fully understand it. It had references to life estates—I had no idea what a life estate was.

I was busy raising a son, running a household, and launching a business. I was adding clients, hiring staff, juggling a divorce—I didn't need to be dealing with this byzantine real estate transaction.

Or maybe I sensed instinctively there was something in those documents that I didn't want to know.

Just to be safe, I asked a lawyer friend to take a look at the will. Charlie was an immigration attorney, not a family law specialist, but he was smart, and I trusted him. I had never told him much about my family. I drew up a rough chart of my family tree, so he could get all the names straight, and faxed it to him, along with my grandmother's will and my aunts' petition to partition.

A few days later, Charlie and I met for dinner at the Pillar House, an elegant restaurant not far from my office. It was a friendly exchange—I would pick up the tab for dinner in return for his legal advice.

"So what's all this about life estates?" I asked.

"A life estate," he explained, speaking slowly and precisely, "under common and statutory law, is the ownership of land for the duration of a person's life." I could feel my eyes looking blankly at him, about to glaze over in abject boredom.

"In legal terms," he continued, "it's an estate that ends at death, when ownership of the property passes from the owner of a life estate, called a 'life tenant,' to ownership by the 'remaindermen,' who are named in the agreement as the ultimate heirs."

"Charlie, I'm sorry. I don't get it. What does any of this have to do with me?"

"Let me put it this way. Your grandmother wanted some, but not all, of her children—including your father—to be life tenants. That meant they could live in the house as long as they wanted to. But they would never own the house. After their deaths, or after they gave up their life estates, the house would be bequeathed equally to the remaindermen."

"Who the heck are the remaindermen?"

"You, Catherine. You and your siblings. The house belongs entirely to you."

I put down my fork and knife. Charlie had my full attention.

"In other words, Catherine, your aunts don't own the house. They don't even own six seven-hundred-and-twentieths of the house. You do. You and your brother and sister. The whole thing, lock, stock and barrel. You've owned that house all along."

His words took my breath away. "No, oh no, that's not possible. No. It can't be."

I was squirming in my chair, pushing my hands toward him, as if shoving the space between us. I was pushing away the strangeness of his words, as if I were refusing another serving of food.

"What's wrong? You inherited a house. A nice one, by the looks of it. What could be bad about that?"

My head was spinning, and my lawyer friend couldn't possibly understand my reaction. He didn't know my history, didn't know how my family had lived. I had never told anyone about that. Forty years in a one-room dwelling, and all the while, my father had every right to live in his parents' enormous house? My siblings and I actually owned that house all along?

How could my family not have known this? Is it possible my father might not have been made aware of his mother's will? How could he not? Even if he had seen it, would he have understood it? Even with a college education and a master's degree in English, I still needed a lawyer to help me decipher it.

So many things were coming back to me.

"You know, Charlie, there were times over the years when my family saw these strange legal notices in the *Milford Daily News*. Something to the effect that anyone with an interest in the property at 7 Hayward Street should come forward. We didn't know it had anything to do with us, so we just shrugged it off. Were those, perhaps, the machinations of my aunts, trying to get control of the property?"

"I think," he said, "it's quite possible your aunts were trying to sell the house and hit a brick wall. They couldn't get a clear title. From what you tell me, they may have been trying to sell it for years. Now they're desperate. They want to get the house off their hands. Here's what I think: they're trying to convince you that you have just a small stake in it, so they can buy you out for less than you deserve."

It was just sinking in. I could have grown up in a large spectacular house, with a lush expansive yard in the middle of town, less than a block away from my elementary school. Surely it would have been the favorite after-school gathering place of all my friends, the ones I never dared invite to Prairie Street. What would it have been like to live there? To have parties there? To play hide and seek in the numerous first-floor parlors and upstairs bedrooms and attic, laughing and running from one room to the next, up and down the elegant stairs?

A beautiful lifetime had been denied to us.

There was more to the will, too. My grandmother also bequeathed to my father all the furniture in her house, for the benefit of us, her grandchildren, and she stated it was her wish that the home remain in the hands of a Marenghi as long as possible. At the time of her death, my father had a house full of children, including a son. Most of his siblings had no children at all. Collectively we would have presented the best hope of carrying on the family name—a very important commodity in an Italian family.

The entire petition to partition, it appeared, was a sham. It named stakeholders in the property that had no rights to the house at all, such as my deceased Uncle Albert's wife and adopted daughter. Albert had a life estate, but a life estate cannot be bequeathed to anyone—it ends when the life tenant dies. It also named Rose and Irene, two other sisters of my father who did not even have life estates; they were each bequeathed a small amount of cash in my grandmother's will, but nothing more.

It was all a subterfuge, a petition to deny, to confuse, to distract and bewilder, and to keep us from knowing my aunts' ultimate aim.

The following weekend, I went to visit my mother and brother at their house. With Steven snuggled against my shoulder, I carefully laid out the papers on their kitchen table, including my grandmother's will. They didn't seem to know anything about it. My mother, who had saved every important document that ever touched her hands, would have surely held onto this if she had ever seen it. She had a cedar chest crammed with all the important artifacts of her life, so full it was hard to close it. But she had never seen this will.

My mother vaguely remembered getting some old-fashioned baby carriages and high chairs when Marcia and Celia were little, but she knew nothing about inheriting a house full of furniture. And she, too, had no idea what a life estate was, or that her husband ever had one.

"Do you know what this means?" I said. "We own the house on Hayward Street! We always have. We could have been living in that great big house all these years. For God's sake, we could have each had our own bedroom. It belongs to us! It belonged to us all along!"

My mother paused for a moment, expressionless, and turned to me. "Do you remember that letter?"

"What letter?"

"Years ago, just after your dad passed. I got a letter, out of the blue, no return address. It always bothered me. It was signed by a so-called 'friend of the family.' It said our relatives were plotting against us, trying to steal something that was ours."

"Oh-h-h-h, I do remember that," I said. "It was weird. A warning, but no specifics. Without knowing what it was about, we couldn't act on it. But now, I wonder…"

"I always thought Mary Speroni sent it. Nonnie was her big sister. She would have known what her sister wanted."

"And it would have made her mad if anyone was trying to go against Nonnie's wishes," I added. "It could have been her. That would make a lot of sense."

Jerry stood up from the table, looking agitated. "I want nothing to do with that house on Hayward Street," he proclaimed. "I have too many bad feelings about that place. I wash my hands of the whole thing."

I looked askance at him. "Jerry, do you know what you're saying? This is exactly what they're hoping we'll do, that we'll just back off and walk away." I feared I had told him the news too quickly. It would take him a while to process this startling information. I was still trying to come to terms with it myself.

"Jerry," Ma said, "maybe we should let Catherine decide what to do. She's the one with a business head on her shoulders."

My mother's comment startled me. I was indeed running a business, but I was never quite sure if she ever even noticed what I did. Every now and then, she surprised me.

"Look," I said, "there's no way in hell we're going to hand this property over to anyone. Those two in Vermont, Chezz in particular—I think they've been trying to sell the house out from under us for years. I'm sure of it. And we're not going to reward them for that. The house is not theirs, and we're not going to let them have it."

"So what do we do?" Ma asked.

"I'll tell you what we do. Nothing. We do absolutely nothing. Lizzie is still living there, and she has every right to. She has a life estate, too. I don't blame her for any of this. She's always been good to us. We wait until none of them wants to live there anymore. They're all old. They're tired of taking care of that place, and they want to be done with it. But until then, we do nothing. We wait."

They both nodded slightly, without speaking. We all sat silently for a while, trying to take in this strange news, occasionally distracted by Steven's squirming against my shoulder.

"I think I'd better get this little guy home," I said.

I stood up and began stuffing my papers back into my briefcase. But before I left, I took a look down the hallway and thought about Marcia. This time I would try to speak to her. I walked up to her bedroom door and softly knocked.

"Marcia! Marcia, it's me. Steven is here. Would you like to come out and meet your little nephew? Marcia? Marcia?"

No response. I waited for a few minutes outside her door, trying to listen for her footsteps, a noise of some kind. Nothing.

I closed my eyes and let out a soft sigh.

A week later, I got a card in the mail from Marcia.

She wrote, in her elaborate and elegant cursive handwriting, that she had heard our voices when Steven and I had come to visit.

"Steven has a beautiful voice," she wrote. "He must be a very beautiful boy."

Her note, with its rare expression of simple human feeling, was heartbreaking. Why couldn't she have come out to meet her one and only nephew, her brother's namesake? She knew he was there, and she knew exactly who he was.

I resolved to try, every time I visited, to persuade Marcia to come out and meet my son. How hard would it be for her to just open the door?

27

AWAKENING

Sometimes my brother came home from work to find my mother, now in her mid-seventies, quietly sitting at the kitchen table, in total darkness. Just sitting alone, doing nothing. She seemed not to notice the darkness had fallen around her until her son walked in and flipped the light switch.

That's how I felt when, a year after splitting from my husband, I suddenly realized I was emerging from a deep depression. I didn't recognize it as such, until I stepped out of it and into the shock of daylight. Suddenly I started noticing things, like the woods around my house, and how lovely and shady they were, with their pine needle carpet, dotted with pink lady's slippers. How could I never have noticed those rare and exquisite wild orchids that were growing there?

There was an amazing variety of birds in the nearby bogs, including swans and blue herons—they came as a total surprise to me. How could I have missed something as glorious as the six-foot wing spread of a blue heron? And those scruffy briars near my driveway—they weren't just briars. They were overflowing with plump blackberries.

It was that way with cooking, too. It was one of my great joys in life, and I hadn't done much of it for over a year. Now I would find myself slicing a purple onion, or tearing garlic cloves from their paper white cocoon, and be overcome with their beauty. Or shrimp, turning from pearly gray to coral pink in the pan. Was there anything prettier than that? So many simple pleasures I had put aside, or forgotten, and suddenly all my senses came rushing back to me, like soldiers coming home from a war.

And the biggest surprise of all—I was suddenly noticing men. I never thought it would happen again. My body had been dormant for so long, I didn't know if it would ever wake up. But it did. I could feel the blood coursing in my veins again. I was acutely conscious of men's bodies underneath their clothes. Men were noticing me, too, as if I were suddenly throwing off torrents of invisible pheromones.

It was December 3, 1993, my 39th birthday. It was a Friday night, and I was feeling like a teenager on her first date. In fact, it was my third date—with one of my clients. There was something slightly scandalous about dating a client. I had always vowed not to do that. It wouldn't be good for my reputation if anyone thought I was using something other than my professional skills to win new business. But in the case of this blue-eyed man, I decided to make an exception. I just wasn't going to tell anybody.

Steven was going to spend the weekend with his dad, part of our shared custody agreement, in which we alternated weekends. I had stopped on the way home from work to pick up Steven from the day care center, and my plan was to drive home, change into my new black dress and strappy high-heeled shoes, drop Steven off with his dad in Cambridge, and continue into Boston to meet my new gentleman friend.

Just as I was driving into the day care center parking lot, I got a call on my cell phone. It was my date for the evening, and he sounded awful. He was suffering from an apparent flu, and he had to cancel. What a crashing letdown! It was too late to make an alternate plan for the evening. So instead of a romantic birthday celebration, I was going to spend my birthday alone.

I already had Steven's overnight bag in the car, so there was no need for me to go home and change. I decided to go straight from day care to Tom's place and drop Steven off. As I strapped Steven into his car seat, I let him know we were going to see Daddy. By now it was a familiar routine. But for some reason, Steven said, "No!"

I was surprised. "Steven, don't you want to see Daddy? I know Daddy wants to see you!"

"No, need to go home with Mommy. Need to go *Mommy's* house now."

I had never seen anything like this before. Steven always seemed happy to be with either parent. But he was so insistent. And I was feeling so low, I didn't feel like arguing.

I called Tom and said, "I don't know what's wrong with Steven, but he really wants to come home with me tonight. Do you mind if I drop him off with you in the morning instead?" Tom did not object.

I drove home with Steven and expected a quiet evening, a quick supper, and off to bed. No sooner had we stepped into the front door than Steven started dashing around the house, like a little madman, as if he were on a mission. What was wrong with that child?

I followed him into the dining room, where he climbed onto a chair and then onto the table, pulled a tall candle from its crystal candlestick, and came running back to deliver it to me.

"Here," he said. "Need to blow a candle."

"What are you talking about, Steven?"

"Need to light the candle and blow. Mummy's birthday!"

I was stunned. How did he know it was my birthday? I hadn't mentioned it. I didn't think he even knew what a birthday was. He was only two years old.

I was completely overcome. "Light the candle, Mummy! Light the candle!" I rummaged through a kitchen drawer, looking for a book of matches, not wanting him to see that my eyes were glistening with tears.

Now Steven was charging off again, this time to the pantry closet, rummaging through the shelves for something else.

"Mummy needs a cake!" I didn't have any cake. Not even the ingredients for a cake. We settled on the closest substitute we could find—a box of breakfast bars with raspberry filling. I pulled out a plate and started unwrapping a few bars, while Steven set to work arranging them artistically on the plate. I returned the candle to its crystal holder and arranged it in the middle of the plate, lit the candle, and we both took turns blowing out the flame while singing the birthday song.

"Yay!" Steven clapped. "Mummy has a happy birthday!"

I wondered if he was thinking and scheming about this all day. How did he know? We lived alone at that time; there was no nanny or anyone else in the house to put him up to this. The only thing I could think of was the fact that I received a bouquet of flowers that morning from my office. I might have read aloud the Happy Birthday greeting on the card, although I don't remember doing so. Whatever tipped him off was a mystery, but that child never missed a thing.

After a dinner of cereal bars and milk, we needed a party. And what does every party need? Balloons, of course. I happened to have a whole bag of them, left over from a previous party, and I set to work blowing up at least a dozen round fat balloons, in rainbow colors, and tying the ends with knots. They were perfect for rubbing against my sweater and making them prickle with static electricity, so they would stick on the wall. The living room walls were studded with festive balloons, with Steven cheerfully insisting, "More balloons! More balloons!"

Even the next morning, Steven had a few more surprises up his sleeve. As I awoke, before getting out of bed or turning on the light in my room, I heard some activity going on outside my bedroom door, just light footsteps at first, and then the doorknob lightly turning. The next thing I knew, Steven burst into the room.

"Surprise, Mummie! Surprise!"

The door flew open and then, with a great whoosh, a dozen balloons came flying into my room, with a giggling little boy behind them. He was sweeping them into the room with his hands, kicking them in, and laughing and jumping in his little one-piece footed pajamas. In a flash, my dark quiet room was transformed into a full-blown party.

I soon realized that this scheming little boy had to have taken at least a dozen trips, up and down the stairs, quietly collecting all the balloons from the living room, one or two at a time—he could carry no more than that while crawling up the stairs. Then he carefully amassed them in front of my bedroom door. At exactly the right moment, he threw open the door and sprang his surprise on me.

Later in the morning, my birthday date called me to apologize for leaving me alone on my birthday the previous night.

"I had a great restaurant picked out for you," he said.

"Oh, it's okay," I replied. "I ended up having an amazing dinner—the best birthday dinner I've ever had. In fact, I'm still celebrating."

28

LOVE

When Marcia passed away on her forty-eighth birthday, I found it strangely difficult to mourn. The woman I had known as my sister had disappeared many years before. Years of mental illness had so ravaged her, she had become unrecognizable. She was already lost to us. It was hard to know when to mark her passing.

Her death came on the heels of another loss—the dissolution of my marriage. She died only a month after the divorce decree was finalized. The two events have since become intertwined in my memory, death and divorce, each an endless season of loss, unrelieved by a clear, defining moment to let one know that the worst has passed.

Knowing I was dealing with a painful divorce, my mother and brother had spared me from the worst of it. So much was happening under their roof that I never knew about. They thought my being the newly single parent of a two-year-old baby, while running a business, was more than enough for me to handle. So they quietly bore the anguish of Marcia's deterioration and never called to tell me about it until my sister was lying on her hospital deathbed.

For nearly two years, barricaded in her bedroom in my mother's house, a self-imposed seclusion, Marcia had never bathed or changed her clothes, and horrific odors emanated from behind her closed door. It was difficult to gauge her condition exactly, but my brother was very concerned. He tried desperately to gain legal custody of Marcia so he could make medical decisions on her behalf. The process proved too slow to do any good.

Then, a cut on Marcia's foot had become dangerously infected, and it was too painful for her to walk on her own. Contrary to all her instincts, she asked for my brother's help—to assist her with taking the few steps across the hall to the bathroom each day. She sat in an old rocking chair, a makeshift wheelchair, and Jerry dragged it across the carpeted floor to the bathroom.

Despite her excruciating pain, Marcia refused to see a doctor. Doctors were part of the grand cabal of conspirators determined to control her brain. The first time my brother called an ambulance, the paramedics left without her, because she refused to go with them. They had no authority to force her. The second time an ambulance was summoned, she was too weak to resist.

The infection on her leg had turned to gangrene.

The last time I saw Marcia alive, she was at Milford Hospital, lying unconscious in her bed, with a morphine drip to dull the pain. Not having actually seen her in years, I found her appearance shocking. Her once-radiant red hair was stringy and colorless, her teeth badly decayed, her body thin and wasted. I remembered her as she was on the day of her high school graduation, a vibrant girl in a black silk shantung dress, her hair the color of a new copper penny.

The gangrene had spread through Marcia's body, and she was dying a terrible and certain death, occasionally gasping and shuddering and completely unresponsive to those around her. I couldn't bear to look at her. I joined Ma and Jerry in a trio of chairs by her hospital bed.

Sitting by Marcia's bed on what would be the last day of her life, I grew impatient and fidgety. I found it impossible to believe that anyone, anyone at all, was still there inside that wasted shell of a human body. I wanted to get up and pace. I frequently offered to go for coffee for everyone, and welcomed the brief escapes.

My mother and brother, on the other hand, were unwaveringly attentive to Marcia. They brought her birthday cards and cake, wished her a happy forty-eighth birthday, and spoke with her continually, even though she never showed any sign of hearing them. My mother sat close to the bed to hold Marcia's hand. Jerry read aloud the birthday cards, big gaudy cards covered with pink flowers and glitter. Their love and tenderness amazed me, and shamed me, especially after all they had been through with her.

Long after I had gone home for the night, they both stayed behind. They wanted to be by her side when she finally died. And they were.

Some months earlier Marcia had entrusted Jerry with some of her papers for safekeeping. Among them was a deed to a burial plot at the Mount Auburn Cemetery, a historic and exquisitely landscaped burial ground in Cambridge. My sister, who never owned a home of her own, who longed for one all her life, had a deed to a gravesite. Her one and only real estate holding. And she purchased it while still a young woman in her twenties. So strange and sad.

Just as I fidgeted in her hospital room, I fidgeted at Marcia's wake. There's no one in that box, I thought. No one at all. Marcia disappeared such a long time ago. I couldn't even bring myself to join the small funeral procession from Milford to Mount Auburn Cemetery, and quietly exited the funeral home alone.

I wondered: Was there something wrong with me that I couldn't express the same loving kindness as my mother and brother did toward my dying sister? I felt nothing. Was it possible that my divorce had so depleted me, I was no longer able to feel anything? Was I heartless? Numb?

Several months later, in December, I awoke early on the morning of my fortieth birthday. Suddenly I remembered how Marcia used to call me every year on my birthday, very early, sometimes distressingly early, at five or six o'clock in the morning, because she always wanted to be the first to wish me a happy birthday. The memory stung me. Fresh grief washed over me like a searing acid rain.

No, I had not forgotten my sister. And I had not forgotten how to love.

29

COUNTERSUIT

When I was three years old, I tagged along one evening when my father drove my mother to see the family doctor. She wasn't feeling well. We used the pick-up truck my father drove home from work every night, since we had no car of our own, and my mother struggled to climb into it. While my parents were in with Dr. Gottlieb, I thought it was great fun to sit all by myself in the doctor's handsome waiting room, with its richly varnished knotty pine paneling, my feet swinging playfully because they didn't touch the floor. So many colorful magazines to look at, too.

Only many years later did I learn that my mother gave birth to a premature baby that night. He was stillborn. They named him Tommy. The doctor placed the baby's lifeless body in my mother's arms, and an ambulance took them both to the Framingham Union Hospital.

No mother wants to outlive her children, but my mother had now witnessed the loss of four: Tommy, Stephen, Celia, and now Marcia. Her two first-born and her two last-born. It was a lot for one woman to bear.

Marcia's long deterioration and death had taken a terrible toll on my mother. She suffered a major stroke shortly after Marcia died. When I saw her in the hospital, she seemed very changed—weaker and frailer, and a bit somber. I had never seen her that way. Despite her hard life, I always thought she had a sweet, childlike cheerfulness, always seeing the bright side of everything. She never really had health problems before. She was always so strong and sturdy. Now in her mid-seventies, the cares and woes of her life were catching up to her. She would begin to experience what her doctor called mini-strokes, each one claiming another little piece of her memory.

My brother Jerry continued to live with her and care for her, sacrificing a life of his own. He always kept his promise, made at the age of twelve, to be the man of the family. He supported the household with his wages, working in the warehouse of a local hair products company, when the Milford Shoe Company went out of business—after more than a century of operation. He had been lifting boxes all day for twenty-seven years. He kept my mother company and drove her everywhere she needed to go—to doctors' appointments, shopping, or just rides to get out of the house. She loved taking car rides to nowhere, just to see something different. It lifted her spirits.

I often drove out to Milford, to give my brother some occasional relief from all the driving, and to give them both a chance to see Steven. No one could make my mother smile the way Steven could. When Steven was old enough to hold a Polaroid camera, he turned the tables on my mother and snapped pictures of her, the inveterate photographer. Each photo Steven took was from the perspective of a small boy looking up, and you saw the face of an adoring grandmother, looking down toward the camera, with a loving expression that no one else could have captured.

I sometimes drove my mother to see the New England fall foliage and all the multitudes of orange pumpkins for sale at farm stands. In summer we might go out for fried clams at the Rosewood, or to Carbone's, a little Italian restaurant where she used to go with my dad when they were young and just starting to date. It didn't matter where we went; any destination seemed to make her happy. If we stopped at a restaurant, there was always the struggle to get Ma to say what she wanted to order. She would stare at the menu and could never decide, never seemed to have any ability to declare out loud what she wanted. Invariably I would have to order something for her.

I tried to see Aunt Lizzie when I was in town, too, at the house on 7 Hayward Street. I often found her outdoors, an old Italian woman energetically pushing a lawn mower, even when she was well into her eighties, her face shiny with sweat and loose strands of her white hair flying in the wind. Or I might find her tending the tall rows of tomato plants in her garden. She loved babies and always beamed when she saw me walk up with little Steven.

"Look, his little arms look like Italian sausages," she said affectionately, pointing out the creases in Steven's plump limbs.

Lizzie was always ready to drop everything and heat me up a bowl of her homemade minestrone, a somewhat bland concoction with lots of cabbage, in the northern Italian style, and no salt because of her high blood pressure.

Once she had set out food for her guests, her habit was to sit at the head of the table and start talking. It was as if someone had wound a key on her back and let her go. Without prompting, without any context or lead-in, Lizzie would start telling something that happened to her many years before. Her stories bored me when I was a child, but as I grew older, they fascinated me.

"My muthuh, you know, she worked picking cranberries. They used to grow a lot of cranberries in Holliston. She took me and Jerry along in the baby carriage."

I was calculating in my head. If my father was a baby, maybe one or two years old, and Lizzie was three years older, the year would have been around 1908. The walk to Holliston had to be three miles. The women then would have been wearing heavy long dresses, unbearable in the sun.

"Back then, you know, the bus cost five cents each way, but Mama, she only made fifteen cents a day, so we walked. You couldn't get the men to do that work, 'cuz it didn't pay nuthin'. So all the ladies did it. They didn't put no water in those bogs, neithuh, like they do now, so the berries all float to the top. Oh, no, it was all dry back then. The ladies dragged these long skinny burlap bags behind 'em, gettin' their hands all scratched and cut, stuffin' the berries in them bags as they went."

"And what did you do while she was working?"

"I watched Jerry. Mama used to lay him on a board and wrap him up tight, like a papoose. That's what they did with babies back then, you know, to keep their legs straight. Then she'd hang him up on a tree, in the shade, and I stayed there with him, watching him."

Swaddling, I thought. My grandmother swaddled her baby, as they did two thousand years ago, and let him swing on a tree branch so she could do backbreaking work for fifteen cents a day.

Lizzie talked about working, herself, too, starting when she was eight or nine years old, long before the era of child labor laws, at the Milford Shoe Company.

"My first day, they put me at a sewing machine and give me two pieces a leathuh. They told me how to stitch the pieces togethuh—paht of a man's shoe. Each time I did that, they told me, drop it inna drawa. I thought, this is easy. Zip, zip, zip, one afta anuthuh. End of the day comes, my drawa is full. Lady next to me, olda woman—she didn't have so many done. The boss fired her right then. They gave me her job afta that."

From that day on, my aunt worked in factories all her life. Like my mother, she was heavy set but solid, as sturdy and muscled as the men who worked beside her, first at Milford Shoe and later at William Lapworth & Sons, a manufacturer of elastic fabrics, whose British-born owner berated her whenever a needle broke on her sewing machine. Later she worked at Archer Rubber, where a chemical spray left a small scar on her cheek. Her final employer was the Stylon Tile Company, known for making pink and black bathroom tiles, which were hard to handle without cutting her hands. She always called her place of work "the shop." She was "working down at the shop."

Before I left her house, she always gave me something to take with me, like a bag of her hand-made swiss-chard ravioli, or if it was close to Christmas, a plate of her own Italian cookies. My favorites were the ceci, little fried cookies that looked like ravioli but were stuffed with sweet chestnut and honey filling, or the ones that looked like bowties, called cenci, dusted with powdered sugar. No matter how busy she was, she never let anyone leave her house hungry or empty-handed.

Once I accompanied Lizzie to the Sacred Heart Cemetery to help her with all the flower baskets she wanted to lay on the gravestones of lost family members. There's something about Italians and cemeteries. I was never attracted to cemeteries, never finding any comfort in visiting the dead, but for most of my family, it was like attending a family reunion. Seeing Lizzie moving among the graves, one would think she was hobnobbing at a cocktail party.

"Oh, look over there, that's Joe. That's Desolina. And oh, here, here's Irene…"

As if she were calling on old friends.

I never faulted Lizzie for all the nonsense about the petition to partition. She was always kind to my family. But my aunts in Vermont, it seemed, weren't through with us yet.

In 1996, another shoe fell in the case of the house on Hayward Street. My mother found a thick envelope from an attorney on her doorstep. Aunt Chezz was at it again. She was suing my mother, Jerry, and me for every penny she and Tillie spent on the Hayward Street house since my grandmother died in 1957. They had a long list of the relatively modest investments they had made—a can of paint here and there, new window screens, plumbing bills, cement repairs, and other simple household expenses over the course of forty years. Not one of the expenditures was for a major home improvement; it was all basic maintenance. They even threw in the cost of my grandmother's funeral, which Chezz had paid for. I was two years old when my grandmother died, and I was being asked to reimburse my aunt for her mother's funeral.

"Well, that's one way to punish us," I told my mother. "Make us pay for her mother's funeral, to get back at us for being her mother's heirs."

There was even a bill for the cost of an estimated fifty trips by car between Milford and the aunts' home in Vermont over the course of forty years, each one 350 miles round trip. Sisters visiting sisters. They estimated the total mileage cost at $5,000. Even phone calls between Massachusetts and Vermont were tallied up at $1,800 over the years.

The total bill: $97,915. And some change.

Apparently this is why we hadn't heard from the aunts in Vermont for a while. They must have pulled out every receipt they could find from every shoebox and file drawer they ever had.

Once again I faxed the document to my lawyer friend Charlie, who quickly examined the bizarre complaint. He called me to explain the situation.

"You aren't obligated to pay anything, Catherine. The people who live in the house, the ones with life estates, are obligated to maintain the property while they live there. On top of that, there's a legal concept called 'waste.' If they don't keep the property in good shape, they are guilty of 'waste.' In other words, they are damaging *your* property. In fact, you're entitled to sue your aunts if they haven't taken good care of the place."

At minimum, he proposed a counterclaim, charging the aunts with filing a frivolous lawsuit, which would force them to pay my legal expenses as a penalty for filing such a suit.

I was comfortable with the frivolous lawsuit counterclaim, but I was not at all interested in suing my elderly aunts for damages or so-called "waste." By then I had more important things to do. My business was growing rapidly. My original business partner had left to become a full-time parent, and I now I was the sole principal with a dozen people working for me. The business was now called "Marenghi Public Relations," or MPR, and it would continue to grow and support my family for years. Steven was now in kindergarten. I had moved from Duxbury to buy a smaller, more manageable cape-style house in Needham, Massachusetts, where the public school system was said to be excellent. My life was very full, and the lawsuit was nothing more than an annoying distraction.

I had never been busier, never worked harder. Every evening, after a full day of work, preparing dinner, and doing the bare minimum of housework, I would send Steven off to bed with a story, a lullaby, and a kiss, and then begin the second part of my work day: sitting at my computer for three or four hours, running reports, writing new business proposals, or doing the most deadening accounting tasks.

Both fortunately and unfortunately, my agency was in the high-technology sector, and business was booming. It was a heady era when business plans were scribbled on the backs of envelopes, and that might be enough for a venture capitalist to commit millions of dollars in funding. Dot-com startups were popping up at a dizzying rate, and I couldn't keep up with all the requests for proposals.

Often, in the middle of populating a spreadsheet with numbers or printing out the latest P&L, I remembered the cutting admonishment from my professor and poet Denise Levertov: "You shouldn't be doing some *job*, Catherine. You know what you should be doing."

No, I was not writing poetry, or doing anything she would call creative. But wasn't it creative to start a business? To imagine a possible future and then assemble it, bit by bit? Wasn't I applying my writing skill in my work, even if a well-crafted press release would never win a Pulitzer Prize? And what about the overpowering responsibility to provide for my son? Wasn't being a good parent and provider an honorable pursuit?

I didn't mind working hard. After all, I was working for my son and myself. But I often wondered how it might have been different if my family were like those of so many of my college classmates, each the latest generation in a long line of successful business people. No one in my family had ever started a business. There was no one from an older generation to ask for advice or guidance on business matters; I had to learn everything on my own, the slow way and the hard way.

It never would have occurred to me to ask my mother about my financial projections, or my profit-and-loss statement. She was a lifelong farmer and homemaker. She just wouldn't have understood.

30

ENTREPRENEUR

Myrtle

It was late in the evening, December 1945. I was sitting at the kitchen table in my pink chenille bathrobe, doing some late-night accounting under the dim lamplight, while Jerry, my husband of two months, was slumped in his armchair, drifting off to sleep. I turned down the radio. Artie Shaw's band was playing one of my favorite new tunes, "Begin the Beguine," and I was softly humming along while I worked. Da da da DA, da da DA...

I knew a thing or two about accounting. It was one of my favorite classes at Becker College. Now I was sorting through an accordion folder of bank passbooks and receipts, and an envelope full of cash and loose change, laying it all out on the table. I learned how to file and organize records when I was in college, and I learned always to keep my receipts.

Now, after carefully sharpening my pencil by shaving off the tip with a razor blade and blowing the pencil shavings into the trash, I tallied up all of our assets in a neat column of numbers on a sheet of notepaper:

RECORD OF MONEY IN CEDAR CHEST
Dec. 1, 1945

Wedding gift from Jerry's mother:	$100.00
Wedding gift from Aunt Rena:	$ 5.00
" " " from Aunt Jennie:	$ 5.00
Christmas club account at bank:	$ 50.00
Bank savings account:	$ 37.00
Cash, paper currency:	$ 43.00
Wedding shower gifts:	$ 30.00
War bond:	$ 18.75
Last pay check:	$ 23.78
Rolled coins:	$ 35.00

And on and on, my narrow tower of numbers grew. When I finished tallying up everything, I had my grand total: $400.14. That was the sum total of our combined assets. It was all we had in the world. Was it enough to bankroll our future?

I did a few projections. Jerry was earning about $30 a week from Draper Corporation, where he was an electric jitney driver. His paycheck was enough to pay the rent, the milkman, the day-to-day bills, without touching our meager assets.

And then I thought we could get the rent lowered from $30 a month to $20. The landlord wasn't doing everything he promised in the rental agreement, and he was making us live through noisy construction in the flat above ours. Ceiling plaster was falling in great chunks on our heads. I thought we had a good case for a rent abatement, and I already had the petition letter drawn up. My husband Jerry would sign the letter, of course; there were some things only a man could do. But ten dollars more in our pockets every month would be a big help.

I had counted up our assets and forecast our expenses. I was convinced we had enough to get by. We could make it work.

Jerry and I had a plan. We were going to start a farm! A flower farm. We were going to grow gladiolus and be the only supplier to florists in the area. We were seeing glads everywhere; they were on magazine covers, in shop windows, in movies. The most popular flower around. Every girl wanted to see her beau arrive at her door with a bouquet of bright red gladiolus. And they were pretty easy to grow, too, even in New England.

I grew up on a farm, and I always had a knack for making things grow, even in the hardest, rockiest soil. I have a Grange certificate in horticulture to prove it! Jerry's a good farmer, too, and we both love flowers. So what could be better than working side by side with the man I adore? We'll be financially independent, we can be our own bosses, and we won't need to suffer our terrible landlord any more.

I had met my future husband when our paths crossed, quite suddenly, at Draper Corporation in Hopedale, Massachusetts. It was the biggest employer in the region, a big sprawling noisy manufacturer of cotton looms, with three thousand employees. Everyone wanted to work there. I had a job in the front office, doing bookkeeping, typing, and shorthand with a gaggle of other college girls like me. I was walking back from lunch one day, taking a short cut across the shop floor, when I saw an electric jitney speeding toward me—it nearly ran me over!

I hopped out of the way just in time, and when I saw the grin on the driver's face, I was sure that man had done it deliberately, just to see my reaction. All I could do was giggle and look away, hoping he wouldn't see me blushing. When I turned around, he was staring straight at me. I never saw such a look. I could feel his eyes on me like hot sunlight on my back as I walked away.

He was waiting for me as I left the office that day. I was hurrying toward the bus when he pulled up to the curb in his car.

"Hey, Toots, you wanna go for a spin?"

No one had ever called me "Toots" before. I liked it. I had always hated my name anyway. Myrtle. It didn't sound like anything nice. When I was ten, I announced to my mother I wanted to change my name to Rosebud. Pink rosebuds were my favorite flower. But my mother told me that Myrtle was the name of a pretty flower, too. *Hmmph*, I thought. Tell that to the little boys who used to tease me and call me Myrtle the Turtle.

This man could call me Toots any time he wanted. And he had a nice black Ford coupe. It wasn't like me to get into cars with strange men, but this time I did. I hopped right in beside him.

We drove around for a while. He told me his name was Gerolamo, but everyone called him Jerry. He came from a big Italian family. He had six sisters and one brother, and his parents were both born in Italy. I came from a big family, too, with seven siblings of my own. Jerry had been working for Draper for eighteen years. He was thirty-seven years old, and I was twenty-four.

On our first date, he took me out to eat at Carbone's, a quiet little family restaurant. I didn't know much about Italian food, so he ordered dinner for me, something on the menu called "manicotti," although it sounded like he was saying "manniGOT." He also ordered me a Tom Collins—I didn't know a thing about cocktails, either. I never drank before. I was hoping he wouldn't see how inexperienced I was with cocktails, with restaurants—and with men.

Looking across the table with the red-and-white-checkered tablecloth, I saw a remarkably good-looking man, tall, strongly built, and darkly handsome. I never saw such black hair, thick and wavy, combed back away from his face with a touch of pomade that made it shine. And his profile—was that what you call an aquiline nose? So distinguished looking. And such deep-brown eyes. I couldn't believe this man was interested in *me*.

I had never known anyone like him. In the little farming town where I grew up, all my neighbors had familiar-sounding English names, and many could trace their family origins back to the time of the Pilgrims. This man was different. His family had barely taken root in American soil. There was something fresh and exotic about him. He even smelled different. He had the woody smell of Camel cigarettes on his fingertips, and his face had the scent of Old Spice shaving cream. I loved the way he smelled.

No matter that he barely had a seventh-grade education; that wasn't his fault. The kids in his family all quit school at an early age, some as young as nine years old, just to support the family. No matter. I thought he had real depth and intelligence, not the kind you learn in schoolbooks. The kind of man who knew specific names of things, like the different kinds of birds, fish, and flowers. I noticed that. And he had a quiet, gentle way of talking, even a little bit shy—just like me.

All he had to do was graze my hand with his fingertips, ever so lightly, and I knew. I just knew. There would never be any other man for me.

It was a wonderful year to be in love. The war was over. Just like that picture in *Life* magazine, where the sailor plants a big fat kiss on a nurse in Times Square—that's how everyone felt that year. It was time to live again, really live. No more rations, no more scraping by, nothing but happy days ahead. It was 1945, the year the whole world was starting over.

I was carrying our first child on our wedding day. I wasn't ashamed. I knew all along we'd be spending the rest of our lives together. And now we were going to start a beautiful gladiolus farm, and watch our fortunes rise and grow like a field full of flowers.

Jerry had found a square acre of land on the outskirts of Milford in an area called Prairie Park Platt. It was on a dirt road that didn't even have a street sign yet. Jerry had heard there was an old Italian couple living there, Rosa and Pietro Tessicini, who had a pig farm, and they were barely scraping by. They weren't keeping up with their taxes and were going to lose their farm to a tax lien. We could get the land for just three hundred bucks, the price of the back taxes. It was a bargain. The land was already cleared, the soil was rich with pig manure, and we didn't need town water—there was already a natural spring-fed well on the land. It even had a little shed that the couple had lived in; we would use it to store our garden equipment.

It was perfect. We snapped up the land, and Jerry started working there on evenings and weekends while still earning wages at Draper. I quit my job—no self-respecting man would let his wife work! So I stayed home in the apartment and kept house, prepared for our baby's arrival, and sewed baby clothes, all the while keeping track of our business expenses. I subscribed to *Florist Exchange* and *Farmer's Monthly* magazines, studied all the ads about flower bulbs and farm equipment, and kept a tally of all the things we'd need to get started. We could get a glass greenhouse for $100. That was a lot of money, but an essential investment. The greenhouse would give us a head start cultivating the gladiolus corms in the early spring, and extend the short growing season.

I found an ad for Champlain View Gardens in Burlington, Vermont, that could ship every kind of gladiolus imaginable. I sent away for their catalog, and nearly devoured every page. I loved the names of the gladiolus varieties. There was American Commander— a name inspired by the war—that was just as red as the stripes in the American flag. There was Algonquin, Red Charm, Lady Jane, Early Rose, Ohio Nonpareil, Salutation, Gold Rush, Marimba, Sensation, Purple Supreme, Candy Heart, High Finance, Mermaid, Blessed Damosel, Rima, White Gold, Blue Beauty. I circled all these names— our future inventory. I would order all of them.

I knew we'd also need fertilizers and soil conditioners, lots of live earthworms, garden tools, and a sturdy Gravely rototiller. These were all among our projected expenses. We had already paid someone $35 to till the soil thoroughly, and now we had to maintain it.

Jerry had grown up gardening, too. His family's house on Hayward Street had a quarter-acre garden with rows of tall tomato plants, each tied to stakes with scraps of rags. Everyone in that family worked to keep up the gardens. There were fruit trees and grape arbors, too, and Jerry had learned from his father Stefano how to make wine from grapes and cherries. He told me their cellar always had dozens of bottles of homemade wine and a root cellar full of butternut squash, potatoes, carrots, and beets that lasted all winter long.

As soon as we got the deed to our future farm, Jerry started pouring a shallow cement foundation for the house. He decided we would save money by building the house himself. He had built a barn once, so he thought he could figure it out. He picked the farthest spot from the main road, where a rocky ledge just below the ground rendered it unfit for planting. That left the deep, rich, fertile land that was close to the road for the gladiolus fields.

When I first saw that foundation, it made me so happy. It was the outline of our future home! It was only about sixteen by twenty, but it looked enormous to me. We would start out simply, and just add to it as our family grew.

℘ℭℛ

Our family started growing more quickly than I would have imagined. Marcia, our first-born, arrived March 28, 1946, with strawberry-blond curls like her grandfather Stefano. We named her after the month she was born, March, but Jerry had violated the old Italian tradition of naming the firstborn children after the father's parents. We made up for that when Celia came along less than a year later, on March 1, 1947, with black eyes and dark hair, looking nothing like her sister. Jerry's mother, Celesta, often went by the name Celia.

Starting out, Jerry and I didn't get a lot of help from our families. Both sides didn't think much of us for marrying outside our own kind. To mix Anglo-Saxon and Italian, Protestant and Catholic, Republican and socialist—you would think we were marrying another species. Each family thought the other was foreign and strange and far beneath them.

The only thing I knew about Italians before I met Jerry was that they seemed to like to listen to opera. I had once heard a recording of Enrico Caruso singing "O Sole Mio." He was a pretty famous Italian, I think. I also remembered that notorious Sacco and Vanzetti trial that made all the newspapers when I was a little girl. Nicola Sacco came from Milford—he even worked at Draper Corporation, as we did—and the judge of the trial, Webster Thayer, came from nearby Mendon, my hometown. My mother's family knew the judge. After he sentenced those two men to the electric chair, I heard that judge was so pleased with himself, he bragged all over town about how he'd "fried those filthy little wops." You wouldn't dare use an ugly word like "wop" or "guinea" in front of Jerry, but my mother said words like that all the time.

And Jerry's family wasn't any better. If you weren't Italian, you quickly got a nickname like "Frenchie" or "Dutchie." If you were Irish, God help you—they hated the Irish most of all. And if you were colored, well, I'll just say if my Italian mother-in-law ever knew there was a colored person within fifty miles, she would lock the doors, draw the shades, and tremble in fear. They didn't know what to make of me, but I certainly wasn't Italian. That was all they needed to know.

When Marcia was born, and then Celia, they were my mother-in-law's first grandchildren, and it softened how she felt about me. We got a few hand-me-downs from Jerry's family, like a very old stroller Jerry had used when he was a baby. It had to have been from the 1800s, a strange wooden contraption with a woven cane seat that served as high chair, rocker and stroller, all in one. We happily accepted these occasional donations; with four mouths to feed, it was all we could do to get by. It was embarrassing to ask either family for anything, and we preferred not to. But then there came a time when we had no choice.

One day Jerry and I were served an eviction notice. We had been withholding our rent payments, and for good reason, I thought. We had filed too many complaints and grievances against our landlord. Now it was really time to go. The apartment was just too small for us with our two daughters. But the house Jerry was building for us was nowhere near being finished, so we needed a place to go in the meantime.

Jerry went to his mother, whom we now called Nonnie, and asked if we could live in the little cottage behind the Marenghi family house on Hayward Street. It was built for guests, a miniature version of the main house, chocolate brown with white trim. The cottage didn't have a lot of space, and there was no bathroom—we'd have to use the fancy little outhouse they still kept out back, to use when they were out gardening, or the small indoor bathroom in the main house. It wasn't much, but it would just be temporary, and it would save us from paying rent.

Nonnie readily agreed to let us move in. Her husband Stefano had passed away some years before, and she lived with three of her unmarried daughters. I think these women liked the idea of having little toddlers around the house again, and they liked to help wash and dress them as if they were baby dolls.

While they watched the babies, it gave me a chance to get over to the farm, which now was on an official street—Prairie Street. I worked right alongside Jerry in the fields, tilling, weeding, and lugging pails of water from the well. Jerry was still working at Draper, so I tried to get to the farm during the week when I could, sometimes bringing the girls with me in that fancy old stroller. They loved running through the tall rows of gladiolus. I couldn't get much done when they were around.

By 1950, the farm was well established. We were getting orders from local florists, who picked up our glads by the truckload, and we sold them right from the farm to anyone who stopped by. We had one regular customer named Harold Moran. I wasn't sure if he was injured in the war or had a clubfoot, but it made me sad to see a young man walking with a cane. He bought a bouquet from us every Saturday afternoon. I thought it would be rude to ask whom they were for. But he was not the only young man who came by. After all, as I would tell my customers, the gladiolus is the flower of love. It comes from a word meaning "sword"—a flower to pierce the heart.

Gradually we moved our things into the house Jerry built. He had finished the wiring, covered the bare walls with plasterboard, and he dug the hole for the outhouse. We picked out a pretty linoleum floor covering, a golden beige covered with big flowers—it looked like cross-stitch needlepoint. He saved a piece of linoleum to cover the seat in the outhouse, so it felt smooth as porcelain when you sat on it. Jerry even laid the pipes to connect the well to the house, so we'd have fresh spring water to drink.

I was amazed at how talented he was, to do all these things by himself. It took him a few years, but it was wonderful to watch the house grow, plank by plank. The first night Jerry and I slept there in our big iron bed, it felt so good having a place of our own. No more landlords, no more living in the shadow of the great Marenghi house. This was a place to call our own.

I didn't care that it wasn't fancy. Our little business was booming, and it could only get better. Maybe we could even buy some more land nearby and expand the farm someday. For now, Jerry was planting with an almost religious fervor, and not just gladiolus, either. So many fruit trees—pears, peaches, plums, cherries, and apples. He grafted five different kinds of apples onto one tree alone; that's the kind of green thumb he has. He planted quince bushes and a little vegetable patch. We even had a beehive that gave us delicious honey. We were just like Adam and Eve in the garden of Eden.

Oh, it was hard work, too, but I was used to that. I had been on a farm most of my life. I didn't mind working hard when I was working for myself.

I took a picture of Jerry once, working in the gladiolus field in mid-summer, when the young plants were barely up to his knees. He hated having his picture taken—I don't know why. Such a good-looking man. So I sneaked a shot when his head was bent down and a large straw hat obscured his view of me with my camera. It was the fourth of July weekend, but Jerry never took a day off, never stopped to rest, shovel in hand and wheelbarrow beside him, his shirt drenched with sweat.

Would anyone ever see the man as I saw him, looking through that viewfinder on my camera? Could any picture capture the enormous love I felt for this man?

හෝෂ

In 1951 I was pregnant again, and I was hoping for a boy. Every man wants a son to carry on the family name, especially an

Italian man, and I was sure this one would be a boy. He felt different, hanging low on my body, and I was gaining weight faster than I did with the girls. Sure enough, on January 2, 1952, I gave birth to a big strapping boy, weighing over ten pounds. We named him Jerry, after his father. But I called him "Tiny."

I knew 1952 would be a special year, and not just because of the birth of our son. It would mark my husband's twenty-fifth anniversary working for Draper.

One afternoon in late spring, Jerry came home from work a little early. He had a letter in his hand, and he thrust it into mine.

"Here, read this."

Holding baby Jerry in one arm, I walked over to the window to get better reading light. The letter, printed on fine Draper stationery, commended Jerry for twenty-five years of service and thanked him. He would be honored in the fall at a banquet, along with other "25-year men," and a few "50-year men." Before I could finish reading, Jerry snatched the letter back.

"It's a friggin' thank-you note. After twenty-five years, that's all I get. A thank-you note."

"Jerry, why are you home so early?"

"Because I felt like it. And I'm not going back. I'm sick of working like a dog."

I was stunned. The timing was all wrong. I had just received a note from our biggest buyer that the demand for gladiolus was waning. The florists were going to pay less money for glads this year. Maybe next year the prices would swing back upward, but that was a big maybe. In the meantime, we needed Jerry's paycheck. The farm income wasn't going to be enough to support us, a family of five. I was hoping he would get a raise this year for working so many years, not give up his job altogether.

I felt myself panicking. My heart was racing. I had to choose my words so very carefully. A man doesn't like a woman to sound smarter than he is. If I reminded him he had five mouths to feed now, he just might've slapped me. I knew what that felt like.

"But Jerry," I said as gently as I could, "couldn't you hold out just a little longer? At least until the banquet this fall? Maybe there'll be a little something they give you then, like some money, maybe a bonus."

"No! I'm sick of it. The same thing, day in, day out. Twenty-five years, and what have I got to show for it? Nothing. I'm never going back to that friggin' place again!"

I bit my lip and set about fixing an early supper. I didn't say another word. I knew better than to speak when he was in one of his moods. The more I thought about it, though, I couldn't help thinking maybe Jerry was right. Between the factory and the farm, he had been working two jobs for seven years, with never a moment's rest. He was tired and needed a change. So maybe we'd have a rough year. Farming always has its up years and down years. If we could get through this one year, living off the farm alone, I knew we could make it work for the rest of our lives.

My fears were calmed the next morning when Jerry went back to work. But now it was just a matter of time. This would be Jerry's last year at Draper—I knew that much. And this was the year that would make or break our little gladiolus farm. But I was optimistic, not just as a farmer. I was a mother, with all the strength of a mother protecting her young. I would never let my babies go hungry.

31

FRIENDSHIP

Because of my experience losing my little brother, I was protective to the extreme when it came to my son. At the first sniffle, I was quick to call the pediatrician. If Steven was hospitalized, which happened with some frequency because of his asthma, I would not leave his hospital room, wearing the same clothes for days, sleeping in an armchair by his bed.

I was always watchful and wary. Whether he was scaling the rocks at the beach in Rockport, or bouncing playfully along with the choppy waves on the deck of the Nantucket ferry, he always heard my predictable refrain: "Careful—don't get hurt!"

How many times did Steven hear me say that? But instead of rebelling against my mother-hen behavior, he was always surprisingly tender and understanding toward me. Once Steven turned to me with the gentlest expression and said, "Mom. It's okay. You don't have to worry."

Steven had more than one guardian and protector. When he was a baby, shortly after my husband and I split, Steven had another woman in his life: Deborah. She was among the close circle of friends that Tom and I had been part of for the previous decade. It was always the same small group that attended each other's parties, rented summer cottages on Cape Cod together, witnessed each other's weddings and baby showers, and stood with each other at funerals. Now our little group was seeing its first divorces, and not just Tom's and mine. Our gatherings had to readjust and reconfigure accordingly.

I had only known Deborah somewhat indirectly, as the friend and longtime roommate of Cindy, who ultimately married our friend Rich. A native of Georgia, Deborah still had a Southern drawl and never stopped saying "y'all," decades after leaving the South. I liked her, but had never spent a lot of time with her. I knew she was a legendary cook, had a knack for growing flowers, dressed stylishly, and had an infectiously gregarious charm.

One Sunday evening in the middle of May 1993, after Tom had dropped Steven off with me, Steven started chattering about his weekend activities.

"I went to Rich's birthday party!" he announced.

Now that was odd, I thought. I was always invited to Rich's birthday parties, and this year I wasn't. He and Cindy were my dearest friends. Why would they not have invited me?

"Dad was there with Deborah," Steven went on. And with a very sly, knowing expression, he added, "Deborah is Dad's *friend*."

"Oh-h-h-hh...I said. "Now I get it."

I suddenly burst out laughing.

"What's so funny, Mom?"

"Oh, nothing, nothing at all."

I was thinking how hard they must have tried to keep that birthday party a secret from me. And Steven, of all people, spilled the beans! They had underestimated this toddler's powers of observation.

It must have been awkward for everyone when Tom and Deborah became a pair. You couldn't invite Tom and Deborah—and me—to the same party, could you? I hadn't really thought about it until then. The next time I spoke with Cindy by phone, I told her I knew about Tom and Deborah.

"But how did you know?" she asked me, sounding somewhat shocked.

"Steven told me."

"Steven told you?" she said nervously.

"Yes. He told me all about seeing them together at Rich's birthday party."

"Oh, Catherine, I am so sorry, we really wanted to invite you but then Deborah is our friend and Tom is our friend and you're our friend, and if we invited you we couldn't invite Tom and if we invited Deborah we had to invite Tom, and if we invited Tom we had to invite Deborah and if you saw Tom with Deborah, it would hurt your feelings and...and..."

Her rapid-fire response was full of anxiety, as well as genuine concern over hurting my feelings.

"Really," I interrupted, "it's all right. I understand. You were in a difficult position. And I want you to know, I don't care that Tom is with Deborah. I don't care."

"Seriously?"

"I don't care. I feel nothing for the man. Honestly. I'm just worried about Deborah. Does she know what she's getting into?"

If Deborah was Tom's woman on the rebound, it was a long rebound. They would be together for the better part of a decade, and Deborah would be a regular part of my son's life. Tom quickly moved into Deborah's apartment in a classic triple-decker in Cambridge, the one she had shared with Cindy since they were roommates fresh out of college. Deborah had lovingly painted and restored the apartment after Cindy left to get married to Rich, and she filled it with a jungle of plants and carefully chosen antique furnishings. She had a second bedroom in her apartment, and she decorated it just for little Steven.

On the alternating weekends Deborah and Tom spent with Steven, she took him for frequent outings in Cambridge, like hot chocolate at Burdick's, a fancy chocolate shop in Harvard Square. The three of them spent afternoons promenading down Memorial Drive, along the Charles River, on those summer Sundays when they closed the road to traffic, and there Steven learned to ride his little two-wheeler bicycle with Tom and Deborah walking on either side.

When Steven's much-loved teddy bear got a tiny rip in its chest, it was Deborah who stitched a heart-shaped patch over it. And when Tom bought a cottage in the New Hampshire mountains for weekend getaways, it was Deborah who planted hundreds of flower bulbs around it and filled the cabin with her cooking aromas, from spicy jambalaya to sweet pecan pies. Deborah hung sheer curtains covered with embroidered stars in Steven's loft bedroom, just so he would always see stars from his bed, and on Sunday mornings, she sent him outdoors with a wicker basket to pick wild blueberries, which went straight into her special "very-berry" muffins. Steven had yet another home and another circle of friends, further extending his already extended family.

In many respects, Deborah was a second mother to Steven. I didn't mind. The worst thing would have been for Tom to find a woman who had no interest in the offspring of a prior relationship. I have overheard so many conversations among women, in airports, in public places, complaining about the "little monsters" from a previous marriage and how they couldn't wait to ship them off to overnight camp or boarding school. With Deborah, I had the comfort of knowing Steven was in good hands when he was away from my home. I was always grateful for that.

On the Friday evenings when I dropped Steven off at Tom and Deborah's apartment, Tom wasn't always home, and sometimes I would spend a few moments chatting with Deborah about Steven, as if we were two mothers trading notes about our shared child. She told me a story once about bickering with Tom about something, when little Steven piped in, taking her side: "Dad! She has a point, you know!" She and I both laughed.

Over time, our friends got past their resistance to having Tom, Deborah and me at the same events. When Cindy threw a big fiftieth birthday party for Rich, they invited everyone from the old circle of friends, including the three of us. There was a particular moment when I found myself chatting with Tom, Deborah, and a gentleman I hadn't met before. When he politely asked me, "Do you all know each other?" I smiled and pointed to Tom and said, "Yes, this is the father of my child."

"Tom and Deborah" had become a phrase that rolled off the tongue, as easily as "Tom and Catherine" had a decade before. So when, in 2002, Tom called me out of the blue to tell me he had broken up with Deborah, I was more than a little surprised. Things had always been a bit rocky between him and Deb, but I thought that was just the inevitable result of two strong personalities living together. Having two homes, one in Cambridge and one in New Hampshire, was not enough to soften that tension. Instead it became a dividing line, with Tom spending most of his time in New Hampshire, especially during frequent bouts of unemployment, while Deborah lived and worked in Cambridge during the week.

"I just told Deborah we're through," Tom announced to me on the phone. "I drove down from New Hampshire to tell her in person. I gave her her walking papers."

I was shocked. It seemed very sudden and expressed very coldly. "Walking papers? But what about Steven?" I said. "Does he know?"

"No, not yet. I thought you might want to know. And you might want to talk to him before he comes up next weekend."

"Tom, Steven has known Deb a long time. This is going to be a shock to him."

"I don't think it'll be a big deal. He'll get over it." I bit my lip and took a deep breath.

"I don't know, Tom. I want you to give Steven a little time to process this. Please don't expose him to any new girlfriend for a while. Could you do that for me?"

"Don't worry about it. Steven will be fine. See you Friday." And that was that.

I immediately talked to Steven. He was stunned by the news, as I had anticipated. What would his every-other-weekend be like now? Would anyone but Deborah sew a heart-shaped patch on his teddy bear?

There was no time for Steven to adjust. On the following weekend, Tom introduced Steven to his new girlfriend, ignoring all my admonitions.

I couldn't control what happened in New Hampshire every other weekend. But there was something I could do.

I called Deborah.

"Deborah, look. I know what happened. Tom told me. And Steven was very upset by the news. You've been a very important part of his life for a long time, and I know that. And I just want you to know—if you want Steven to continue being part of your life, he and I would both like that. You are welcome in our house any time."

And that was the beginning of a beautiful friendship.

Deb, Steven, and I would often be seen together, the three of us having dinner at a restaurant, traveling to the beach, or even attending events at Steven's school—if we knew Tom wasn't going to be there. After a couple years, Deb and I got together without Steven, forming a more direct friendship of our own. For a while there was the inevitable purging of shared demons. Grousing about an ex-husband was a remarkably satisfying thing to do with someone who knew exactly what I was talking about. But we got past that stage pretty quickly and found ourselves moving to more positive topics.

We both loved cooking, traveling, gardening. We were both strong, capable, self-reliant, able to wield a hammer and nail as easily as a wire whisk and a sauté pan. We both had experienced the loss of a father early in our lives—mine in death, hers in divorce—and we both had mothers who struggled to raise us as single parents. And we found in each other a sense of joy, a love of living, that neither of us had found in our lives with Tom.

She would become my favorite traveling companion, always up for any new adventure. I delighted in introducing her to people as the ex-girlfriend of my ex-husband, just to see their scandalized reaction. But the description did not do her justice. She was quite simply my friend. The one who would call spontaneously to say, in her quintessential Georgian phrasing, "Hey, y'all, how would you like to get into some devilment?"

Just as new growth springs from a burnt forest, so did many such friendships spring for me from the ashes of divorce.

32

MYSTERY TOUR

"Mom, my teacher today didn't know how to pronounce the word *Chihuahua*. She was reading aloud to the class and said 'chi-*hoowa-hoowa*'! "

I burst out laughing. "Steven, what did you do?"

"Well, I didn't want to embarrass her, so I showed her the word in the dictionary after class."

"And what did she say?"

"She still didn't believe me! She still thinks it's supposed to be chi-*hoowa-hoowa*!"

We both laughed. No one could make me laugh like Steven. He was now nine years old, and I was no longer surprised to hear he might be more proficient at language than some of his teachers. Two years earlier, when he was in second grade, his teacher insisted he had a learning disability because his mind wandered off in class. I had a different theory: I thought he was bored. He was a gifted child whose rich imagination was far more interesting than what was going on in class.

But no one was going to believe a mother's highly biased opinion. So I had Steven formally tested. He had no learning disabilities. What we found instead was that, at the age of seven, Steven was reading at a high-school level.

Blond and brown-eyed, he reminded me sometimes of my little brother. Silly and whimsical one minute, serious and scholarly the next, an old soul in a young body. Someone with such an agile mind, he could mix a character from a Wagner opera with TV superheroes like the Mighty Morphin' Power Rangers, all in the same sentence. And woe to you if you spoke down to him as if he were a child.

I once made the mistake of assuming a boy in kindergarten would not know one musical genre from another. He was going through an "opera phase," when he liked to belt out songs in a goofy operatic tone—a little Pavarotti in the making. And so I called him over to listen to the radio. Patti Lupone was singing the theme song from "Evita" in what sounded like an operatic style.

I said, "Listen, Steven. Opera! Your favorite!"

Steven looked up at me with a deadpan expression. "Mum, it's not opera. It's called a *show tune*."

I didn't know how a five-year-old would know that, but I tried to never repeat the mistake of talking down to him again.

Best of all, Steven was a marvelous traveling companion, and we saw quite a few places together. My PR business was doing extremely well, now employing twenty-four people full-time, and it gave me the means to spend money on travel. I didn't buy expensive cars or clothes or jewelry, but the shared experience of traveling with my son, I thought, was a very good investment.

I liked to pick him up from school on a Friday afternoon, and instead of going home, I would say, "We're going on a magical mystery tour!" He would try in vain to guess where we were going. Not until we were on an airplane would I tell him we were headed to England, or Disneyworld, or Mexico. I loved the fact that he was always up for any adventure. And he never wanted to stay at the hotel; even if we were at a posh resort, he wanted to venture out and see how the local people lived. He wanted to see what the native food was like, what coins and currency they used, and what toys the children played with.

One Saturday morning in the fall of 2000, we drove out on a magical mystery tour to Milford. Not every destination could be London, after all. That was part of the mystery. Nearly eight years had passed since I first learned of my grandmother's will, and Steven and I were going out to see my grandmother's house. I had learned from Jerry that the house on Hayward Street had been abandoned. Lizzie had moved to Vermont, where she and her two sisters were now living together in an assisted living facility. Lizzie was ninety-four years old, Chezz was eighty-nine, and Tillie was seventy-eight. The sisters had held onto the house for a long time, and finally they were all just walking away.

The year was 2000, and the house on Hayward Street was finally ours.

The night before driving there, I had pulled out my grandmother's will to read it once again. This was a woman who died just before my third birthday. But reading my grandmother's wishes again, it was if she were speaking to me from the grave, more than forty years after her death.

"It is my wish and desire that if at all possible, the said real estate shall remain in the name and hands of a Marenghi for as long as possible."

Now, it appeared, the house had come into the hands of two Marenghis—my brother and me. We were the last of my father's children, and I wanted my son—the namesake of my brother and grandfather—to see what was left to us.

With some trepidation, I picked up the keys from my brother and drove over to Hayward Street with Steven. Pulling into the narrow driveway, framed by my grandfather's great stone gateposts, I was shocked by the appearance of the house. It looked shabby and badly in need of painting. A sapling peach tree had taken root under the front porch and was growing out through the floorboards, blocking the front steps.

We started with the cottage in the back. I thought my parents once stayed there after they were married, but I didn't know the circumstances. Every time I asked my mother about it, her memory was hazy, or she deflected the question. I couldn't imagine anyone living there. Although it was a pretty and well-constructed little building, it seemed more of a one-room storage shed, with a potbelly stove and a soapstone utility sink. It had a fine stone basement, too, where we found a very old and weathered wooden wine press. My grandfather must have used it to make wine. I would have liked to keep it, but it was huge—I'd have nowhere to put it.

Another find in the cottage basement was a rectangular brick of solid white marble, about a foot long and four inches wide and deep. It had the name "Catherine" engraved on it. I guessed it might have been the original marker on my Aunt Catherine's grave. She was buried in Sacred Heart Cemetery in the Marenghi family plot, next to my grandparents and my father, and this looked like the kind of marker one would put at the foot of a grave. It was chipped a little on the corners and apparently had been replaced. Certainly a stone with my own name on it was not something I could leave behind, so I placed it carefully in my car.

Besides the cottage and garage and a rather elegant outhouse, there was also a huge barn. I wasn't quite sure what it was for, but that was our next stop. The barn had a large garage-style door and a cement floor, something you could drive vehicles into, maybe horse-drawn carriages at one time, but now it was absolutely empty. Its design had a familiar look. Just like the house I grew up in, the barn had stairs against the back wall that terminated abruptly against the lower side wall. I had to step up sideways to mount the first step. Was this where my father got the idea for the design of our house? Or maybe he wasn't envisioning a house at all? Maybe he thought he was building a barn or a guest cottage, with the future house to be built in front of it, just like his parents' house? Whatever it was, this barn was clearly used for more than storing animals or hay.

Steven followed me up the steps to the barn's upper loft. There we found old pictures of movie stars like Cary Grant and Jimmy Stewart, tacked to the walls, crumbling pages from fan magazines, now yellowed and water-stained. Maybe the Marenghi children used this place as a clubhouse of sorts, a place to listen to the radio, or just to get away from their parents?

Now on to the main house, which we saved for last. I had never seen the whole house. Mostly visitors were received in the kitchen, and I only got a glimpse of the small parlors off the main hallway. But I had never seen the house in its entirety. I remembered another section from my grandmother's will:

"To my son, Jeremiah Marenghi, I give and bequeath all of my household furniture; but in trust, nevertheless, for the benefit of his children who may be living at the time of my decease."

I had no idea if any of her household furniture would be left behind. I remembered the massive oak kitchen table, the throne-like chairs with red velvet seats in the hallway, an ornately carved upright piano, and a mahogany dining room set, with at least a dozen chairs, all with woven cane seats. As we pushed open the kitchen door, I soon had my answer: nothing remained. Absolutely nothing. The place was stripped bare.

I began to remember other things, great mirrored armoires, and a vintage Victrola with boxes of records, each the size of a dinner plate and a quart-inch thick, with songs like "Yes, We Have No Bananas," and "I Don't Want Her, You Can Have Her, She's Too Fat for Me." And the elaborate birdcages, quaint cupboards with little decals, linens with handmade lace, fainting sofas, room upon room of precious heirlooms. All of it ours. All of it gone.

The rooms all seemed so small. Not one of them was as ample as my memory of it.

There were several bedrooms on the second floor. Some seemed barely big enough to hold a bed, and the closets were all tiny. There was no bathroom on the second floor at all. The only toilet was in a small powder room on the first floor, under the staircase, and a more primitive one was in the basement. The only shower was in the basement, too. Not an attractive layout at all.

I peeked into every bedroom on the second floor, trying to imagine who slept where. The slightly larger room in the back was most likely my grandparents'. I wondered: did my father share a room with his brother Albert, back when they were called Bartolomeo and Gerolamo? They were the only boys in the family and they were close in age, with just a few years separating them. Surely they must have shared a room. Two boys, growing up in close quarters, in beds that would have been inches apart, listening to each others' dreams, talking about girls as they lay in the dark, and looking to all the world like twins. What could have ripped them apart, so that they never spoke to each other for most of their adult lives?

And the girls—Elisabetta, Cesarina, Cotilda, Irene, Caterina, and Rosa—were surely bunked together in some way, especially since the house often accommodated relatives visiting from Italy. I had seen this documented in the US Census records from 1910, 1920, and 1930, each one showing two or three additional boarders with the last name of Marenghi. The house would have been full of noise—chattering sisters, clanging pots and pans in the kitchen, the Victrola blaring Italian opera. You couldn't turn around without brushing your elbow against someone.

It would have made Celesta sad to see her house so quiet, stripped to the bare walls. She so wanted another generation of Marenghis to fill these rooms with familial noise. But each of her children married and went their separate ways. Albert didn't talk to Jerry. Chezz and Tillie split off to become the Vermont faction. Irene and Rose married, and after getting next to nothing from their mother's will, I can only assume there was nothing to hold them there and moved away. Lizzie lived in this house with her husband, after marrying late in life, and lived her final thirty-five years alone, as a widow. And my eponymous aunt Catherine—who knows what became of her. No one ever talked about Catherine. I only knew that she died young, a couple years before I was born.

I moved on to the attic on the third floor, an enormous space, but it had a brick chimney right in the middle of it that looked as if it would fall over if you leaned on it. In my mind, I was tallying up how much it would cost just to do essential repairs, and bring the systems up to code, let alone update the floor plan into a more modern style. My instincts told me the house would have to be sold. I did not have the time or money to completely restore the place, and even if we could get a loan, it might not be worth it. I feared it was too ambitious an undertaking for me or my brother to take on. The words *white elephant* came to mind.

I would have to come back another day with a building inspector to take a closer look at the plumbing, heating, and electrical systems, and all the structural elements, and get a full assessment. We would then have a better idea of what we would do with the house. It had been in the "hands of a Marenghi," as my grandmother put it, for one hundred years. But I had no desire to live there. I was happily settled miles away in a house with my son, and my mother and brother were happy where they were in their pristine modern house on Prairie Street. We could keep the place and rent it, but it would require massive renovations.

We would wait for the final appraisal and then decide.

33

FINAL WALK-THROUGH

The following Saturday, while Steven was with his father, I came back to Milford alone to do the final walk-through with the home inspector. As it turned out, the inspector was a school classmate of mine who had lived in the town all his life and remembered the house well.

"This used to be the nicest house around," he recalled. "What a shame, the way they let it go." He remembered my Aunt Lizzie and how hard she had worked in her gardens, always wearing a brightly flowered apron. He also remembered the old Bing cherry tree, now long gone, with its sweet, reddish-black fruit; its branches extended over the stone wall, so you could sneak a few cherries if you were walking by.

The inspector snapped pictures and took notes on a clipboard as we walked through the house. From what he could tell, the house had not been updated in at least fifty years, maybe more. The light switches on the walls were of the old push-button style, possibly a hundred years old. Odd that I never noticed them before. The single phone hookup was a pronged outlet for a rotary phone—not a single modern phone jack in the house. Nothing was up to code. No smoke detectors of any kind, and the furnace in the basement was caked with a thick asbestos shell, which would have to be professionally removed. It would cost a fortune.

We spent a lot of time in the basement, looking at the plumbing, furnace, and electrical systems. He shook his head.

"You're looking at six figures, easy, to fix up this place. The asbestos removal alone will be a killer."

While he was taking notes by the furnace, I was poking around what was probably the most intriguing part of the house. The enormous cellar had a slatted wooden gate at one end, where I found an old root cellar with wooden bushel baskets, stacked up neatly, even the dried remains of a gourd or two. And at the other end, I was delighted to find an old wine cellar, with a heavy wooden door that once was padlocked. Training my flashlight on every corner, I found several enormous wooden bins, about six or eight feet wide and four feet tall, each filled with hundreds of dusty old wine bottles, arranged on their sides, piled one on atop the other. If there was ever any doubt my grandfather made his own wine, here was the proof. But now the bottles were dried out and rattled with dry, blackened dregs. Other than these relics of wine making, not a thing was left behind in that old house.

I had a thought to keep a few of the wine bottles, just as a small souvenir. So I started rummaging through the bottle bins, pulling out bottles in shades of dark green and brown, trying to find the ones with the prettiest shapes. I had poked through three or four of the bins when something caught my eye.

It was a thin, dusty scrapbook, wedged behind one of the wooden bins, only visible after I pulled some bottles away. I pulled it out and brought it upstairs to take a closer look at in the daylight. I dug some tissues from my purse to brush off years of spider webs and dust. I laid it down on a deep windowsill to see it in the best light.

It was a cheaply made scrapbook, covered with a thin, cream-colored leather, frayed at the corners, and bound together simply with string. A lithograph of large flowers against a dark background, showing yellow and white chrysanthemums and a single red zinnia, was pasted to the front cover. The pages were yellowed and dry. I carefully opened the cover.

It was a scrapbook of a family horror. The pages told the long-buried story of my Aunt Catherine—and what became of her.

I had always known I was named after my father's younger sister, but I knew nothing about her. I had only seen one picture of her, a snapshot of a slim young brunette with wavy hair, posing in a prim white blouse and a long tweed skirt. She was standing with her brother Albert in front of his brand new 1952 deluxe Ford sedan. It was a black-and-white photo, but the car appeared to be a soft pastel color, perhaps a gray or a creamy light blue. Catherine and Albert had broad smiles; they both seemed quite pleased by his handsome new car.

That was the only image I had ever seen of Aunt Catherine. No one had ever told me what happened to her. No one had wanted to talk about it. I was about to find out why.

The first page of the scrapbook held a yellowed newspaper clipping from the *Milford Daily News*, dated June 2, 1952. The headline was enormous, seventy-two-point type, clearly a big, front-page story. It read, "Crash at Intersection Kills Milford Woman."

The story reported a horrific collision at the intersection of Routes 140 and 16 in Milford. The driver of one of the cars was Albert Marenghi, my uncle. His young wife, Lucy, was seated in the middle of the front seat, back at a time when cars had a single continuous bench seat in the front, and no one ever used seatbelts. And his sister Catherine, my aunt, was in the front seat, passenger side.

The "Marenghi trio," as the article described them, was headed eastbound on Route 16 after going to a drive-in movie theater; it was about 11:30 on a rainy Saturday night. They were crossing the intersection when a drunk driver, heading north on Route 140, came barreling toward them—never seeing the stop sign—and smashed into the passenger side where Catherine was seated. The impact sent both cars spinning, and Catherine was thrown from the car. Ironically, the accident occurred just a few yards away from the Milford Hospital, where the unconscious Catherine was taken immediately. Albert, Lucy, and the drunken driver suffered only minor scrapes and bruises, but Catherine suffered massive internal injuries, a lacerated lung, a fractured skull, a torn leg, and broken ribs.

She never regained consciousness. Two hours later, at 1:30 Sunday morning, Catherine was gone. She was twenty-six years old.

The article had three large photos, one of them showing a white 1951 Chevrolet, driven by the man who ran the stop sign. The Chevrolet had crumpled front fenders, and its hood was bent upward like a tent. A second photo showed Albert's 1952 Ford, which, the article noted, had only three thousand miles on it. The Ford's passenger side showed the impact of the crash, and the passenger door was nearly torn off. Eerily, it was the same car I'd seen in the only picture I ever had of Catherine, standing in front of that same passenger door, with Albert smiling over her shoulder.

The third large photo was a portrait of Catherine Marenghi, her smiling face looking fresh and clean-scrubbed, her dark eyes very similar to my sister Celia's. I wondered what she saw with those eyes. Did she ever see it coming? Did she turn those eyes over her right shoulder, at 11:30 p.m., and see the oncoming headlights?

The newspaper story carried an elaborate schematic drawing of the fatal intersection, with an X in the form of an iron cross at the point of impact. According to the article, Albert was driving very slowly through the intersection, about twenty miles an hour, because of the rain and poor visibility. "If I had only been going a bit faster," he reportedly said, with bitter irony, "we might have avoided the crash."

The next page of the album carried additional news clippings about the events that followed, including the drunk driver's hearing at District Court. He was charged with "driving under the influence of liquor, driving to endanger, and speeding." Bail was set at $1,000—a very large sum at the time.

There were also articles about the longstanding controversy over the intersection, which had seen another fatal crash just two months earlier, and repeated calls to install a stoplight. Finally, a small clipping about Catherine's funeral noted that the services took place at the Marenghi home on 7 Hayward Street, followed by a high mass at Sacred Heart of Jesus Church; the clipping named the six pall bearers, and I thought it was very telling that neither of her brothers was among them. Albert and Jerry would have been obvious choices for pallbearers, two strong young men, but for reasons I can only guess, in their shock and grief, they couldn't bring themselves to do it.

The next page contained a page from a company newsletter. Catherine's employer, the Telechron clock factory in Ashland, published a brief note on Catherine's death, misspelling her name, amid a flurry of wedding and birth announcements from other employees. And a neatly hand-written list of 213 funeral attendees was carefully preserved and tucked inside an envelope.

All of this was neatly documented, sealed in a scrapbook, and hidden away in a wine cellar. I only came upon it by chance. Some future owner of this house might have tossed it out with the wine bottles, and no one would have ever seen it again.

It was all starting to make sense. The story my brother told me about my father's nervous breakdown in the early 1950s, before I was born, and his rumored visit to a psychiatric clinic. Surely this was the event that pushed him over the edge, that left him so shattered. And was this the cause of a permanent rift between two brothers, Albert and Jerry, and a permanent taking of sides among their sisters? Did my father blame Albert for not driving just a little bit faster on that rainy night, just as Albert reportedly blamed himself? So much anger and hurt. So much that was never spoken of, never forgiven. All wrapped up in a terrible scrapbook, hidden beneath the raw basement timbers of that long neglected house.

A young and much-beloved daughter and sister was taken without warning while still in her prime, and the family was never completely whole without her. Would the Marenghi family have been so fractured if Catherine had lived? If my father never experienced that crippling loss, would he have had the strength and the will to be a better provider for his family, build a bigger and better house for his wife and kids? Would we have been so poor?

Would my father have moved his young family to the house on Hayward Street, which he had every right to do, if Catherine's lifeless body had never been waked there? Or were there just too many ghosts, too many bitter memories, for him to live under that roof? How would my family's history have been different if that accident had not happened? Would I even have been born, if Albert had crossed that intersection just five seconds sooner?

A million little intersections, a million little chances to change the future, to go left or go right, faster or slower, and no way of knowing which of those choices will matter.

Of all the things that define us, it's not the things we know, the stuff we can measure out and document and parse by the inch or the mile. It's the great unknowing, the things we never see or hear or grasp, that pull the hardest on the driver's wheel, and send us veering, lurching, stalling. And sometimes crashing.

34

MEMORY

"You're so pretty. Do I know you?"

My mother looked at me with a sweet, blank expression from her wheelchair at the Sunbridge nursing facility, her home of five years. It was less than half a mile from the plot of land she tilled for most of her life.

"I'm your daughter, Ma. I'm Catherine."

"Oh, for heaven's sake!" She was genuinely delighted with the startling good news that she had a daughter.

"And this is your grandson, Ma. His name is Steven."

"A grandson? I have a grandson? Well, how do you like that!"

It was Christmas Day. Jerry, Steven, and I had come to bring her a movable feast. I was holding three Tupperware plates with snap-on dome lids, stacked one atop the other, each laden with turkey and gravy, mashed potatoes, jellied cranberry sauce, and all the vegetables I could cram onto the plates. All of it was prepared at the house on Prairie Street nearby. Steven and Jerry each came bearing my home-made pies—mincemeat, her favorite, and an apple pie for the boys.

We gathered round her like a Christmas tree, festooning her with our offerings, hoping these tastes and smells might jog some long-buried memory of Christmases past. Would she remember the turkeys she roasted in a speckled blue pan in a wood-fired oven? The olive and pickle trays, the celery sticks she filled with a mixture of cream cheese and chopped green olives? Or perhaps my little brother's sweet high voice singing, "Over the river and through the woods, to Grandmother's house we go!" Somehow everything was new and unfamiliar to her. Like a Christmas tree, she had been lopped off from the roots of her memory.

My mother passed away peacefully in that same nursing home in March 2009, at the age of eighty-nine. The once robust farm girl had shrunk to ninety-five pounds. At the moment she passed, my brother and I, her two remaining children, were flanking her at her bedside, each of us holding one of her delicate hands as she gasped her last breath.

I spoke at her funeral about how she lived a life of almost unbelievable hardship, but how, in spite of it, she always maintained a childlike sweetness, and a cheerful optimism about the future. I think that's one of the many gifts my mother gave me—an unswerving faith in the future.

My brother and I had covered her casket in pink rosebuds, her favorite flower. I decided I would plant a pink rosebush in her memory, and place it close to my house. It was a home I had recently purchased in Marblehead, an ocean-side town north of Boston, a few months after my mother died, and I was always sorry she never got to see it. The house was built in 1682 and rebuilt in 1765. I thought my mother would have loved it, with its wide-plank pumpkin pine floors and ancient fireplaces. If houses define us, I would love to think this strong, enduring structure, rooted firmly in history, looking directly into the sun, would leave its mark on me.

A few weeks after moving in, on a mid-August day, I was surveying the front of the house looking for a place to plant the memorial roses, and I was shocked to see a rosebush was already planted there, bursting with pink blooms. Where did it come from? I hadn't noticed any roses when I bought the house two months earlier. I was standing looking at it, with a baffled look on my face, when my neighbor Dorothea, an avid gardener, put down her garden shears and stopped by.

"Oh, Catherine, aren't they amazing? They bloomed last May, before you moved in, but this is the first time I ever saw them bloom a second time in one year."

I told her the story of my mother's love for pink roses, and how I was planning to plant them in her memory.

"I don't know how I could have missed seeing the rosebush before," I told Dorothea. "Maybe it was all green, and its flowers gone by, at the time when I bought the house."

Dorothea touched my arm and whispered, "It's your mother. She's looking down on you. That's what made them bloom again. She's giving roses to *you.*"

My mother gave me much more than that. No matter what I've done in life, I've always felt the warmth and reassurance of her pride in me. I hope she would have been proud of this book.

35

THE CEDAR CHEST

It was made in the 1930s, an Art Deco design with sleek rounded corners, and rich mahogany and walnut burl veneers, carefully matched to form a diamond pattern on the top. It was once a hope chest, back when young girls had such things, lovely when it was new, but after seventy years of use, the veneers were badly peeling. Now it was just a very battered old box, packed solid with linens, photos, papers, coins, books—my mother put her whole life into it.

My mother had acquired the cedar chest before she was married in 1945. It had always fascinated me when I was a little girl. In our shabby little house, this extravagant piece of furniture stood out as a single point of shining elegance. It was my mother's special box, the place where she kept all her secrets.

In 2013, I was helping to clean out my mother's house to prepare it for sale. My brother had lived there alone since my mother entered the nursing home, since 2005, some five years before she died, and now the large property was just too much for one person to manage. While my brother went through my mother's clothes and books, I volunteered to tackle the cedar chest. It must have been decades since anyone, including my mother, had dug through it.

I found an amazing trove of artifacts, arranged in layers like geological strata, each capturing an era in my mother's life the way layers of silt preserve centuries of fossils. Most of it I had never seen before, but it all enriched and enlightened this story in profound ways.

For one thing, there were books, mostly frayed and water-damaged, including a surprising collection of poetry. My mother and I shared a love of Emily Dickinson. How I wish I had known that sooner!

I found her college yearbook, too, from Becker College, class of 1940. My mother had always downplayed her education, saying she had some secretarial training, but Becker was then a respected business college, like Babson or Bentley, something I had never appreciated before reading her yearbook. There were so many handwritten notes from her classmates, page after page: "To a swell kid." "You will surely be successful in all you do." "Hardworking, demure, and a grand sense of humor." "May you always be as happy as you were at Becker."

The woman everyone knew as a barefoot farmer in a tattered dress had a college degree, and her life might have been very different had she married one of those handsome young men who signed her college yearbook.

At the very bottom of the chest was a slender white satin negligee with a silk rose at the low neckline—surely the very thing she wore on her wedding night. It had a long lacy robe to match, hand-crocheted, with tiny satin-covered buttons. Both pieces were stained and crumbling from age, and they must have been the first things my mother had placed in her hope chest. I held the delicate garments up to myself in the mirror, imagining how my mother might have looked in them.

As I pulled things out of the cedar chest, I carefully separated them into piles. One was for World War II artifacts. There were war ration books, with pages of unused coupons—so typical of my mother to save things to the last and never use them. Was she saving them for the next world war? And my father's original draft notice—I had always wondered why he never fought in the war. Turning it over, I saw the word REJECTED stamped diagonally in red ink across the back. Apparently he had failed his physical—something about a chronic fatigue issue.

Among the legal and financial papers, I placed the original deed to the land where my family lived before it even had a street name, purchased through a tax foreclosure in 1945. The carbon copy from the money order was still intact. And I found my mother's tally of their marital assets when they bought the land, carefully itemized, written in pencil on a sheet of notepaper. The young couple had a grand total of $400.14 to their names.

I found fragile letters and cards, birth and death certificates, insurance policies, and pay stubs. There were dozens of receipts from the milkman alone, dating from the 1940s, which I carefully separated into a single stack. Envelopes that once contained my father's income tax returns were covered with my mother's notations, recording how every penny was spent. She was the accountant of all things.

Hundreds of photos and negatives, some of them going back to 1900, were all jumbled together alongside cheap Polaroids from decades later. One picture of my father I had never seen before, probably from the 1930s, showed a handsome young man posing in front of a Ford roadster. He was dressed in his hunting clothes, with tall leather boots laced up the front, and a freshly shot stag was draped over the front fender of the car. He was a good-looking man—not at all like the world-weary, gray-haired father I remembered. I could see what my mother saw in him.

My mother had taken several photographs of my family's tiny original house as a work in progress, as my father was building it, in the late 1940s. I could see the mismatched pieces of lumber tacked to the roof, all different widths and lengths, before he sawed the ends to even them off. Just as I suspected, he had terribly shoddy materials to work with. It was a wonder anyone ever lived in that makeshift one-room structure, let alone a family of seven.

She had pictures of the other house, too, on 7 Hayward Street, Milford, where my father and his large Italian family were raised. That grand old house would inhabit my story in a way I could never have foreseen.

And it was there, in that cedar chest, that I first began to learn about the gladiolus farm.

It started with sepia-toned pictures I found of my two older sisters, toddlers at the time, wandering through a field of gladiolus in 1949. The field stretched from Prairie Street over most of an acre, all the way back to the old shed we used as a barn. There was a picture of my father, too, a tall man in a wide straw hat, standing next to a wheelbarrow, shovel in hand, with gladiolus blades up to his knees. His work-shirt was drenched with sweat.

I knew nothing about the gladiolus farm for most of my life, even though I grew up on the land where thousands of these exotic flowers once bloomed. I never understood those occasional anecdotes I had heard growing up, random comments here and there, about how my parents once grew gladiolus. I assumed they were simply part of a flower garden. But what I saw in these pictures was no flower garden. This was a working farm. And its cash crop was gladiolus.

The cedar chest told the story. I found all the detailed invoices for gladiolus bulbs, or corms as they're called, and the names of their extraordinary varieties: Gold Rush, Marimba, Candy Heart, just to name a few. There were bills for loam and live earthworms and soil conditioners, and order forms for trade magazines like *Farmer's Monthly* and *Florists Exchange*. There were receipts for farm equipment and a glass greenhouse, and copies of their invoices to florists. They must have supplied all the florists in the area.

I gained a startling new appreciation of my mother, not just as a farmer, but as a businesswoman. I had started a business once, but so had she—we were both entrepreneurs. I had just never seen her that way. On bits of paper and the backs of envelopes, she recorded her revenues and projected her expenses—just as I would do years later with an electronic spreadsheet. She subscribed to trade magazines, just as I would, decades later, for my own business.

And in 1986, forty years after my parents started their flower farm with high hopes and dreams of a better life, the place where we finally broke ground for a new house was the very spot where row upon row of towering gladiolus once bloomed.

I wish I could have seen the gladiolus farm as it once was, in the late 1940s, blazing with color on stalks nearly six feet high. By the time I was born in 1954, the gladiolus fields were long gone, plowed under, and forgotten, and the land was mainly a source of subsistence crops for my struggling family. My parents spoke little about their history, and the story of the glad farm was something I would only piece together years after both parents were gone.

I've since learned that the gladiolus was a wildly popular flower in the 1930s and 1940s. Flamboyant gladiolus bouquets, often arranged in fan-shaped vases, were the height of elegance. You can see them in old black-and-white movies, if you look closely, in the stylish apartments that formed the backdrop behind Norma Shearer or William Powell. In the 1950s, though, for whatever reason, the gladiolus fell from favor. The gladiolus market plummeted, and the flowers were used primarily as inexpensive fillers in funeral and wedding arrangements after that.

It would have been a difficult period for my parents and their glad farm. The florists started paying less each year for their flowers, and with everything else conspiring against my parents, their glad farm was doomed to fail. In recent years, the gladiolus has seen something of a resurgence, some fifty years too late for my parents.

This downward spiral in the gladiolus market was happening while my father was wrestling with the shocking death of his sister Catherine in 1952, another event I knew nothing about until many later years. It was the same year my brother Jerry was born, giving my father the joy of his first son and also the stress of another mouth to feed when their farm income was dwindling. It was also the year my father worked his twenty-fifth and final year at Draper Corporation. The letter congratulating him on his twenty-fifth anniversary was buried in my mother's papers. The same letter that I imagined filled him with rage and despair after all his labors had come to so little.

It was a turning point in my father's life. Shortly after that terrible year, my father suffered what was then called a nervous breakdown, what we might now call depression or post-traumatic stress. He was physically and emotionally exhausted. Seeking psychiatric treatment in the early 1950s was extremely rare, especially for people of limited means, and for a proud Italian man, it was unheard of. But that's exactly what my father did—indicating the depth of his suffering.

Cleaning out my mother's cedar chest, I found documents to prove it, including a letter from the psychiatric clinic where my father was treated, the indiscreetly named Southard Clinic for the Indigent Mentally Ill in Boston. The letter from Southard referred to my father's initial "request for help," some eight months before I was born. All this would help explain the deeply troubled, deeply downtrodden man I knew briefly as my father.

⅄℡™

The houses that form the backdrop to this story are no longer in my family's hands. My mother, brother, and I sold my grandparents' large home on Hayward Street, Milford, shortly after my aunts abandoned it. The appraisal made it clear that the cost of bringing it up to modern standards was too much for us. The crude house my father had built on Prairie Street, Milford, starting in 1946, was demolished shortly after the new house was built in 1986. And that newer house, the one I financed, along with the land under it that was once a glad farm, was sold in 2013.

The house that cradled my early years had a powerful effect on my family's psyche. It was debilitating for some of us. In my case, the house lit a fire under me, propelling me out into the world.

How deeply our homes define us, so much more than we define them. Whenever I travel some rural New England road and see a shabby house on some isolated plot of land, I wonder if a little girl lives there, a girl like I once was, with no choice in the home she was born to.

Most people just look away, thinking the people who live in such places deserve their fate. They assume the inhabitants must be lazy, or impaired in some way. The idea that such houses might contain hard-working, loving families is rarely considered. But sometimes, despite all good intentions, something just goes terribly wrong. It might be something that happened in another lifetime. And it sets the course of a family's history for generations.

So much if what I now know about my parents was revealed to me in 2013, in a matter of a few short months. The relics stored in my mother's cedar chest were jigsaw pieces of my family's early life, telling me what my mother and father never spoke of, helping me complete their complex mosaic.

It was also the year my wonderful son Steven graduated from Columbia University with high honors while his proud parents, my ex-husband and I, sat side-by-side looking on. Seeing him ascend the platform to receive his diploma, his sky-blue Columbia gown flowing loosely over his tall lean frame, my eyes glowing with tears of love and pride, I could feel the presence of another Stephen, a dusty little boy with bare feet. I thought for a moment that if I turned my head, I could see him, seated beside me, my sweet little brother, his sun-tinted face smiling up at mine.

My son Steven, namesake of my brother Stephen, named in turn for my grandfather Stefano, was living proof of that simple idea that comforted me, that saved my life, after my brother's death so many years ago. As it turns out, I was right. Life, precious life, always wins over death. Life gets the last word.

- END -

FAMILY PHOTOS

Myrtle Ann Thomas, c. 1937
Mendon High School graduation photo

Jerry Marenghi, c. 1937

Jerry working on 4th of July, c. 1948

Jerry Marenghi with daughters
Marcia (l) and Celia, c. 1949,
7 Hayward St., Milford, Mass.

The house Jerry Marenghi built on Prairie Street, as a work in progress.

The old Gravely plow

Marcia (r) and Celia in gladiolus field, c. 1948

Marcia, Jerry, Celia (l-r), c. 1954

Jerry, Catherine, Ma, c. 1955

Jerry and Catherine in new
Christmas clothes, c. 1958

Stephen, c. 1968

Catherine and Stephen, c. 1967

Crash At Intersection Kills Milford Woman

Newspaper clipping from *Milford Daily News*, June 2, 1952, with accident scene reconstruction below

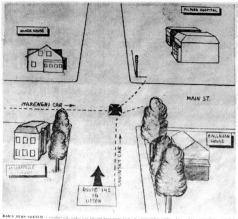

The new house erected on Prairie Street, Milford, in 1986 on a former gladiolus field

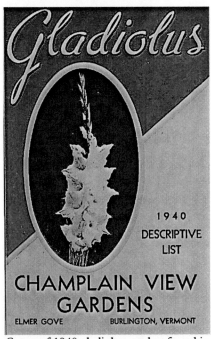

Cover of 1940 gladiolus catalog found in Myrtle Marenghi's cedar chest in 2013

About the Author

Catherine Marenghi brings to her writing a poet's sensibility and the clear eyes of a journalist. In addition to her memoir and award-winning poetry, she has written two nonfiction books. A native of Massachusetts, the granddaughter of Italian immigrants, Catherine writes with a profound sense of place and a fascination with the power of house, home, and family bonds. She divides her time between New England and Mexico.

CPSIA information can be obtained
at www.ICGtesting.com
Printed in the USA
LVOW12s1709230318
570967LV00003B/570/P